EDUCATION FOR MINISTRY

Reading and Reflection Guide, Volume C

Living as Spiritually Mature Christians

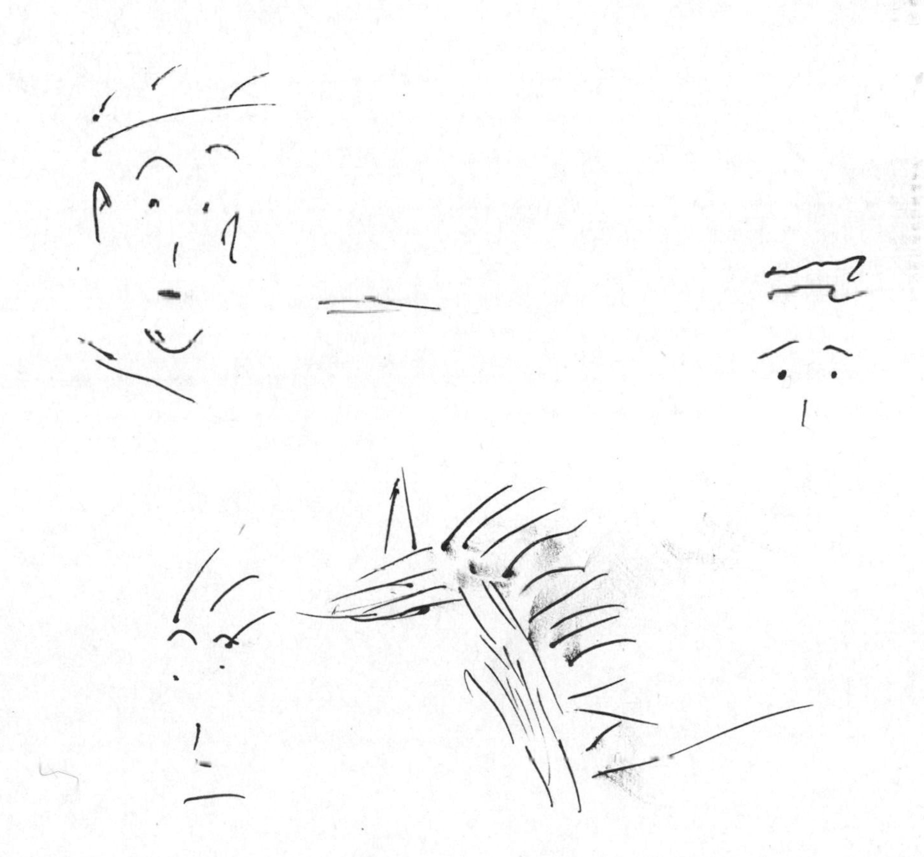

EDUCATION FOR MINISTRY

Reading and Reflection Guide, Volume C

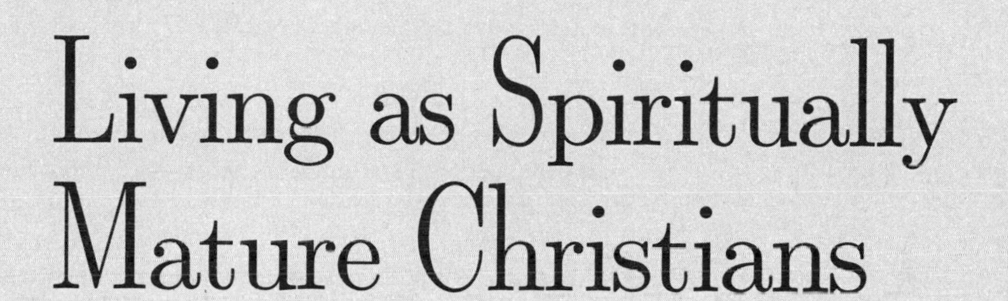

Living as Spiritually Mature Christians

Morehouse Publishing, 19 East 34th Street, New York, NY 10016
Morehouse Publishing is an imprint of Church Publishing Incorporated.
www.churchpublishing.org

Cover design by Laurie Klein Westhafer
Typeset by Beth Oberholtzer

Library of Congress Cataloging-in-Publication Data
A catalog record of this book is available from the Library of Congress.

978-0-8192-2920-5 (pbk)
978-0-8192-3288-5 (ebook)

Printed in the United States of America

Contents

Unit Four: Integrating Belief, Behavior, and Doctrine

Second Interlude Unit: Knowing Who We Are

Unit Five: Vocation: A Way to Love in Permanent White Water

PART II: RESOURCES

Supplemental Readings in the Christian Tradition

Resources for Spiritual Autobiography and Listening

Resources for Reflecting Theologically

Resources for Community Life

Acknowledgments

A revision by definition is not *sui generis*. Although this series of Reading and Reflection Guides may look different from previous editions of EfM materials, although it may be organized differently, it is nonetheless built on a framework that has evolved over the nearly forty years of Education for Ministry. Those who have some years of acquaintance with the program will recognize what the new format owes to components developed for its predecessors, among them parallel guides, common lessons, and the many variations of EfM's central discipline of theological reflection.

The developers of those foundational components are by now nearly legion and include not only founder Charles Winters and succeeding leaders like John de Beer and Edward de Bary but also the many EfM coordinators and trainers whose work with mentors all over the globe and over time has shaped the program.

The principal author of Reading and Reflection Guide, Volume C: *Living Faithfully as Spiritually Mature Christians*, the third in the cycle of four guides, is Rick Brewer, who has a long history of writing and curriculum design in EfM. Other contributors to this volume include Angela Hock Brewer and Karen M. Meridith. In addition, several of the essays and resources included in this *Guide*, some adapted, others left as originally published in the previous edition, have long been a part of the EfM program, designed and written by a number of contributors over the years. We are grateful for their work and know that we can look to the future of EfM only because we stand on the shoulders of giants.

Karen M. Meridith, series editor
Executive Director of Education for Ministry
Sewanee, Tennessee
March, 2015

About the Author

Richard E. Brewer (Rick) is a retired Episcopal priest who served in parochial ministry and in adult Christian formation for forty years. A graduate of The University of the South and General Theological Seminary, he has lived in Oklahoma most of his life and served as priest and educator in Tulsa and Stillwater Episcopal churches. Additionally, he developed and directed the Deacon Formation Program for the Episcopal Diocese of Oklahoma.

Rick first learned about EfM in 1975 from Dr. Charles Winters, the originator and first director of the program. He has been a trainer since 1978, a coordinator, a mentor, and interim assistant director for the EfM program. He conceived and edited the Common Lesson series for the first revision of the materials. He coauthored the Parallel Guides and numerous common lessons with the Reverend John de Beer. He, along with Angela Hock, co-wrote *Practically Christian: A Guide to Practical Christian Prayer, Action, and Reflection*. They co-directed Opportunities for Adult Christian Education and Spirituality (OACES), Inc. which developed a variety of adult Christian formation learning guides and a comprehensive ministry formation program for the Episcopal Diocese of Nebraska. For over a decade he participated in the Progoff Intensive Journal program. Rick brings this extensive experience in adult Christian formation to the revision of the new materials for EfM.

Program Overview

The Education for Ministry (EfM) program is a four-year study and group reflection process for the formation of Christian ministry through the development of knowledge, attitude, skill, and identity as Christians. Published texts and essays provide the primary knowledge content in the study of the Christian tradition.

The first year studies the Hebrew Scriptures (Old Testament). The second year offers a study of the New Testament. Year Three provides study of Christian (church) history. Theology, ethics, and interfaith encounter constitute study in the fourth year.

Texts for Each Year

- **Year One:** *A Short Introduction to the Hebrew Bible, 2nd Ed.* by John J. Collins. *The Holy Bible,* Old Testament and Apocrypha.
- **Year Two**: *Introducing the New Testament* by Mark Allan Powell. *The Holy Bible*, New Testament.
- **Year Three:** *Christianity: The First Three Thousand Years* by Diarmaid MacCulloch.
- **Year Four**: *Theology for a Troubled Believer* by Diogenes Allen. *The Christian Moral Life: Practices of Piety* by Timothy F. Sedgwick. *My Neighbor's Faith* edited by Jennifer Howe Peace, Or N. Rose, and Gregory Mobley.

Note: The most recent Oxford Annotated edition of the New Revised Standard Version of the Bible is recommended, but any translation may be used as long as it includes the Apocrypha. Paraphrased Bibles are not recommended for study.

The Interlude Texts for Volume C

- *Jesus and the Disinherited* by Howard Thurman
- *We Are Theologians*: *Strengthening the People of God* by Fredrica Harris Thompsett

Reading and Reflection Guide

A *Reading and Reflection Guide* provides weekly reading assignments, reflection questions, and additional supportive resources for the group.

- The entire group uses the same *Guide* each year–Volume A, B, C, or D. Each volume has a particular focus: Volume A, "Living Faithfully in Our

World," works with the contexts of a person's life; Volume B builds on "Living Faithfully in an Intercultural World"; Volumes C and D explore "Living as Spiritually Mature Christians" and "Living our Journey into God," respectively.

- Each volume contains **Part I**, the reading and reflection assignments, and **Part II**, supporting materials, such as methods of spiritual autobiography and theological reflection.
- Five primary units in each volume have six sessions each.
- Two interlude units in each volume have two sessions each.
- An organization session at the beginning and a closing session at the end bring the total to thirty-six sessions in a year.

Focus of the *Reading and Reflection Guide* Units

The first session of each primary unit is either an essay or other material for all in the group to read to help set the stage for the focus of the unit:

- **Unit One**–identity and meaning (individual, corporate, and historical);
- **Unit Two**–theological reflection as a life skill; orientation to attitudes to prayer, worship, and spirituality;
- **First Interlude**–a spirituality of liberation;
- **Unit Three**–spirituality, prayer, and worship;
- **Unit Four**–integrating behavior and belief into a congruency that supports faithful living;
- **Second Interlude**–ecclesiology: knowing who we are;
- **Unit Five**–vocation: hearing the call and passion of our lives in relation to God.

PART I

The Guide

Week One: Orientation and Organization

The following outline provides ideas for beginning a seminar year. Online groups will have some differences, but the basic ideas of planning the group's organization, orienting to the year's Reading and Reflection Guide, and beginning to get to know the other group members are the same.

Welcoming

Each person briefly introduces himself or herself–name, year in EfM, what drew them to participate.

Worship

A Form of Prayer for Groups or Families[1]

1. The Preparation

Light a candle or candles on the table or in the worship area. The one who lights them says one of the following:

Leader God is our light and our salvation, and in his name we light these candles. May they remind us of
the beauty of his truth and the radiance of his love. May our hearts be open to the light of Christ now and at all times.

All ***Lord, in your mercy, let there be light.***

Or

Leader O God, you command a light to shine out of darkness. Shine in our hearts that we may be as
lights in the world reflecting the glory of Jesus in our lives.
All God is light and in him is no darkness.

All ***Lord, in your mercy, let there be light.***

The Collect of the Day may then be said.

3. Praise

Here may follow a psalm, hymn, song, or instrumental music.

4. Readings

One or more passages of scripture may be read.

1. Reprinted from pages 687–693 of the *Book of Alternative Services of the Anglican Church of Canada.* Copyright 1985 by the General Synod of the Anglican Church of Canada. Used with permission.

5. Response

Any of the following may follow the readings: silence, discussion of the scripture passage or theme of the day, reading of a related work of literature, telling of a related story, study of special material from the parish, diocese, or national Church, discussion of family concerns in the light of scripture or the theme of the day.

6. Intercession

Prayer may be offered for the Church . . . and all in authority, the world, the special needs of the group, those in need, and the departed. The following litany may be used, or a seasonal litany or other prayers; or individuals may offer their own prayers, silently or aloud.

Leader Let us pray together to the Lord, saying, "Lord, hear our prayer."
All ***Lord, hear our prayer.***

Leader Loving God, we thank you for your many gifts to us, for the love which brings us together, for the earth which provides for our needs, for the new life you have given us in Jesus Christ, (for . . .).
All ***Lord, hear our prayer.***

Leader We pray to you for our Christian family (especially for . . .), [for all people of faith], and for grace to grow in your love.
All ***Lord, hear our prayer.***

Leader We pray to you for our world, for all its cares and needs, and for all who lead us and care for us, (especially . . .).
All ***Lord, hear our prayer.***

Leader We pray to you for those in need, for the sick and the lonely, for the hurt and the frightened, and for those who live without hope (especially . . .).
All ***Lord, hear our prayer.***

Leader We pray for those we love who have died, that you will surround them with your care and love (especially . . .).
All ***Lord, hear our prayer.***

Leader We pray for one another, asking you to bless us, our friends, and our relatives. Bless the places where we work, and bless our homes and our life together.
All ***Lord, hear our prayer.***

Members of the [group] may wish to share in personal prayer. Then may be said,

Leader Let us remember before God our selfish ways, the things we have done wrong, the sorrows we have caused, the love we have not shown.

Silence for reflection is kept.

All ***Most merciful Father,***
forgive us our sins against you
and against each other.
Strengthen us to overcome our weaknesses,
that we may live in love
as you would have us live,
for the sake of Jesus Christ our Saviour. Amen.

7. The Lord's Prayer

Leader As our Saviour taught us, let us pray,
All ***Our Father in heaven,***
hallowed be your name,
your kingdom come,
your will be done,
on earth as in heaven.
Give us today our daily bread.
Forgive us our sins
as we forgive those who sin against us.
Save us from the time of trial,
and deliver us from evil.
For the kingdom, the power,
and the glory are yours,
now and forever. Amen.

8. Conclusion

Leader Jesus said, "I am the light of the world; whoever follows me will not walk in darkness, but will have the light of life." *Amen.*

Checking-in

Each participant is invited to respond to one of the following:

- Describe a moment of joy this past week.
- Describe a moment of challenge this past week.
- Describe a moment when someone ministered to you this past week.

Or use some other way to open up awareness of one another and what is happening in each other's lives.

Organizing

Distribute materials for the year–all textbooks and the *Reading and Reflection Guide, Volume C.*

- **Year One:** *A Short Introduction to the Hebrew Bible, 2nd Edition*, John J. Collins.
- **Year Two**: *Introducing the New Testament*, Mark Allan Powell.
- **Year Three:** *Christianity: The First Three Thousand Years*, Diarmaid MacCulloch.
- **Year Four**: *Theology for a Troubled Believer*, Diogenes Allen. *The Christian Moral Life: Practices of Piety*, Timothy F. Sedgwick. *My Neighbor's Faith*, Jennifer Howe Peace, Or N. Rose and Gregory Mobley, editors.
- **Interlude Books for each participant***: Jesus and the Disinherited*,, Howard Thurman. *We Are Theologians*, Fredrica Harris Thompsett.

Look through the *Guide* to get a sense of how the weeks and units are laid out. A chart of the year's assigned readings is in Part II, pages 155–158. Note that supplemental readings for certain weeks are in Part II, and program expectations are outlined in pages 161–164.

Discuss, ask/answer questions about the *Guide.* The work assigned to be completed before each seminar meeting is in Part I. In addition to the overview chart and supplemental readings, Part II offers a number of resources participants may find interesting or helpful.

Returning participants may offer suggestions for study and preparation.

Learning Goals and Needs

Participants identify what they hope to do as part of their participation in EfM this year.

Covenant /Norms

Questions to consider when forming norms:

What environment will best facilitate your goals for this year?

What commitments will you make to your fellow travelers on this journey?

**Respectful Communications Guidelines from the Kaleidoscope Institute, (KI), found on page 240 in Part II of this Guide, may serve as a base for the group's norms. Groups are encouraged to establish an agreed upon set of norms or standards for how the group members will relate to one another during their year together.

Other KI tools for gracious communication may be of interest. See pages 237–240 in Part II.

Seminar Calendar

The group may wish to set a schedule or calendar for the thirty-six seminar weeks that includes sharing

- Worship
- Spiritual Autobiographies
- Theological Reflection

Holiday breaks

Anything else that needs to be scheduled?

Deepening Connections

Invitation for each to tell a bit more about yourselves may help begin the building of relationships. Where did you grow up? What's the most interesting place you have ever been? What three well-known people would you like to invite to dinner? What is your favorite music/art/type of food? How would you describe yourself besides stating relationships such as spouse, parent, employee/boss/student, sibling, and offspring?

Closing Prayer

All: Say the following words of Hymn 394 from The Hymnal 1982 *or select a hymn from any hymn source.*

Creating God, your fingers trace the bold designs of farthest space;
let sun and moon and stars and light and what lies hidden praise your might.
Sustaining God, your hands uphold earth's mysteries known or yet untold;
let water's fragile blend with air, enabling life, proclaim your care.
Redeeming God, your arms embrace all now despised for creed or race;
let peace, descending like a dove, make known on earth your healing love.
Indwelling God, your gospel claims one family with a billion names;
let every life be touched by grace until we praise you face to face.[2]

2. The Hymnal 1982 (New York: The Church Hymnal Corporation, 1985), 394. Used with permission.

UNIT ONE

Spiritual Autobiography and Listening

Week Two

The *Reading and Reflection Guide* is for each participant's work between seminar sessions. Since EfM is based on principles of adult learning, participants who complete the work each week prior to the seminar meeting will find their learning enhanced.

Assignments for all year levels generally have three parts. First, the reading assignments for each year level (Years One–Four) are listed, followed by a suggested Focus on significant terms, names, or concepts. Then the Respond section poses an idea that all participants can relate to from their week's study. Finally, the Practice section invites all participants to actually practice skills such as listening or theological reflection. At certain times, in the initial week of each unit and in the interludes, all year levels will be reading a common essay or text.

Mentors may find ways to incorporate participant's weekly work into the seminar sessions. This is most easily done by using the Respond or Practice sections, since they are integrative, as jumping off points for discussion or reflection, but it is not required. Mentors and groups are free to find other ways to integrate their learning into the regular practice of theological reflection.

ALL YEARS

Read

Spiritual Maturity: Living Authentically as an Adult Christian

Those who carry out the work of ministry in the world need support, guidance, knowledge, and vision. The Letter to the Ephesians offers one vision for Christianity, bringing the people of God "to maturity, to the measure of the full stature of Christ." (Ephesians 4:13) To serve the world intentionally in Christ's name means that each Christian needs to find a personal way into God's incarnating actions that bring growth and maturity.

> Human maturity has an elusive quality to it. By definition, *maturity* means full development. But there are so many aspects to human development–physical, intellectual, emotional, social, spiritual–that its attainment across the spectrum is clearly beyond our reach. Indeed, with the possible exception of the physical, even a single dimension of maturity will ultimately elude us. We can always aspire to greater maturity; we can always entertain the possibility of

more personal integration, more wisdom, more love of God. Maturity is a goal that has no defined end point.[3]

Through this year in EfM we will be considering what it means to be a spiritually mature Christian. As Neil Parent notes above, the term "maturity" is ambiguous in that it has several simultaneous meanings, each dependent on the context in which it is used. Adding the adjective "Christian" amplifies the ambiguity because there are variant expressions of Christianity.

To live as an adult Christian in today's world requires, in part, striving for wholeness, acting wisely, assuming responsibility, and living authentically. Throughout the year the topics of adulthood, wisdom, integration, authenticity, and wholeness act as lenses to bring into focus a vision for living in the world as spiritually mature followers of Jesus Christ, especially for how that identity blossoms when nurtured and challenged by biblical, historical, theological, and ethical learning.

Ellen Wondra, professor of theology and ethics at Bexley-Seabury Seminary Federation in Chicago and editor of *The Anglican Theological Review*, gives a snapshot of the purpose of theological education:

> There are at least 289 theological colleges, seminaries, training programs, and other institutions of theological education in the Anglican Communion worldwide. Two hundred and eighty-nine, according to the Anglican Communion office. All of them have a fundamental purpose in common, regardless of their widely varying curricula, pedagogies, constituencies, and resources: they are all dedicated to **"equip[ping] the saints for the work of ministry, for building up the body of Christ, until all of us come to the unity of the faith and of the knowledge of the Son of God, to maturity, to the measure of the full stature of Christ"** (Eph. 4:12–13, emphasis added).[4]

The Education for Ministry Program is among those 289 theological learning enterprises and shares the purpose Wondra describes.

Spiritual maturity, like physical and emotional maturity, has a trajectory. "When I was a child, I spoke like a child, I thought like a child, I reasoned like a child; when I became an adult, I put an end to childish ways. For now we see in a mirror, dimly, but then we will see face to face." (1 Corinthians 13:11–12) But unlike physical maturity, which has a set and attainable final form, moving from spiritually childish to spiritually adult ways proceeds toward a goal that is striven for, but never fully attained. "For now we see in a mirror, dimly" applies to an understanding of Christian maturity. Christian adulthood, therefore, is an ideal for which one strives, knowing that goal–given the limitations and complexity of human life–is essentially never fully apprehended nor completely realized.

---

3. Neil A. Parent, ed., *Educating for Christian Maturity*, Department of Education, United States Catholic Conference, (Washington, D.C., 1990), 1–3.

4. Ellen K. Wondra, "Editor's Notes," *Anglican Theological Review* 90:4 (2008), 689.

Dimensions of Maturity

The physical life has distinguishable development. As a person grows, physical growth progresses along predictable lines. An infant moves through measurable phases that indicate healthy progressions of maturity. The growth continues within significant measures that assure "normal" growth. However, exactly when full development occurs is somewhat elusive. A person tends to grow in height after other physical characteristics have reached the full physical potential. An eighteen-year-old male may reach sexual maturity before he has reached his full height. A female's body reaches maturity sooner than a male body, indicating sexual differences impact physical maturity. Once the physical growth is completed the body continues to develop differently. Cultural and social standards shape what such physical aging means. Do the physical characteristics of a ninety-year-old person demonstrate maturity or an atrophying of maturity? How the question is answered depends in large part upon the ways in which a culture views youth, elders, and the cycle of life.

Feelings such as love, fear, joy, anger, delight, and frustration (along with many other feelings) comprise one's emotional life. How a person lives within the realm of emotions discloses the degree of emotional maturity. An emotionally mature person understands and manages her/his emotions in ways that result in behavior and attitudes that contribute positively to a situation.

What does it mean to be intellectually mature? If mature means fully grown, questions immediately surface. Is a person's intelligence a fixed aptitude throughout life? Or is it developed in stages? Is intelligence an ability that has meaning only in given circumstances? Further, are there multiple intelligences, such as described by Howard Gardner?[5] If so, does each kind of intelligence develop or are they innate givens? Intellectual maturity points to an individual's competence in reasoning, creating, deciding, and applying in ways that convey an in-depth understanding of areas of interest. Within the arena of Christian ministry a person demonstrates intellectual maturity as one reflects carefully and critically within life situations in ways that increase and enhance the ability to discern God's self-revelation and action.

Social maturity refers to how a person relates to other people. Cultural norms establish a proper way to relate to other people whether they are family, friends, neighbors, acquaintances, or strangers, and individuals are socialized to function responsibly within the standards and norms of that particular society. A socially mature person recognizes that different cultures, communities, organizations, and families have differing practices that govern acceptable behavior. Social maturity refers to the ability to participate with integrity while in different social settings.

---

5. For information on the theory of multiple intelligences see Howard Gardner, *Intelligence Reframed: Multiple Intelligences for the 21st Century*, (New York, New York: Basic Books, Inc., 2000).

Ambiguity abounds when describing spiritual maturity. A fully realized spiritual maturity–for Christians, attaining the "full stature of Christ"–is always just beyond our reach and thus continually eludes us. Spirituality's biblical etymology rooted in words like "wind" and "breath" increases its ambiguity exponentially. Spiritual maturity cannot be easily defined; however, it can be intimated and experienced. Phenomena associated with spiritual maturity are best communicated through analogy, symbol, metaphor, and images–the "stuff" of poetry and the fine arts.

The markers of physical, emotional, intellectual, social, and spiritual maturity occur throughout life. The dimensions of maturity are interrelated yet they develop independently. Physical maturity does not guarantee emotional maturity. A person may demonstrate intellectual development beyond his or her age, yet remain socially immature. The expression "this child has an old soul" suggests that progress toward spiritual maturity may show within any developmental stage. In addition, maturity has a fluid quality that can appear to come and go. Clichés such as "second childhood" or "mid-life crisis" intimate a dynamic quality of maturity that progresses and regresses.

Christian Maturity

The measure of Christian maturity weaves together all of the above dimensions of maturity in relation to an understanding of Jesus as the model of the fully mature human.

> Every age and culture must apply the model of Jesus to its own times and circumstances. The question of what constitutes Christian maturity must be answered afresh by each generation. What first-century Christians in Antioch thought about being Christ-like would be vastly different from those in pre-Reformation Europe or from those of us in the United States at the close of the twentieth century. Christians in every era and location seek to model Christ out of their own experiences of the world, with their different needs and responsibilities, with their vastly different self-concepts.[6]

Through this year together in EfM we will be using a conceptual framework that guides the application of "the model of Jesus" to our own times and circumstances. Each of the five units of the *Guide* contributes to the building of an authentic, adult Christian faith.

Mature followers of Christ strive to live authentically within all levels of life. Practical theologian Johannes Van der Ven names three levels sociologists have used for analyzing human behavior: the micro-level refers to the individual's specific and peculiar circumstances; the meso-level is the communal and institutional dimensions of living; the macro-level includes global pluralities.[7] These three levels help create a more

---

6. Parent, *Educating for Christian Maturity*, 3.

7. Johannes Van der Ven, *Education for Reflective Ministry* (Louvain/Grand Rapids: Peeters/Eerdmans 1998), 11–13.

comprehensive understanding of the meaning of coming to "the full stature of Christ."

At the **micro level**, the personal or individual level, particularities shape the meaning and values that make each person distinctive. The specific time and place of birth, DNA makeup, and other individual distinguishing characteristics work together and contribute to the uniqueness of each person while particular persons, actions, events, and physical experiences shape an individual's identity. Each individual encounters persons who model what it means to be an adult. Wisdom figures, whether known through direct relationships or encountered within the literature of childhood, adolescence, and adulthood also are formative. Further, cultural activities and events communicate values in each decade of a person's life, introducing figures, experiences, and ideas that convey notions of maturity. Often, developing an understanding of what it means to be an adult comes through negative as well as positive experiences

Human beings are individuals, yet much more. Each person has a corporate identity fashioned by the givens of the individual life mediated through institutions and social patterns. When a person is viewed at the **meso level**, the communal dimension of human nature comes to center stage. Institutions–family, religion, school, government, business, among others–help produce the self that is "we." It is important to attend to the institutional realities of a particular society, for they reveal the influential factors that form a person's assertions about reality. Directives that come in the form of "should, must, and ought" shape the moral environment of a person's life. Viewing life from the standpoint of the meso level highlights the contours of a community's ethical geography.

At the **macro level** is a person's global, planetary context situated in the greater physical universe. Satellite technology that can picture the entire planet astonishes us with a sudden view of the macro level of life. Social media graphically illustrates that humans live within a global, interrelated reality while instant communication through mobile technology helps bring the macro level into nearly constant awareness. Earthquakes along the Pacific Rim affect daily life across the globe. Wars and the refugees they produce contribute to devastating conflicts in the intercultural fabric of the human family. Environmental concerns are heightened as a person sees our blue planet against the black background of interstellar space and realizes that viewing the earth from outer space is in actuality a long view in which all the particularities of day to day life exist. In less than a minute, a person with the Google Earth app on a smart phone can experience all the levels of human experience that Van der Ven describes.

The concept of micro, meso, and macro dimensions of life can be a useful tool for forming a more inclusive and comprehensive understanding of Christian maturity. With greater clarity about how values, assumptions, and desires shape the world at the individual, institutional, and global levels comes greater ability to envision what being intentional about growing into "the full stature of Christ" looks like in daily life.

Listening as a Way into Christian Maturity

Tucked away within the United States Department of State website is a resource written to help adolescent international students handle stress. In the chapter on communication the authors introduce "active listening":

The most common problem in communication is not listening! A Chinese symbol for "To Listen" is shown below. It is wise beyond the art. The left side of the symbol represents an ear. The right side represents the individual–you. The eyes and undivided attention are next and finally there is the heart.

"TO LISTEN"

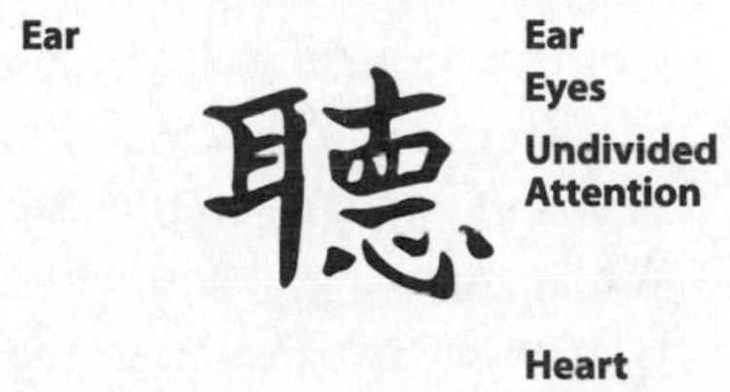

Ear

聽

Ear
Eyes
Undivided Attention
Heart

This symbol tells us that to listen we must use both ears, watch and maintain eye contact, give undivided attention, and finally be empathetic.[8]

Deep listening requires the convergence of ears, eyes, and heart in undivided attention. Anyone who has been given undivided attention knows the power of that level of listening. A person who desires to be heard, especially about a heart-felt matter, experiences such listening as a profound service. To listen with undivided attention opens the door for ministry.

Listening as a skill can be learned and practiced, but listening also is an attitude–a way of being in the world.

> The ability to listen depends not in the first place on any particular skill or technique, but on a fundamental respect for one's partner in conversation. Listening is thus a moral act. Listening is an act of attending to the other that discloses the strangeness of otherness, disrupting our comfortable self-images and threatening to undo our everyday experience of ourselves (and others) as familiar and basically unified personalities. Not listening becomes a way of securing ourselves from encounter with the mystery of otherness. Listening exposes us to our own desires not to want to share of ourselves. Listeners are required not only to welcome the strangeness of the other but to risk self-disclosure in the act of listening, for the listener must at some point recognize and then expose to the other his or her own strangeness–and not only to the other but to one's own self.[9]

---

8. Henry J. Nicols and Susan M. Baum, *Tool Kit for Teens: A Guide for Helping Adolescents Manage Stress for American-Sponsored Overseas Schools*, Overseas Schools Advisory Council (Washington, D. C.: Department of State, 2003).

9. Lloyd Steffen, Listening Point, *Christian Century*, November 21–28, 1990, 1087.

As emotional and spiritual maturity deepen, a person increases in the capacity and willingness to be present with another in silence. The ability to listen attentively extends beyond the other person; it increases the propensity to listen to oneself as well. The combination of listening attentively to self and others in turn increases the disposition to listen for God. Other virtues, such as patience and humility, grow as well.

Seeking Christian maturity demands our moving toward wholeness, exploring how to act wisely, becoming more willing to accept responsibility and to live authentically and gracefully. Listening deeply and attentively is foundational for living authentically with others and cultivating relationships that guide one through the complexities of human behavior.

A person cannot listen to everything at once and therefore listening is selective. Listening also requires focus that attends to specifics. We listen to and listen for different things when we give our attention to someone or something, and so the listening experience operates on multiple levels. While attending to another the listener may notice comments and emotional nuances that are applicable to her or his own individual life.

Listening requires interpretation and each situation shades what is heard. Communication happens contextually, at Van der Ven's micro, meso, and macro levels. Listening involves attending to the individual characteristics and style of another's self-expression. The tenor of the voice, facial expression, and gestures comprise a specific medium of communication on the micro level of experience. A person speaks with an accent from a distinct culture or environment, using vocabulary and idioms from a larger cultural context shared by ethnic groups at the meso level of experience. At the same time, on the macro level, the big picture context of nation or hemisphere always plays in the background. National and global realities influence how one interprets and understands issues in the two other levels, individual (micro) and institutional (meso).

Ministry matures as the attitude and skill of listening integrate the three contextual levels into the interactive process of communication. Wholeness, authenticity, and wisdom have room to grow as people become attuned to the macro, meso, and micro levels present in every conversation. As a person knows more about the Christian heritage, cultural realities, and personal beliefs and experience, the potential for ministry matures.

Lloyd Steffen, chaplain at Leigh University in Pennsylvania, who has spent years in helping young adults grow into maturity, believes that the wise listener listens from a theological perspective.

> We are in need of a theology of listening, for a willingness to listen ultimately expresses an attitude of love. Christians believe that Jesus listened to God and to those he encountered in his daily life. We do neither. If we listened to one another we should be inviting one another into new forms of relationship based on openness and respect and a willingness to share ourselves. If we listened for God, we should spend our time not praying for ourselves but listening to our prayers to see what we are saying not to God but to ourselves. The

heart is a great mystery. Christians believe that God knows the human heart (and we do not), for that heart is where God's omniscience lies. God does not need to be informed about our wants and needs. It is we who need to know what we want, what we fear, what we love.

Ultimately, listening for God is like listening to one's own self, and that is no easy task. Listening for God requires the kind of listening to the self that makes up any moment of confession and self-examination. Listening for God requires that we learn to be critical of ourselves, since so much of what we want interferes with what our religious traditions tell us God wants, which is simply that we love one another and trust that the spirit of God shall be with us. For the listening point is what Jesus wanted for us–that place where "they should perceive with their eyes, and hear with their ears, and understand with their heart, and turn for me to heal them" (Matt. 13:15).[10]

Anglican theologian David Ford advocates expanding "doing theology" beyond the dominant voices that issue affirmations of "right belief" and directives of "right action":

> One caricature of theology is as a neat, unquestioning package of dogma in which there are affirmations that say "Believe this!" and commands that say "Do this!" That is theology in what grammarians call the indicative and imperative moods. These are in fact the dominant moods of a great deal of theology, and they are as vital to theology as they are to life. A man and woman getting married are right to exchange basic affirmations: "I do," "I will." A fire-fighter at a blaze is right to order: "Clear the building!" But affirmations and commands by themselves do not make for good theology any more than they do for good living. Before the marriage comes the mutual questioning, the exploration of whether it is the right move, and above all the discernment of whether the desires of each are sufficiently in harmony. After marriage there are (one hopes) years of living out the promises, with a great deal of further questioning, experimental trial and error, and the further shaping and education of desires. The fire-fighter's order is not arbitrary, but comes from years of training, practice drills, and experience, learning to ask the relevant questions and to take decisions after assessing situations in line with the overarching goal of saving lives.
>
> Likewise in Christian theology: there are endless questions to be asked as minds and hearts are stretched in trying to do justice to the wonder of God and God's relationship to all creation–past, present, and future. There is an overarching desire for God and the purposes of God. Between the questioning and the desiring, and weaving into them in fascinating, ever-new ways, are the experiments with possibilities, the affirmations of truths and commitments, and the imperatives that guide judgments and decisions.[11]

---

10. Ibid., 1088.

11. David F. Ford, *The Future of Christian Theology* (Oxford, UK: Wiley-Blackwell, 2011), 68.

Questions, especially those that dare enter the deep of human consciousness, explore “the wonder of God” to uncover and cultivate humanity’s yearnings. Desiring and inquiring, seeking to do justice to wonder and holiness, open avenues into experimenting with “fascinating, ever-new ways” to know God. Exploring possibilities encourages emerging practices that uncover and affirm truths and commitments. Imperatives, grounded in secured affirmations, enliven faith that embraces the maturing mind, heart, and soul of individual and communal life. Humankind’s triad of perspectives (individual, institutional, and globally inclusive) magnifies theological insight and awareness so that Christians can more fully encompass maturity and wisdom.

Ford’s approach to theology offers a possible framework for developing a balanced theology of spiritual maturity as an adult Christian.

- **Desires**–interests that an individual holds
  *What do you **long or yearn** for?*
- **Questions**–inquiries that are raised and that motivate and guide increased learning
  *What do you **wonder about or doubt**?*
- **Explorations**–experiments available for “hands on” practical experience
  *What **possibilities** do you **want to explore or test**?*
- **Affirmations**–positions held as true and that are valued
  What are you coming to **believe or affirm**?
- **Imperatives**–commands that call for action
  What **should, ought, or must you do**?

Throughout the coming weeks, one or more of these lines of thought will guide the formation of knowledge and action in seeking a way to “the full stature of Christ.”

Focus

Define: physical, emotional, intellectual, social, and spiritual dimensions of maturity; micro, meso, and macro levels

Respond

What connections did you make to the ideas presented in this week’s Read and Focus sections?

Note questions raised and affirmations discovered.

Consider and write about how you listen for God’s presence, and what gets in the way of your doing that.

Practice

Constructing a Spiritual Autobiography

Note: The Education for Ministry program is based in the Christian tradition and generally the participants are part of that tradition, though representing a variety of denominations. However, sometimes other faith traditions may be represented in a seminar group, or group members may have been part of other traditions in the course of their spiritual journeys. This spiritual autobiography format makes room for the possibility of including other expressions of faith.

Before beginning the assignment, please read "Spiritual Autobiographies–Some Guidelines" on pages 198–199 in Part II of this Reading and Reflection Guide. It is expected that every participant in EfM will share a portion of her or his spiritual autobiography each year. Your mentor will work with the group to construct a schedule for presenting spiritual autobiographies, usually spread across several weeks of seminar meetings.

- Imagine the metaphor of an artist's palette to represent your experience of maturing in faith.
- Name the "colors" that have gone into your personal maturing process: the people, events, resources, locations, and so forth that have been part of personal growth in knowing God.
- Colors can represent various moods and levels of energy. Try assigning an actual color to each of the people and circumstances that you identify.
- Identify when each color was added. Note how that person or circumstance or resource played a part in a personal journey of faith maturity.
- "Mix" your palette/life by writing about the desires you have felt in relationship to God, the things you have tried, the questions you have raised, the affirmations and commitments of faith you have made, and the imperatives for action and decisions that you hold.
- An artist creates with a result in mind, a finished product at the end–a picture, a weaving, a sculpture. However, in the work of maturing in a relationship with God, the creative process itself may be more important than achieving an end. What do you think?
- What picture or sculpture or other work of art would represent your journey of faith maturity?

Week Three

A resource for broadening and deepening biblical study is the Oxford Biblical Studies Internet site. **All EfM participants have subscriber's access to this resource**, which has articles, maps, timelines, a variety of biblical translations, illustrations, and numerous other items. Articles on biblical interpretation are particularly supportive for Year One participants. Also, notice that the **site contains the *New Oxford Annotated Bible*.** Reach the site with the following Internet address:

oxfordbiblicalstudies.com

The login ID is **efm-sewanee** and the password is **ministry**.

Looking ahead: There will be large chunks of text reading in various weeks throughout the year, as well as opportunities for deepening understanding offered in the *Reading and Reflection Guide*. The practice of looking ahead can help you plan time to comfortably complete the study.

YEAR ONE

Read

Collins, Preface to the Second Edition, Abbreviations, Introduction, Chapter 1, "The Near Eastern Context" and Chapter 2, "The Nature of the Pentateuchal Narrative," pages xiii–40

Looking ahead: In order to provide opportunity to read a substantial portion of the Year One primary source, the Bible's Old Testament, the Year One reading assignments will sometimes be long. Please think about what you will have to do in order to provide enough time for yourself whenever possible. For example, if you have a long commute each day or if you are someone who enjoys audio-books, you might consider listening to an audio recording of the Bible passages assigned.

Focus

Define: anthropomorphic, Torah, Pentateuch, Julius Wellhausen, Hermann Gunkel, Rolf Rendtorff, Gerhard von Rad, Erhard Blum; sources in the Hebrew scripture, e.g. documentary hypothesis, J, E, P, and D sources

What multicultural dimensions existed in the context of the Near East as "the story" begins?

YEAR TWO

Read

Powell, Preface and Chapter 1, "The New Testament World," pages 9–46, and Chapter 2, "The New Testament Writings," pages 47–62

Focus

Define: Essenes; Zealots; Mishnah; Talmud; Hellenism; apocalyptic thought; Septuagint; types of criticism; Dead Sea Scrolls testament; apostolic; catholic; seven categories of New Testament writings; Justin Martyr's account of Christian worship; canon; stages in the transmission of the Gospel Tradition; Marcion; exegesis; hermeneutics

In the section "Exegesis and Hermeneutics," Powell states, "All the exegetical methods and academic disciplines described above are used by people who operate with different hermeneutical assumptions and interests. The methods themselves are simply tools that are employed for very different purposes by people with different attitudes and goals [60]."

Describe the cultural context for those living at the time of the New Testament events and writing. Compare and contrast to the current local cultural environment.

YEAR THREE

Read

MacCulloch, Acknowledgements, Introduction, and Chapter 1, "Greece and Rome," pages xxiii–46

Focus

Until recently, church historians have primarily traced Christian history as the movement from Jerusalem, through the Roman Empire, and on to Europe, steadily moving westward to the New World. MacCulloch takes a more global approach, presenting Christian history along three paths: the movement west from Jerusalem that became the Western-Latin expression of Christianity; the path into the Middle East and Far East; and the Eastern Orthodoxies of Byzantine empires.

What is gained or lost in MacCulloch's approach?

Define: Christians of the Middle East; Latin-speaking Church; Orthodoxy; repentance and conversion; Bible as central text of Christianity; "[b]ooks are the storehouses for human ideas"; historical truth; conventions used throughout MacCulloch's book; *Logos*; *Hellas*; *polis*; *ekklesia*; Plato's influence on Christianity; Hellenistic Greece; *res publica* (republic); Roman Republic; imperial monarchy

Name desires, experiments, questions, affirmations and/or imperatives that MacCulloch's discussion raised for you (refer to Week Two, page 18, to refresh your understanding of the terms "desires, experiments," and so forth).

YEAR FOUR

Read

Allen, Preface, "Introduction: What is Theology?" pages ix–xxiv

Focus

Identify Allen's six motives that draw people to Christianity.

Reflect on which of the motives have been present in your response to Christianity.

How do those motives relate to your attraction to other groups, causes, or interests?

Name desires, experiments, questions, affirmations and/or imperatives that Allen's discussion raised for you (refer to Week Two to refresh your understanding of the terms "desires, experiments," and so forth).

ALL YEARS

Respond

Group Life

Read "Group Life: The Seminar" on pages 234–236 in Part II. Any type of group proceeds through identifiable phases of maturing, whether the group is constituted for a short or long term. A group's life begins, deliberately or otherwise, with the work of getting to know one another, of finding a place among people who may or may not already know one another–Inclusion. Then there is a period of determining what authority each person has in the group, how each can contribute to the life of the group, how differences are responded to–Control. As those phases are successfully accomplished, people begin to have a sense of support and care for another, to feel good about one another and how things are going–Affection.

As the life of a group draws to completion, such as nearing the end of a seminar year, the phases work in reverse, with questions such as how will we stay in touch (Affection), what needs to happen to continue the group in the future (Control), and who will be back, graduate, or be added (Inclusion).

Consider how the Inclusion phase is being addressed in the seminar group.

Identify how your participation in EfM could support maturing in the knowledge and love of God.

Practice

Continue to work on a spiritual autobiography that identifies the "colors" of your life as you have matured in faith.

Week Four

YEAR ONE

Read

Genesis 1–11;
Collins, Chapter 3, "The Primeval History," pages 41–50

Focus

Define: primeval; Genesis's two creation stories; *'adam*; Atrahsis myth; Epic of Gilgamesh; Sons of God (Genesis 6); Enuma Elish

Stories delight and entertain in various forms and styles. Myths, epics, legends, novellas, and fables each tell some tale that interests as it instills values, guidance, and meaning. Often values live implicitly within the listeners, only to surface in moments of crisis that call for decisive action. Some myths explain why things are as they are, others prescribe "right" behavior, while others venture into explanations as they establish meaning.

Some fundamental questions addressed in stories are "what is truth and can I know it, what endures, what is real, is there purpose to my life, where did we come from and where are we going?" Stories offer answers to basic concerns.

What family stories or personal experiences have contributed to your social, intellectual, or faith maturation?

YEAR TWO

Read

Powell, Chapter 3, "Jesus," and Chapter 4, "The Gospels," pages 63–101

Focus

Define: The two doctrines of Jesus; kingdom of God; themes in Jesus' teaching; the historical Jesus; gospel as a literary genre; parables; miracle stories; pronouncement stories; passion and resurrection narratives; sayings of Jesus; the synoptic puzzle (*aka* problem); the Q source; Griesbach hypothesis; *Diatessaron*

What stories in your family or your experience have contributed to your social or intellectual maturation? To your faith maturation?

YEAR THREE

Read

MacCulloch, Chapter 2, "Israel," pages 47–73

Focus

Define: Maccabees; Tanakh; Apocrypha; the first and second exiles; Samaritans; the first and second temples; Septuagint; Hellenized Jews; creation out of nothingness; development of the notion of afterlife and individual soul; Hasmonean dynasty; Sadducees; Pharisees; Essenes; Zealots

Chapter 2 concludes Part I, "A Millennium of Beginnings," in which MacCulloch traces the social and intellectual "seeds" of Christianity. The two histories (Greco-Roman and Israel) continually influence Christian life and thought.

The following quote appears near the bottom of page 50 of MacCulloch's *Christianity: The First Three Thousand Years* : ". . . even through their hardest and most wretched experiences of fighting with those they love most deeply, [Israel is] being given some glimpse of how they relate to God."

MacCulloch connects this struggle with Jacob's formational struggle with the angel of the Lord at the River Jabok. This way of drawing meaning from experience allowed Israel to view history through the eyes of faith. History became the arena in which they could see God at work, bringing them into being as a people bound to God. Some consider this a re-writing of history only, merely a means of self-justification. There is plenty of room for that view. However, this is also a way of interpreting history, of seeing God at work in the life and experience of an individual and a group; this is salvation history–history that tells the story of God's work of redemption.

Reflect on how that concept of salvation history resonates in your life.

YEAR FOUR

Read

Allen, Chapter 1, "The Holy One of Israel," pages 3–18

Focus

Define: henotheist; monotheist; transcendence; immanence; *mysterium tremendum et fascinans*; Otto; Anselm; intellectual repentance; holiness

Allen writes that we know about God "because God makes God's self known or reveals God's self *in what God does*" (17).

Identify what God has done in your experience that reveals something about God.

ALL YEARS

Respond

List the favorite stories you have heard or read in your life. Include movies and plays as well as books.

What is similar across the list?

What values seem to be consistent in those stories?

What stories have you rejected?

Practice

Listen to the stories around you during the week, from your family, friends, your coworkers, and people in stores you frequent. What concerns are expressed? What hopes do you hear?

How do you discern truth in what you hear?

Week Five

YEAR ONE

Read

"The Priestly Creation Story" essay found in Part II, pages 166–183, of the *Reading and Reflection Guide*

Looking ahead: The Week Six reading assignment is Genesis 12–50 and a chapter in Collins. It takes about one and one-half hours for a moderately-paced reading of all of the Genesis assignment.

Focus

Define: covenant; Baals, cult; Sabbath, *ex nihilo*; Zoroastrianism; Manichaeism; dualism; Plato; Neo-Platonic; *via negativa*

The Priestly Creation Story in Genesis 1:1–2:4a poetically presents a doctrine of creation and offers a doctrine of God. This guided study of the story draws out meaning in this ancient poem, showing God as Wholly Other yet present to creation. God transcends all that is, thereby providing a corrective to all forms of dualism. Many theological difficulties get untangled by the implications in the story.

The Priestly Creation Story is a mature statement of Israel's belief about God and the relationship of all that exists to God. Describe the development of your personal view of the relationship between God and creation, that is, between God and all that is not God.

YEAR TWO

Read

The Gospel according to Matthew *(Try to read this gospel in one or two sittings.)*

Focus

Define: Pharisees, Sadducees; Mount of Olives; Messiah; King Herod; sermon on the mount; Matthew's miracles of Jesus; John the Baptist; Matthew's parables of Jesus; the Transfiguration; lament over Jerusalem; the Resurrection; the commissioning of the disciples

The Gospel writers tell the story of the Good News of God in Christ. The Gospel in its entirety communicates the story. However, seldom do people hear the entire story; they experience the scripture either verse by verse or in short pieces they hear within worship. Such reading is like watching a trailer of a film and believing you have seen the movie. Individual scenes make little or no sense without the context of the story. So too it is important to know the entire Gospel, allowing you to experience its drama. Once you have a sense of Matthew's story, you are positioned better to interpret individual scenes, teachings, and events.

What is your favorite account of Jesus' ministry in Matthew's gospel?

What account is most troubling to you?

Describe your response and explore from where that arises; that is, is the discomfort related to something you have been taught or believe or have come across in some other way?

YEAR THREE

Read

MacCulloch, Chapter 3, "A Crucified Messiah," pages 77–111

Focus

Define: cluster of words (*evaggelion*, *evangelium*, *Gospel*); Julius Africanus; epiousios; parables; *abba*; *Kyrios*–"Jesus is Lord, the word for God"; Paul of Tarsus; *epistole*; Paul's use of the word "church"; Johannine Christ; Jewish revolt and fall of Jerusalem. Learn the pronunciations

Change disrupts continuity. New ways of speaking and even newer ways of behaving create unrest. Yet, without continuity change evaporates into nothingness. Society's reordering of itself after chaotic change provides the stuff of history. Change in the eastern region of the Roman Empire eventually upset the Roman Empire's social order. The history of Christianity began with seemingly insignificant events. The importance of those events became clear through the lenses of experience and hindsight.

Describe your attitude towards change.

Explore what might be responsible for that attitude.

YEAR FOUR

Read

Allen, Chapter 2, "Holiness for Today," pages 19–27

Focus

Compare Isaiah's vision of God with Moses's encounter with God.

Define: Simone Weil; Jean Vanier; absolute value

State in your own words the justification of the claim that "human beings are significant, have dignity, and have absolute value" (27).

Sometimes, the most important work of maturation involves accepting one's own worth. Describe your journey of maturation in this area.

What price have you paid?

What reward have you known?

ALL YEARS

Respond

Sometimes, the ministry that one engages is a ministry to self. Attending to one's personal growth in relationship to God is part of that ministry.

What does this week's study help you to understand about the ministry needed for yourself in order to facilitate your growth in your relationship with God?

Describe your image of a relationship with God.

Practice

Review your autobiography. How does that story reflect your image of a relationship with God?

Where do you see that image of relationship with God exhibited in others?

Week Six

YEAR ONE

Read

Genesis 12–50

Collins, Chapter 4, "The Patriarchs," pages 51–62

Looking ahead: Next week the reading assignment is Exodus 1–15 and Collins, Chapter 5.

Focus

Define: the Patriarchs; Abraham; Sarah; Isaac; Rebecca; Jacob; Rachel; Leah; Benjamin; Joseph; Miriam; pharaoh at time of Joseph; Jethro; Horeb

Reading the primary text–the Bible for Year One–is essential to understanding scripture. Your reading forms the basis for understanding what scholars and others say about the text. Dr. Robert Denton, professor of the Old Testament at General Theological Seminary often reminded students that they would be amazed by how much the text illuminates the commentary. Each person has unique experiences that shape how he or she interprets scripture. While the work of biblical scholars is enormously valuable, only the individual can bring a distinctive experience to the learning process. Then, as experience enters into dialogue with what scholars have written, deeper learning occurs. For this reason we suggest reading the Bible assignment before reading the survey text chapter.

Identify: Legends–etiological, ethnological, etymological, ceremonial; Hermon Gunkel; *Sitz im Lebem*; *bris*; Abraham Cycle; Jacob Cycle; Joseph Story

What light did the commentary shed on the biblical text?

Describe the process of spiritual growth that you could see in the whole of Genesis.

YEAR TWO

Read

Powell, Chapter 5, "Matthew," pages 103–123

Focus

Define: five speeches of Jesus; Beatitudes; binding and loosing of the law; *oligopistoi*; Eusebius; *Ecclesiastical History*

What light did Powell's commentary shed on the Gospel of Matthew?

How did you respond to the commentary?

YEAR THREE

Read

MacCulloch, Chapter 4, "Boundaries Defined," pages 112–154

References to primary sources are sprinkled throughout the chapter. Read two or three of the sources, which can be found in Bettenson's *Documents of the Christian Church* and online. Christian Classics Ethereal Library, www.ccel.org provides numerous documents of the church. For example, http://www.ccel.org/ccel/richardson/fathers.viii.i.iii.html presents *The Teaching of the Twelve Apostles, Commonly Called the Didache.*

Focus

Define: *Hermas* (*The Shepherd*) and the *Didache* online or in Bettenson (if you have purchased that book) or elsewhere and read what you can or want; Letter to Philemon; *Didache*; gnosis, Gnosticism, Nag Hammadi; Docetism; key points of difference between gnostic and Jewish attitudes; Marcion; Diatessaron; *presbyteroi*; *diakonos*; *episkopoi*; the importance of Antioch and Jerusalem in the early church; Clement; Ignatius; Victor; Stephen of Rome. Become familiar with pronunciation.

Describe the value and the price of boundaries in terms of growth and maturation.

YEAR FOUR

Read

Allen, Chapter 3, "The Maker of Heaven and Earth"; Chapter 4, "Limits of Science," pages 28–43

Focus

Define: Gerhard Von Rad; Israel's cosmology; Augustine's examination of time; contemporary cosmology; relationship of creation and salvation

State the difference between a biblical view of creation and a scientific view of the universe.

Distinguish between the origin of the universe and the purpose of creation.

ALL YEARS

Respond

Numerous world and personal events color all that this work of ministry education and formation is about. Uncertainty has a face. Fear, hope, anger, and suspicion grow in the face of uncertainty.

How does what you are learning in the EfM study and reflection address moments of mounting anxiety?

Practice

The following is an exercise in very informal theological reflection.

Create a picture that captures a personal anxiety.

Write one or two paragraphs about that image.

What prompts anxiety for someone in that image? What would someone in that image fear?

From your study, what ideas or people have you discovered that would help someone in that image make sense of things when they are anxious?

What past experience comes to mind that helps you deal with anxiety?

What do you believe or hope for about anxiety and Christian maturity?

Who can you think of in your culture that could offer wisdom for someone in the face of anxiety?

Notice discoveries you have made.

Sit quietly with any prayer that may surface in response to what you wrote.

Week Seven

YEAR ONE

Read

Exodus 1–15
Collins, Chapter 5, "The Exodus from Egypt," pages 63–72

Focus

Define: Manetho; Hyksos; Hecataeus; Rameses II; Habiru; *Yam Sup*; Passover; "charter myth"; history; legend; folklore; founding myth; YHWH; Adonai (Lord); *HaShem*; *'ehyeh 'aser* (I AM WHO I AM); *'ehyeh*; *eimi ho on* (I am the one who is); absolute Being; YHWH is on the side of the weak; "salvation history"

Name the images/metaphors for God that the writer of Exodus used to tell the story of God's action of liberation for the children of Israel. Select two or three of the images for God and explore the qualities of God the image reveals.

How is the relationship between God and creation/humankind/Israel maturing?

YEAR TWO

Read

The Gospel according to Mark
Powell, Chapter 6, "Mark," pages 125–145

Focus

Define: John Mark; intercalation; major themes in Mark; messianic secret; *inclusio*

Every discussion, written or spoken, draws on some material. The content (images, story, and ideas) comes from sources that may be other writings, personal experiences, or beliefs held. Make note of the sources that Powell uses throughout his discussion of Mark.

YEAR THREE

Read

MacCulloch, Chapter 5, "The Prince: Ally or Enemy," pages 155–188

Focus

Define: *parousia*; *Apostolic Tradition*; Celus; *in catacumbas*; Origen; Plotinus; Mani; Manichee/Manichaean; Diocletian; Syriac Church; Osrhoene; Dura Europos; Armenia; Ephren; *Odes of Solomon*; Trdat (Tiridates)

Christianity not only survived but grew under the wave of persecutions from 100 to 300 CE. The understanding that people are willing to suffer and die for what they believe wields powerful inspirations. When religious conviction is stronger than the fear of pain and death, people notice. It's as if the persecutors' sword sharpens one's beliefs into passionate convictions. Clarity comes whenever a person discovers relationships that matter more than death. The witness born from martyrdom has transformative power for both believers and non-believers.

What evidence of martyrs, if any, can you think of in your time and place?

How do those actions reveal something of maturing in a relationship with God?

YEAR FOUR

Read

Allen, 5 "What is Meant by 'God,'" pages 44–53

Focus

Define: universe as everything but God; hiddenness of God; cosmological argument for existence of God; faith as above reason

Answer Allen's question, "What is meant by God?"

How has that answer changed as you have matured in your relationship with God?

ALL YEARS

Respond

Summarize your learning from the unit's study.

What stands out for you as a key discovery in these first weeks of EfM?

What have you learned about listening?

Using a few words for each category, describe the micro (individual), meso (institutional), and macro (global/cosmic) levels of your life. Refer to Vander Ven's categories on pages 13–14 in Week Two if you need to refresh your memory.

What do you value, assume, and seek for yourself and others?

Compline

The Lord Almighty grant us a peaceful night
✠ and a perfect end. **Amen.**

Our help is in the Name of the Lord;
The maker of heaven and earth.

O God, ✠ make speed to save us.
O Lord, make haste to help us.

Glory be to the Father, and to the Son, and to the Holy Ghost: as it was in the beginning, is now, and ever shall be, world without end. Amen.

Alleluia.

Psalm 134 *Ecce Nunc*
[1] Behold now, bless the Lord, all you servants of the Lord, *
you that stand by night in the house of the Lord.
[2] Lift up your hands in the holy place and bless the Lord; *
the Lord who made heaven and earth bless you out of Zion.

Glory be to the Father, and to the Son, and to the Holy Ghost: as it was in the beginning, is now, and ever shall be, world without end. Amen.

Thou art in the midst of us, O Lord, and we are called by thy Name: Do not forsake us. *Jeremiah 14:9, 22*
Thanks be to God.

Into thy hands, O Lord, I commend my spirit;
For thou hast redeemed me, O Lord, O God of truth.
Keep us, O Lord, as the apple of thy eye;
Hide us under the shelter of thy wings.
Lord, have mercy upon us.
Christ, have mercy upon us.
Lord, have mercy upon us.
Our Father...but deliver us from evil. Amen.

O Lord, hear our prayer.
And let our cry come unto thee.
Let us pray.

r example, home,

ıgh these areas.

ce, from the world

:s, or doubts.
ıined and what com-

ıat you especially
areas of your life.

Be present, O merciful God, and protect us through the hours of this night, that we who are wearied by the [illegible] eternal changelessness; through Jesus Christ our Lord. Amen.

Keep watch, dear Lord, with those who [illegible] watch, or weep this night, and give thy angels charge over those who [illegible] weary, bless the dying, soothe the [illegible] shield the joyous; and all for thy love's sake. Amen.

Guide us waking, [illegible] awake we may watch [illegible] may rest in peace.

The Song of Simeon *Nunc Dimittis*

Lord, ✠ now lettest thou thy servant depart in peace, according to thy word. For mine eyes have seen thy salvation, which thou hast prepared before the face of all people, to be a light to lighten the Gentiles and to be the glory of thy people Israel. *Luke 2:29-32*

Glory be to the Father, and to the Son, and to the Holy Ghost: as it was in the beginning, is now and ever shall be, world without end. Amen.

Guide us waking, O Lord, and guard us sleeping; that awake we may watch with Christ, and asleep we may rest in peace.

Alleluia, alleluia, alleluia.

Let us bless the Lord.
Thanks be to God.

The almighty and merciful Lord, Father, Son, and Holy Spirit, ✠ bless us and keep us. Amen.

UNIT TWO

Theological Reflection as a Life Skill

Week Eight

ALL YEARS

Read

Seeking Meaning

When something happens, those involved in the moment almost immediately begin searching for the meaning or significance of the event. Questions of "Why did this happen?," "Why me?," "Why not me?," "What does this mean?," or "What might I do?" surface. A young boy who constantly asks "What does that mean?" may hear from a weary parent, "Does everything have to have a meaning?" The child's immediate, "What do you mean by that?" is met with a smile.

Human beings seem to have the need for meaning-making hard-wired into our brains. How the sky looks at night or in the morning elicits an adage: "Red sky at night, sailor's delight. Red sky at morning, sailors take warning." Such sayings meet a basic human concern to have confidence in or knowledge of the future. Even in St. Matthew's Gospel when Jesus reminds people of their desire to "read the times" he says, "When it is evening, you say, 'It will be fair weather, for the sky is red.' And in the morning, 'It will be stormy today, for the sky is red and threatening.' You know how to interpret the appearance of the sky, but you cannot interpret the signs of the times." (Matthew 16:2–3)

Desire to know the future is but one side of the desire to make meaning out of the raw experiences of life. Past events are sometimes interpreted and re-interpreted when present circumstances change and bring unexpected surprises or unwanted encounters. Searching for the meaning of present realities may change how past events are understood while a shift in present situations also can reshape how the future is envisioned.

Theological reflection is one way to find meaning in daily life in relation to God. Reflection is a natural process done regularly to make sense out of experience; theological reflection centers that meaning-making around concerns that are ultimate. The ongoing practice of individual and group theological reflection through the EfM year provides a way to become more skilled at viewing daily life through a theological lens. The process used in EfM to facilitate theological reflection developed out of observing how seeking, inquiring people discover meaning and value that is pertinent to living more faithfully and maturely as a Christian. The terms used in the EfM reflection process may be unfamiliar at first, but the realities to which they point are part of the universal human experience.

Theological Reflection as a Search for Wisdom

Theology, like other "-ologies," speaks of the search for knowing and knowledge. Specifically, as used in EfM, theology is knowing God as God has been revealed through the Christian tradition. EfM's approach to theology is part of a stream of practical theological learning that found expression as theological education faced a crisis in the concluding decades of the last century, forcing a reexamination of its aim. One of the first scholars to carefully rethink the purpose of theological education, especially within seminaries, was Edward Farley, who extended the meaning and purpose of theological education to include the acquisition of "sapient knowledge" or practical wisdom. For Farley, theological learning seeks wisdom within the existential concerns of everyday living. He summarized his understanding of theological education in an interview for *The Christian Century* in February 1998:

> My point is that theological education cannot be reduced to the learning of clerical skills or to scholarly knowledge. . . . My assumption is that all Christians are inevitably engaged every day in existential responses to the world, and that theology concerns the wisdom by which one brings the resources of a religious tradition to bear on the world. This task calls not for indifference or innocence or naïveté but wisdom–the ability to assess what is going on and to appraise new possibilities. To put it another way, in living out of the inherited symbols and narratives of one's faith, one isn't just applying dead truths to a living situation. Instead, one is embodying or incorporating oneself into a living tradition. That's a creative act and an interpretive act, an act of theological understanding.[12]

In the discipline of theological reflection EfM lays the foundation for a person to begin the life-long process of seeking theological understanding in the service of ministry. In the words of Farley, the task is one of "incorporating oneself into a living tradition." In EfM the discipline of theological reflection is a primary means of embodying a dynamic, vibrant, living tradition.

If the purpose of theological study is "sapient knowledge"–that is, learning how to live more wisely–then understanding wisdom is of paramount importance. David Ford writes:

> The pursuit of wisdom is found in most civilizations and their religious, philosophical, and cultural traditions. Even when the word "wisdom" is not used, it is often present through concerns for sound, intelligent judgment and decision making, prudent discernment of priorities, long-term flourishing of people and societies, the avoidance of foolishness and stupidity, and the combining of knowledge, values, and appropriate practices. Most of us would agree that wisdom is to be desired in a parent, a leader, a counselor, a teacher, and indeed in any responsible role and in everyone's life. At its best, it not only seeks

12. *The Christian Century,* February 1998, 113–115, 149.

overall meaning, understanding, and truth, both broad and deep, but also tries to connect this with practical responses to specific situations. Because both understanding and situations change, wisdom needs to improvise continually.[13]

Wisdom (sapient knowledge) joins meaning, understanding, and truth with practical responses to specific situations. Not a possession to be gained, wisdom is rather a lover's pursuit. The Wisdom of Solomon broadens the meaning and speaks to the experience of seeking wisdom.[14]

Wisdom is radiant and unfading,
and she is easily discerned by those who love her,
and is found by those who seek her.
She hastens to make herself known to those who desire her.
One who rises early to seek her will have no difficulty,
for she will be found sitting at the gate.
To fix one's thought on her is perfect understanding,
and one who is vigilant on her account will soon be free from care,
because she goes about seeking those worthy of her,
and she graciously appears to them in their paths,
and meets them in every thought.

The beginning of wisdom is the most sincere desire for instruction,
and concern for instruction is love of her,
and love of her is the keeping of her laws,
and giving heed to her laws is assurance of immortality,
and immortality brings one near to God;
so the desire for wisdom leads to a kingdom.
Wisdom of Solomon 6: 12–20

Wisdom comes from God: "Therefore I prayed, and understanding was given me; I called on God, and the spirit of wisdom came to me" (Wisdom of Solomon 7:7). The passage continues until it becomes clear that wisdom not only is given by God but is indeed an aspect of God's own self. Thus wisdom is not only a gift from God but the gift of God to the seeker.

For she is a breath of the power of God,
and a pure emanation of the glory of the Almighty;
therefore nothing defiled gains entrance into her.
For she is a reflection of eternal light,
a spotless mirror of the working of God,

13. David F. Ford, *The Drama of Living* (Norwich, UK: Canterbury, 2014), Kindle Edition, location 529–535.

14. In the Bible the Wisdom of Solomon is found in the Apocrypha in the Protestant tradition, but is included in the Hebrew Scriptures in the Roman Catholic and Orthodox traditions. Learn more at Oxford Biblical Studies Online www.oxfordbiblicalstudies.com.

and an image of his goodness.
Although she is but one, she can do all things,
and while remaining in herself, she renews all things;
in every generation she passes into holy souls
and makes them friends of God, and prophets;
Wisdom of Solomon 7:25–27

Theological reflection, when seen as the pursuit of wisdom, the "breath of the power of God and a pure emanation of the Glory of the Almighty," is thus a spiritual discipline for seeking an ever-deepening relationship with God.

All relationships, especially in a culture of complexity and rapid change, require some degree of improvisation. The continual flux of society presents new and even unprecedented questions, concerns, and issues that require a person to learn in the moment. Peter Vaill characterizes living in the world as navigating "permanent white water." A professor of business management, he initially drew out the implications of the metaphor to apply them to the education of managers, describing the attitude a person must assume to function well in the contemporary world. Successful navigation in a "white water world," according to Vaill, requires practicing integrated learning disciplines to discover insights and implications in the midst of day-to-day activities.

Vaill then extends his vision of learning beyond the category of business management.

> I have chosen to write mainly about the world of work, but are we going to say that family life is exempt from white water? Recreational life? Devotional and spiritual life? Life as a citizen of a community and nation? Life as a participant in various voluntary groups? Life as a sports fan or participant? Retirement life? . . . Since turbulent conditions appear everywhere and pervade our lives in both time and space, learning in permanent white water conditions is and will continue to be a constant way of life for all of us–thus the phrase *learning as a way of being.*[15]

As EfM evolved, participants gradually came to understand that theological learning relevant to complex and ever-changing lives must be an ongoing endeavor. Remember David Ford's insight: "Because both understanding and situations change, wisdom needs to improvise continually."

Improvisation, in this sense, is not making things up on the spot. It is a fresh expression pertinent to a specific moment that is created out of a dialogue with knowledge developed by Christians who have gone before us. *Learning as a way of being Christian* is an apt phrase to describe the way into the wisdom found in Christian maturity.

15. Peter B. Vaill, *Learning as a Way of Being: Strategies for Survival in a World of Permanent White Water* (San Francisco: Jossey-Bass Publications, 1996), 42–43.

In 2004, then Archbishop of Canterbury Rowan Williams addressed the Centre for Anglican Communion Studies (CEFACS) on theological education, where he raised the question, "What does it mean to be a theologically educated person?"

> So in thinking about what is Theological Education I want to think about what a theologically educated person might be like. . . . Now I want to suggest that a theologically educated person is somebody who has acquired the skill of reading the world, reading and interpreting the world, in the context and framework of Christian belief and Christian worship. . . .That means that a theologically educated person is not someone who simply knows a great deal about the Bible or history of doctrine but somebody who is able to engage in some quite risky and innovative interpretation, and who is able, if I can put it this way, to recognise holy lives.[16]

Reading the world; engaging in "risky and innovative interpretation;" and knowing what an exemplary life looks like–all lived in the context of doctrine and worship–are results that can be gained from careful study and courageous reflection done within a learning community such as the EfM seminar group.

Theological Reflection in EfM

> At a basic level, one is confronted with the question: how can I discern how to act faithfully in the world if I do not reflect on both my faith and my experience of the world? When looked at in this way, theological reflection can be said to be fundamental to living faithfully in the world: it is the process through which we constantly deepen our understanding of ourselves, others and God and of how we integrate this understanding in our lives so that what we do becomes congruent in any given context with who we are as people and as communities of faith. In this view, theological reflection is not something that theologians do, nor is it merely an intellectual exercise; rather theological reflection lies at the heart of the Christian commitment to live faithfully in the world for the sake of the world that God loves.[17]

Simply put, theological reflection is considering one's life "in the context and framework of Christian belief and Christian worship" in order to "live faithfully in the world for the sake of the world that God loves."

The method for theological reflection in EfM follows a progression in four movements: identify, explore, connect, apply.

First, an individual or group ***identifies*** *a distinct topic on which to focus.*

Next, the individual or group ***explores*** *the focus by examining it through a theological framework.* The traditional terms for this kind of framework draw

16. http://rowanwilliams.archbishopofcanterbury.org/articles.php/1847/cefacs-lecture-birmingham-centre-for-anglican-communion-studies

17. John Reader, Victoria Slater, Helen Cameron, *Theological Reflection for Human Flourishing: Pastoral Practice and Public Theology* (Norwich, UK: SCM Press, 2012), 2.

themes from systematic theology. Creation, sin, judgment, repentance, and redemption describe one pattern commonly recognized as recurring through the story of God's people. Another way to conceptualize them includes terms such as wholeness/goodness; brokenness/alienation; recognition/awareness; reorientation/repentance; and restoration/redemption. This way may help us see the framework in terms of a more universal human experience.

Exploration leads to *relating **(connecting)** the focus to sources of wisdom* such as Christian scripture, theological teaching, hymns, liturgy and other writings of Christians throughout history. Additionally, other connections can be made to cultural sources of wisdom from literature, the arts, music, drama, or simply in the words of "a parent, a leader, a counselor, a teacher, and indeed in any responsible role and in everyone's life."[18]

Finally, the reflection considers ***application** to one's life.* Australian theologian John E. Paver observes that reflecting theologically increases the awareness of God's presence in daily life.

> As a method for integration, theological reflection's primary focus is one that happens at the intersection of what one believes and how one lives out that belief, and the centre of the process is in the discovery of the movement of the spirit of God in human experience. In addition it seeks to know how God's presence makes a difference to one's ministry.[19]

The discovery of God's presence in human experience and how that presence makes a difference is the life-blood of theological reflection. Without this fourth movement, theological reflection may be just an entertaining, or boring, exercise with little relevance to daily living. Over time the regular practice of theological reflection contributes to an integration that moves a person more fully toward theological maturity.

What is the purpose of theological reflection? The question that might better be asked is "What are the *purposes* of theological reflection?" Brett Morgan, an Anglican priest from Australia, identifies several conceptions of theological reflection that resonate with EfM's approach to theological reflection as a life skill for ministry:[20]

- Theological reflection as an educational method for integrating theory and practice
- Theological reflection as a way to develop insight
- Theological reflection as a process to inform action
- Theological reflection to develop consistent thinking
- Theological reflection as a discipline for critical activity

18. Ford, *The Drama of Living*, Kindle Edition, location 489.

19. John E. Paver, "Formation and Transformation in Theological Reflection," *Ministry, Society and Theology*, Vol. 10, No. 2, 1996, 94.

20. Brett Morgan, "What are we looking for in theological reflection?" *Ministry, Society and Theology*, Vol. 13, No. 2, 1999, 6–12.

Each of these purposes contributes to a needed set of skills for ministry that accrue as a person regularly practices theological reflection.

The *SCM Studyguide to Theological Reflection* defines theological reflection as "a process of coming to know God through reflecting on God's world in the light of resources from the tradition."[21] Participating in the EfM program week by week brings increased knowledge of the Christian tradition. Knowledge grows as human beings are able to make distinctions, and it is with considerable justification that "to know" has been equated with "to distinguish." When our distinctions are not clear, our knowledge is confused.[22] Practice in making clear distinctions helps reduce confusion and increase knowledge.

Theological reflection in EfM relies on a four-source model to guide reflection. A source is that from which something is drawn. When someone asks, "Where did you get that idea?" the inquirer wants to know the origin of the material. As people within a group discuss a topic, it is important to make distinctions in the responses, especially regarding the source from which one draws in responding or reflecting.

EfM uses four basic categories to infer meaning: **Christian Tradition; Culture/Society; Action (personal experience/behavior); and Position (personal beliefs/opinions)**. A person's proficiencies in reflecting theologically are dependent on clearly distinguishing these four sources.

The first fundamental distinction to understand is that the four sources can be grouped into two categories: data from outside a person and data from within the person–*their* knowledge and *my* knowledge. The Tradition and Culture sources refer to knowledge that comes from outside an individual. Action and Position are sources derived from within a person. A document or artifact either belongs to a faith Tradition or a Culture (or a combination of the two sources). One's reaction to the content of the document may evoke a memory of an experience (Action source) or elicit an opinion or belief (Position source).

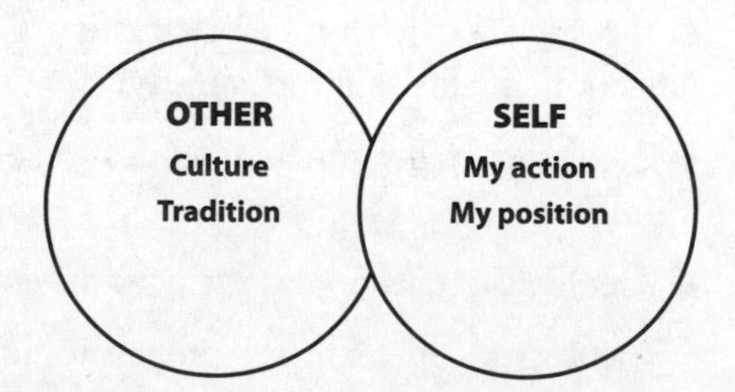

It is not helpful to get too tied to "this belongs to Cephas and this belongs to Paul" thinking, attempting to be "right" about which source some-

21. Judith Thompson, Stephen Pattison, Ross Thompson, *SCM Studyguide to Theological Reflection* (London: SCM Press, 2006), 57.

22. Arthur A. Vogel, *God, Prayer & Healing* (Grand Rapids, MI: William B. Eerdmans Publishing Company, 1995), 36.

thing may reflect. There are other ways to think about these sources. The reality is that while one may recall something learned from a school book or prayer book (Culture or Tradition), that learning does become integrated into the self in some way. The point is to recognize that it is possible to turn to each of these sources to help make sense out of something that has prompted a question such as "What's this about?" or "What am I to do?"

Within the two basic categories further distinctions are made. The ideas, narratives, images, and facts that come from outside a person are considered to have either the Christian tradition as their source or some aspect of the shared culture. One identifying characteristic of either the Tradition or Culture source is that the content exists independently from the individual self. For example, a quotation from the Bible or a line from a contemporary poet has a voice independent of the individual who is reading either. Each exists outside the reader and may have existed before the person and will continue after the person is gone. Much of the material from the Tradition source and/or the Culture source comes from those who have gone before the one who reads or hears them.

Ideas, images, and stories that an individual holds come from the Self category. The specific, unique experience that a person has (according to the EfM vocabulary) comes from the Action source. The meaning the person makes of the experience creates the person's Position source. When a person reads a passage from literature the content may evoke memories of a past experience or elicit an opinion about it. A memory of a past experience would be considered as coming from the Action source and the person's opinion about its truth or validity from the Position source. These connections are part of the attempt to make meaning or sense out of what one reads, hears, or experiences.

When a point of reflection arises, such as reading or hearing something that gives pause, or taking part in an activity or having something happen that causes one to ask questions of meaning or purpose, then it is important to know how to discern the sources in order that they may be brought into conversation with one another so that new or fresh meaning emerges. Identifying sources is a first step in reflection. That reflection becomes theological when questions arise about the nature of creation, of humankind, of temptations and judgments, of the possibility for repentance and restoration. Inviting connections to the four sources opens new perspectives. As the sources each find expression, a fresh meaning or insight often occurs.

The meaning may be in the form an assertion or affirmation of a truth; in understanding what should or must be done; in a better and more significant question; in a sense of needing to explore or give the "insight" a try; or in uncovering of a deep desire, interest, passion, or yearning. It is from affirmations formed, imperatives uncovered, questions clarified or deepened, explorations invited, or desires voiced that an individual can see implications for ministry in daily life. Theological reflection experienced over time can move one toward becoming an authentic, wiser, more mature practicing Christian.

Reaching Christian maturity is not a singular event, but a life-long process. Wisdom for living is a matter of growth over time. Maturity and wisdom result from continual engagement of learning, experiencing, reflecting, and striving toward the integration of all levels of human life. The intentional and deliberate engagement with individual, social, and global concerns, questions, and issues moves one toward wholeness and integration within an ongoing relationship with God within the Christian community. It is an incarnating process guided by the "breath of the power of God" within Christian learning and worship.

Focus

Define: existential; sapient knowledge; four movements of theological reflection; theological perspectives; wisdom; theological reflection; four source model

Respond

Describe ways in which you have grown in wisdom.

The unit's introductory essay makes the case that theological reflection happens naturally when a group or individual experiences something that causes them to ask some questions in a search for meaning, in an attempt to make sense of a circumstance. State your understanding of the purpose of formal theological reflection and how it proceeds.

Identify some ways in which the skill of theological reflection might be necessary to Christian ministry.

Practice

Image and metaphor are often the best language for talking about God or an experience of God. Shepherd, fire, wind, and father are some metaphors that have been used in this way. In theological reflection, image and metaphor can help a group find a common language or a universal language, rather than to remain focused on one individual's experience. When all in a group can identify with a more universal image, the tendency to problem-solve and give advice is also lessened.

Images can be used to represent feelings and thoughts that someone has in a given moment. For an individual or a group, progressing from a set of thoughts and feelings to an image helps to open an experience to a larger, more universal context.

As a way to practice just the skill of creating images or metaphors from thoughts and feelings, use the following sets of thoughts and feelings to create images that reflect those dynamics.

FEELINGS: ANGRY, SAD, TIRED **THOUGHT: I CAN'T DO THIS ANYMORE**

Sit quietly with these thoughts and feelings. What is it like when you have them? Feel their heat, their color, what they smell like, taste like, where you feel them in your body.

Create a picture of those thoughts and feelings. When you have those thoughts and feelings, it is like_________: For example, someone might say, "When I feel that way, it's like a dying fire."

Name times when life seemed like that image you have created.

FEELINGS: JOYFUL, EXPECTANT, WONDER **THOUGHTS: IS THIS REAL? I CAN'T WAIT!**

Sit quietly for a few minutes with those thoughts and feelings. Think about what it's like when you feel that way. Feel what the heat, color, smell, or taste of those feelings is like. Where do you feel those thoughts and feelings in your body?

Create a picture of those thoughts and feelings. When you have those thoughts and feelings, it is like_________. Example: Someone having those thoughts and feelings might say, "It's like finding treasure."

Name times when life seemed like that image you have created.

Write briefly about a time when life felt like the picture you created above.

What do you discover?

Listen for metaphors in the talking or writing of others or yourself this week.

A list of some additional reading on theological reflection is on page 204 in Part II of this Guide.

Week Nine

YEAR ONE

Read

Exodus 16–40
Collins, Chapter 6, "Revelation at Sinai," pages 73–84

Focus

Define: Mosaic/Sinai covenant; the distinction between covenant and contract; Hittite treaties; Assyrian treaties; vassal treaty; theophany; Baal; Asherah; Festival of Unleavened Bread; Sukkoth; Book of the Covenant; apodictic law; casuistic law; Yahwist Decalogue; ritual Decalogue; unwritten (oral) law

The opening essay in Unit One describes a way of understanding spiritual maturity as that of a life of striving for wholeness, acting wisely, assuming responsibility, and living authentically. In what way did the covenant contribute to Israel's maturing faith?

YEAR TWO

Read

The Gospel according to Luke

Focus

What do you understand to have been Luke's purpose in writing this gospel and what is your evidence?

The opening essay in Unit One describes a way of understanding spiritual maturity as that of a life of striving for wholeness, acting wisely, assuming responsibility, and living authentically. Who matured in faith in this gospel and how did that occur?

YEAR THREE

Read

MacCulloch, Chapter 6, "The Imperial Church," pages 189–228

Focus

Define: Constantine; *Hagia Sophia*; Helena, Athanasius, Basil, Arius, Miaphysites, Nestorius; dates: 312, 325, 481; *homoousion, homoios, hypostasis, ousia, Theotokos*; monasticism; *The Acts of Thomas*; Councils; Chalcedonian Definition

The opening essay in Unit One describes a way of understanding spiritual maturity as that of a life of striving for wholeness, acting wisely, assuming responsibility, and living authentically. Name some examples of how the church was maturing in faith at this point in history and who or what contributed to that.

YEAR FOUR

Read

Allen, Chapter 6, "Nature as Witness and Innocent Suffering," pages 57–67

Focus

Witness

Define: three elements of witness; nature's witness; inner witness; Testament; Job; *Vindicator*; William Temple

What or who has provided witness of God to you?

How has that witness contributed to the maturing of your faith?

ALL YEARS

Respond

This unit adds theological reflection as a skill that supports maturing in faith. This week, all four years studied about significant events in the life of people of faith, individually and corporately. Identify aspects of theological reflection in what you studied this week.

In what ways would you identify that the Church (the big C church) is maturing in faith?

Practice

This practice focuses on the two "interior" reflection sources, Action/Experience and Personal Position/Belief using Van der Ven's three levels for examination.

Identifying the Action/Experience Source

Responses in the following areas concern a piece of the Action source to which you might turn when sorting out the meaning of something that has affected you.

Micro level (individual)–particular persons, actions, events, and physical experiences shape an individual's identity.

Name one person who has significantly contributed to your growth as a Christian, someone to whom you might turn (or have turned in the past)

for guidance or wisdom. This person may be someone you personally know or have known, or be a figure you have encountered through reading or other means.

Meso level (regional)–the communal dimension of human experience. The institutions of family, religion, school, government, business (among many other givens) produce the self that is "we."

Name one aspect of your community or regional environment that has significantly contributed to your growth as a Christian, for example, a group or institution that would help you find meaning in a circumstance.

Macro level (global)–the social and intellectual era out of which a person comes.

Name one aspect of the global environment that has significantly contributed to your growth as a Christian.

Identifying the Personal Position/Belief Source

The micro, meso, and macro dimensions of life influence how Christian maturity can be understood and developed. What is valued, assumed, and sought after shapes the world in which an adult Christian lives.

What values or assumptions about God have you formed? These represent a piece of the Positon/Belief source from which you draw in response to things that happen in your life.

If possible, identify some sources that have influenced these assumptions at the micro, meso, and macro levels.

What have you become aware of about yourself as you worked through this piece of a reflection? Are there images that came to mind? How did the Christian tradition contribute to your responses?

How does this awareness relate to how you minister in the world around you each day?

Week Ten

YEAR ONE

Read

Leviticus
Numbers
Collins, Chapter 7, "Priestly Theology: Exodus 25–40, Leviticus & Numbers," pages 85–96

Focus

Define: Tabernacle; sacrificial system; Day of Atonement; stories of Nadab and Abihu and of Korah; impurity laws; Holiness Code; relationship of ethics and holiness; Cultic Calendar; Book of Numbers

Use the spiritual maturity areas of striving for wholeness, acting wisely, assuming responsibility, and living authentically to connect the role played by laws and codes to Israel's maturing relationship with God.

YEAR TWO

Read

Powell, Chapter 7, "Luke," pages 147–167

Focus

Define: Theophilus; "the beloved physician"; Luke's Gospel in relationship to the "Acts of the Apostles"; the major themes in the Gospel of Luke; passages from Luke widely used in Christian liturgies

What interests or concerns you in Powell's presentation of Luke's Gospel?

What do you think makes the Gospel of Luke sacred literature?

What part might this gospel have played in the Christian community's maturing in faith?

YEAR THREE

Read

MacCulloch, Chapter 7, "Defying Chalcedon (kal-**SEE**-dun): Asia and Africa)," pages 231–254

Focus

Define: *The Life of Balaam and Joasaph*; Tome of Leo; *Henotikon*; Jacob Baradeus; Syriac Orthodox Church; Armenian Church; *Trisagion*; Dyophsite Christians; failure of the Marib Dam; School of the Persians in Edessa; "Mar Thoma" Church; Thomas Christians

Note: An eBook English translation of *The Life of Balaam and Joasaph* can be found at http://omacl.org/Barlaam/

Identify a central opposition that one individual or group had to Chalcedon.

What part might the Chalcedonian statements have played in Christian maturity?

YEAR FOUR

Read

Allen, Chapter 7, "Innocent Suffering and Life Beyond Death," pages 68–73

Focus

Define: transformation of suffering; suffering as punishment for sin; prosperity as mark of righteousness; wrong doing results in suffering; injustices of innocent suffering prompt affirmation of life beyond death; omnipotence–can do anything; almighty–having authority over all things; the problem of natural evil

Describe your understanding of a relationship between transformation of suffering and Christian maturity.

ALL YEARS

Respond

Laws and codes serve purposes and sometimes prompt defiance.

Name some circumstances of that conflict in your life. These would be times when you were part of challenging a "law" or "code" in some way.

Practice

THEOLOGICAL REFLECTION BEGINNING WITH A PERSONAL EXPERIENCE

Practice is necessary to refine any skill. To continue practicing theological reflection, use the time before the next seminar session to reflect on a personal circumstance of conflict over a law or code that you were able to recall in the Respond section.

The movement of theological reflection is: Identify a focus, Explore the focus, Connect the focus to other areas/sources, and Apply learning.

Identify a focus.

In writing, describe the conflict you recalled in the Respond section. This places you in the Action/Experience source of your life; you recall something you've experienced or done.

Narrow the narrative by looking for a point in the conflict that had high energy.

Name your thoughts and feelings at that point of energy.

Draw a picture of a metaphor that illustrates what it was like when you had those thoughts and feelings. Think about color, sensation, heat/cold, location in your body of energy or tension. When you have/had those thoughts and feelings, it's as if. . . .

Explore the focus with theological perspectives.

Continue the reflection using your picture and considering these questions.

A reflection takes on theological strength by viewing the image/picture, issue, or matter through some theological lenses, asking questions concerning the nature of the world, the relationship of God to the world, the nature of repentance and forgiveness, the nature of human community, or the quality of redemption and restoration of relationship. These are also known as theological perspectives, sometimes identified by the terms Creation, Sin, Judgment, Repentance, and Redemption/Resurrection.

In the picture you created, what kind of interaction do you see?

How is that interaction revealing goodness or brokenness?

What kind of relationship does God have with those in that world?

What kind of relationships exist in that picture?

What crises are suggested in that picture?

What would persons in that kind of picture-world hope for?

Connect to other sources.

What personal beliefs (Position source) come to mind as you reflect on the picture and the world it captured?

Who or what in the Christian story (Tradition) or the world around you (Culture) helps you make sense of the world in the picture? In those sources, who are the wisdom figures or groups to help or guide you in a moment like you pictured?

Apply learning.

Theological reflection remains only an interesting exercise if learning is not embodied in ministry.

What prayer would you offer to God as a result of your reflection?

Name two areas in which you have the opportunity to minister in your life.

How will this reflection make any difference as you live in those areas?

How has your EfM study given you a way to view the circumstances of your life?

Week Eleven

YEAR ONE

Read

Deuteronomy
Collins, Chapter 8, "Deuteronomy," pages 97–108

Focus

As you read Deuteronomy in your Bible, define the Mosaic covenant and notice how the covenant underwent renewal and reinterpretation.

How does the Mosaic covenant's renewal and reinterpretation relate to the process of maturing in knowing God?

YEAR TWO

Read

The Gospel of John

Focus

Make note of anything you had to look up and any surprising ideas or images that you found in reading John's Gospel. Especially note how John's Gospel presented the message of Jesus.

Compare John's proclamation of good news (*kerygma*) with the other gospel evangelists' proclamations.

YEAR THREE

Read

MacCulloch, Chapter 8, "Islam: the Great Realignment," pages 255–285

Focus

Define: *Qur'an*; *al-ilah* (Allah); how Christian *divisions* contributed to Muslim conquests; Mosques of Umar (Dome of the Rock); John of Damascus; Timothy I; Ta Qin monastery; Bishop Alopen's writing; Khan of the Keratis' vision of St. Sergius; Kublai Khan and Dyophysite Christianity; Christians of Bagdad; North African Church; Coptic patriarchs; Ethiopian Christianity; *The Miracles of Mary*; Prester John myth

YEAR FOUR

Read

Allen, Chapter 8, "Suffering from Nature & Extreme Human Cruelty," pages 74–84

Focus

Define: David Hume's view of the natural world in relation to humanity's well-being; the Stoic Epictetus's view of humankind in relation to nature; Iulia de Beausobre and her experience with suffering at the hand of human cruelty; God's love in the midst of suffering; two possible responses to the Holocaust

ALL YEARS

Respond

What issues of Christian maturity would you say are present in this week's study?

Which level might those issues be related to: micro/individual, meso/institutional, or macro/global?

Practice

THEOLOGICAL REFLECTION BEGINNING WITH THE CHRISTIAN TRADITION

Identify the focus or a primary point of your EfM study this week.

Explore the primary point by identifying the theological perspectives of the world, sin, judgment, repentance, and/or redemption reflected in that focus. Apply any of these or similar theological questions to your consideration.

What view of the world is present in that focus?

What brokenness or sin does that focus address or reveal?

What questions or crises does that focus respond to or contribute to?

How does that concern or focus lead to repentance or reorientation?

How does that concern lead to restoration to a creative life?

What does the focus say about forgiveness?

What concern about God does the focus address?
Move to the other sources

Connect by stating how the focus is present in today's world *(Culture)*.

What book or movie has dealt with this focus?

Compare and contrast the connections to the world around you with the above exploration of the focus.

What issues or concerns do you become aware of?

What personal experiences (Action) have you had that relate to this focus?

State one or two personal beliefs (Position) you have about the focus that surfaced in this reflection.

How did those beliefs form?

When has it been difficult for you to act on those beliefs?

Apply

If you could do just one thing about the concerns that surfaced in this reflection, what would that be?

Week Twelve

YEAR ONE

Read

Joshua
Judges

Focus

As you read the Book of Joshua, note the concerns of the people. Especially think about how the narrative presents the nature of God and how that understanding of God shapes their understanding of the world and of themselves.

What challenges or support for your relationship with God do the Book of Joshua and/or Judges present to you?

YEAR TWO

Read

Powell, Chapter 8, "John," pages 169–189

Focus

Define: Book of Signs; Book of Glory; Logos; beloved disciple; abundant life; Paraclete; Sacred Heart piety; Raising of Lazarus; Washing the Feet; *Christ of Saint John of the Cross*

Major themes in John's Gospel to identify: true revelation of God; Jesus as God; Glorification of Jesus in his death; world and Jews; loving one another

What challenges or support for your relationship with God does Powell's reflection on the Gospel of John present to you?

YEAR THREE

Read

MacCulloch, Chapter 9, "The Making of Latin Christianity," pages 289–318

Focus

Define: The Rome of the Popes (300–400)–*Papa*; catholic; Latin Rite; St. Lawrence; Bascilica of St. Peter; Damasus; Jerome; Vulgate

A Religion Fit for Gentlemen (300–400)–Faltonia Betitia Proba; Prudentius; Ambrose

Augustine, Shaper of the Western Church–*Confessions*; Monica; Manichaeism; *tolle lege*; Donatists; *City of God*; Pelagius; 410 CE; Augustine's analogy of Trinity; double processions of Holy Spirit

Early Monasticism in the West (400–500)–Martin; Sulpicius Severus; *capellae*; Cassian; Benedict; Rule of St. Benedict

What challenges or support for your relationship with God does MacCulloch's historical review of the Church present to you?

YEAR FOUR

Read

Allen, Chapter 9, "The Sacrifice in Creation," pages 87–95

William Porcher Dubose's essay "The Trinity," in Part II of the *Guide*, pages 184–191

By the time that Dubose had written his essay on the Trinity, he was near retirement from a long, productive, and challenging career as a professor and dean of the School of Theology of the University of the South. Before he arrived at the university he served as a soldier and then as chaplain in the Confederate Army. Wounded several times and confined as a prisoner of war, Dubose knew the dark side of humanity. Upon his release as a POW, he read his own obituary–having been reported as killed in action.

His brilliance, apparent throughout his writing, resulted in an international reputation as one of, if not the most, original and creative American theologians of the time. Dogma and experience, which DuBose understood as part of the meaning of incarnation, were in constant dialogue in all his writings.

Focus

Define (from Allen): Power of God; creator's self-renunciation; connection between God's creative self-sacrificing and human moral action; *de facto* person and moral person; doctrine of Trinity in relation to doctrine of creation; Dorothy Sayers; Iris Murdoch; W. H. Auden; Dante; Bonaventure

Define (from DuBose): *logos*; *telos*; grace of the Son; *gratia gratiata*; *gratia gratians*; love is grace *potential*; grace is love *actu*; three constituents of the gospel; *ex pare Dei*; *salvation salvans*; *ex parte hominis*. Briefly list or outline the main movements in Dubose's essay.

What part might grace play in spiritual maturation?

ALL YEARS

Respond

Name five characteristics or hallmarks that would be evident in someone who is maturing emotionally.

Name five characteristics or hallmarks that would be evident in someone who is maturing spiritually.

Practice

THEOLOGICAL REFLECTION BEGINNING WITH A PERSONAL EXPERIENCE

Read through the entire reflection outline first. Let your mind and heart receive images and memories naturally. Keep clear for yourself what the overall movement of reflection is: Getting a focus, Exploring the focus theologically, Connecting other "voices" that confirm or challenge the focus, and Applying the results to ministry in daily life. A written outline might suggest a lock-step approach, which cannot be further from the intention. Reflection is conversation, either between the individual and God or a group and God. Allow that conversation to unfold in its own way, using the outlines as guides to deepen prayerful consideration.

Identify a focus by starting from Personal Experience, describing a moment in your life when you sensed that you were maturing spiritually, even if it was just a hint of that sense.

Pick the particular moment when something occurred that gave you a sense of maturing spiritually.

Name two or three strong feelings you had at that moment and two or three thoughts at that time of awareness.

If you recall first a feeling, identify a thought that was present with that feeling. Likewise, if you recall a thought first, identify a feeling that connects with the thought. This is sometimes an easy way to get at the distinction between thoughts and feelings for a reflection.

Now form the metaphor. Take those two or three thoughts and feelings and make them into a picture or image. Ask yourself, "What is it like when I feel/think that way?"

Work to get an image that is not simply another experience. Something like, "It was like falling in love," could be an actual experience you had. If so, just think about that time, too, but still work for a metaphorical expression. A metaphorical example of thoughts and feelings that contain joy might be something like, "It was like joining a celestial dance," that is, a symbolic representation of thoughts and feelings.

Explore the focus (image or metaphor) first by telling the story of that image. Write the story.

Apply theological perspectives to the image/story. What kind of world does your image-story describe?

What is creative or good about that world?

What would damage or disrupt that world?

How are God and that world related?

Connect the focus to other sources by asking how your image relates to Culture, Christian Tradition, or Position (personal belief). For instance, is there an example of your image happening in your local community or geographic region? Is there an example of that image being threatened in your culture in some way?

Is there an example of your image in the stories or prayers of the Church?

Make notes about the connections that occur to you.

What do the connections imply for spiritual maturity?

Apply insight and learning to ministry. Would you want to bring your image more fully into the life you lead? If so, what support would you want?

What would prevent you from extending the image into ministry in the world?

What commitment are you willing, even hesitantly, to make about ministry in light of this reflection?

Week Thirteen

YEAR ONE

Read

Collins, Chapter 9, "Joshua," and Chapter 10, "Judges," pages 109–138

Focus

Judges in the Hebrew Bible are more aptly described as warlords than magistrates. Collins notes that the selection criterion for a judge is might. What purpose does that criterion serve for Israel?

As you step back into the time of Judges, why do you think these stories would have been recorded and valued?

State how the people of Israel understood God to be present at the time of Joshua and Judges.

YEAR TWO

Read

The Acts of the Apostles
Powell, Chapter 9, "Acts," pages 191–213

Focus

Note the key points in the differences and the goals of Paul and Peter.

Define: the role of the Church in Jerusalem; Stephen; the relationship between Paul and the Roman Empire

What does Luke's Acts of the Apostles reveal of Paul's maturing in the faith?

How is that journey familiar or foreign to your experience?

YEAR THREE

Read

MacCulloch, Chapter 10, "Latin Christendom: New Frontiers," pages 319–362

Focus

MacCulloch organizes five hundred years of Latin Christian history around several areas:

- Changing Allegiances: Rome, Byzantium, and Others
- Mission in Northern Europe (500–600)

- Obedient Anglo-Saxons and Other Converts (600–800)
- Charlemagne, Carolingians, and a New Roman Empire (800–1000)

Identify key persons and events related to each historical era, especially noticing how MacCulloch's presentation sheds light on the "human capacity for relationship."

What image might describe the Church during the historical period of 500–1000 CE?

YEAR FOUR

Read

Allen, Chapter 10, "The Incarnation as Sacrifice," pages 96–106

Focus

Define: God's self-limitation; incarnation as sacrifice; "dwelling place of God"; Kierkegaard's allegory in *Philosophical Fragments*; concept from geometry to point to Jesus' divinity and humanity; miracles ("signs of wonder," "deeds of power," "mighty works") and natural science

How does Allen's reflection on the Incarnation deepen or challenge your understanding of that central teaching of the Church?

ALL YEARS

Respond

One way to think of Incarnation is as Presence, the Presence of God. In your study, what impact did the Presence of God have on the lives of those who had that experience of God?

Practice

THEOLOGICAL REFLECTION BEGINNING WITH A PERSONAL EXPERIENCE

Identify a reflection focus.

Recall a time in your life when you believe you experienced the Presence of God.

Make some notes about the experience.

Locate the central moment of the experience, when your awareness of God's Presence was most vivid.

Name two to three attendant thoughts and feelings in that moment.

"It was like_________." Draw a picture that represents that moment's thoughts and feelings or make a brief statement of six to nine words.

Explore the focus image or statement.

Bring theological perspectives to the reflection.

Study the image or statement in silence. Let the "voice" of the image or statement become present.

What questions about the image/statement surface for you? List those and your responses.

Identify the type of theological questions those are. That is, are the questions about the nature of the world, the nature of God, the relationship of God to the world, the nature of mercy, of grace, of hope, and so forth?

Connect to other sources of meaning in your life.

When life is like that image/statement for you, how do you make sense of the experience?

What wisdom do you draw on for understanding? Who or what have you studied in the Christian tradition or the world around you that can "speak" to you or teach you about a moment like that?

What do you deeply believe about the experience you had? What doubts and hopes are present for you? Where do those feelings originate?

Apply insight/learning.

Sit quietly with the image, exploration and connections, perhaps lighting a candle as you reside with the reflection.

What prayer begins praying in you? Try to write that down.

How does the theological reflection support or challenge one commitment in your life?

FIRST INTERLUDE

A Spirituality of Liberation

Week Fourteen

A note about language: While we now might choose different terms (African American, non-gendered terms for God, more expansive use of pronouns when referring to humans, and so on) we must also remember that Thurman published this book in 1949, thus its language reflects his time. Please do your best to read with a generosity of spirit so that, despite language that may sometimes bring you up short, you can hear what this modern Christian prophet has to say to the Church today.

ALL YEARS

Read

Thurman, *Jesus and the Disinherited*, pages vii–47.

Focus

FOREWORD:

Not liberation theology but a spirituality of liberation; connection to anticolonial movement; who are the disinherited today?

JESUS—AN INTERPRETATION:

A poor Jew in a minority group in dominant culture; survival terms for the disinherited; distinguishing culture from religion; nonresistance–imitation or isolation; resistance–physical expression of inner attitude; the three hounds of Hell; Christianity vs. "religion of Jesus"; Christianity as a religion of the powerful and dominant; Christianity as other-worldly; Paul's security (Roman citizen) vs. Jesus' insecurity (no citizenship); the Gospel's message to the weak and oppressed; the Kingdom of God/Heaven as Jesus' alternative

FEAR:

Power over as one-sided violence; disregard for personhood; threat of violence as weapon; fear as a safety device; segregation and fear; physical, psychic, and spiritual consequences of fear; Jesus' alternative: identity as Child of God = sense of integrity

ALL YEARS

Respond

Thurman notes that

> The masses of men live with their backs constantly against the wall. They are the poor, the disinherited, the dispossessed. What does our religion say to them?[23]

Recall Edward Farley's assertion that "theology concerns the wisdom by which one brings the resources of a religious tradition to bear on the world."[24]

> The urgent question was what must be the attitude toward Rome? Was any attitude possible that would be morally tolerable and at the same time preserve a basic self-esteem–without which life could not possibly have any meaning? The question was not academic. It was the most crucial of questions. In essence Rome was the enemy; Rome symbolized total frustration; Rome was the great barrier to peace of mind. And Rome was everywhere. No Jewish person of the period could deal with the question of his practical life, his vocation, his place in society, until first he had settled deep within himself this critical issue.
>
> This is the position of the disinherited in every age.[25]

In the context of seeking spiritual maturity, we have noted that such maturity demands wisdom, wholeness, and integration. Thurman's "hounds of Hell" may allow the disinherited to survive in the face of "Rome" in any age, but they work against wholeness. What wisdom can be drawn from your religious tradition to encourage the restoration of wholeness to the disinherited today?

Practice

THEOLOGICAL REFLECTION BEGINNING WITH A PROVOCATIVE WORD[26]

Identify

Thurman asks what the Christian tradition has to say to the disinherited since the interpretation of that tradition has long been in the hands of the advantaged and privileged. Consider Thurman's word, "DISINHERITED." In the context of this book, who are they?

What revelations on the meaning of DISINHERITED do you have? Anything it denotes or connotes? What feelings are evoked for you by this word?

---

23. Howard Thurman, *Jesus and the Disinherited* (Boston: Beacon Press, 1976, 1996), 3.
24. *The Christian Century,* February 1998, 113–115, 149.
25. Thurman, 12.
26. Adapted from a design by Patricia Bleicher, EfM mentor.

Explore

Next, ask the six "journalist's questions" about the feeling(s) the word conveys:

WHO was involved when you were feeling _____________________?
(Action . . . tell the stories from your life)

WHAT image comes to mind about the feeling(s) ____________________?
(Explore this image–its reflection of Wholeness, Brokenness, Recognition, Reorientation, and/or Restoration)

Connect

Go to the other sources we use to help explore meaning

WHERE does this image come from and WHERE is it found in society?
(Source/Culture)

WHEN does this image come up in the Bible, lives of saints, hymns, and so forth?
(Source/Tradition. . . explore the world of tradition)

WHY is this image manifest in our lives?
(Source/Position)

HOW might God redeem any negatives in this image?
(Hope in Christ)

Consider insights and implications from reflecting on this image.

What have you learned for the next time you feel the feelings that evoked this image?

Apply

Write a collect using the outline:

Dear God . . .	(naming of God's aspects)
You . . .	(connect situation of the image to that aspect)
We pray that . . .	(petition of our hearts)
So that . . .,	(result we desire)
	Amen.

Week Fifteen

ALL YEARS

Read

Thurman, *Jesus and the Disinherited,* pages 48–102

Focus

DECEPTION:

Defensive tool of the powerless; ethical, moral, and spiritual aspects of deception; the strategy of compromise; the dilemma–a focus on how not to be killed cheapens life; sincerity/truth at any cost as Jesus' alternative; Psalm 139 as ethical imperative; sincerity in human relations = sincerity in relation to God

HATE:

Christianity too sentimental about hate; contact without fellowship; unsympathetic understanding = ill will; hatred by the disinherited born out of bitterness; hatred and moral disintegration; hatred and the illusion of righteousness; Jesus' alternative is love because hatred destroys the hater

LOVE:

Jesus' central love-ethic; all are neighbors; loving the enemy at three levels–personal, tribe, empire; overcoming segregation in the church; the context of common humanity; love possible between two freed spirits; dropping the barrier between strong and weak, powerful and powerless; ethical dilemma the same for privileged and underprivileged; forgiveness is mandatory

ALL YEARS

Respond

In the final chapter, Thurman writes that loving the enemy operates at three levels–personal, tribe, and empire. What examples from the Gospels does Thurman use to illustrate how Jesus chooses love at the micro, meso, and macro levels? What other examples from the Christian tradition come to mind?

As noted earlier, viewing life from the standpoint of the meso (group/tribal) level highlights the contours of a community's ethical geography. Think of examples in contemporary culture/society of

- failure to choose love
- choosing love despite community opposition

What are the ethical considerations in each case?

Practice

Read The Cycle of Gospel Living on page 237 in Part Two of this Guide.

Imagine you are at dinner with Eric Law and Howard Thurman, and the topic has turned to the disinherited. Eric has just explained his Cycle of Gospel Living. What do you think Thurman would say to Law? How might Law reply? What sources do they use to reach their positions? What would you say to each of them? From what sources do you draw?

If you like, write some dialogue for this dinner party scene.

UNIT THREE

Developing a Sustaining Spirituality

Week Sixteen

ALL YEARS

Read

Prayer and Worship

In Education for Ministry we explore our call to be ministers in the world beyond the walls of the institutional church, a challenging call to be sure and one that demands our spiritual growth until finally we "come to the unity of the faith and of the knowledge of the Son of God, to maturity, to the measure of the full stature of Christ" (Ephesians 4:13). To seek maturity as a follower of the Christ we must be grounded in a spiritual life that sustains us in the challenging work of ministry.

One way to develop a sustaining spiritual life is through forming a *habitus* of prayer, worship, and service. Participating in liturgies and rituals fosters growth in the knowledge and love of God.

Challenges and Opportunities in Contemporary Society

A sustaining spirituality provides encouragement (places a heart in us) in the face of unprecedented challenges and opportunities. Since each person lives in the particularities of a place and time, it is essential to reflect carefully and critically on the present moment of history to discern better the ways in which God acts.

Contemporary society is marked by anxiety-producing forces such as rapid change, instant communication, technological advances, and random violence. Rapid change creates situations that generate persistent uncertainty. Instant communication raises our awareness of tragic events spanning the planet. Technological advances, especially in the medical field, may compel unparalleled and stressful ethical dilemmas. Random violence, even in places assumed to be safe, seems to stir unrelenting terror. A culture of violence has emerged marked by anxiety, distress, apprehension, and terror.

And yet forces producing anxiety may also prompt opportunities for increasing compassion, justice, and human flourishing. Social media can help new relationships form and broken ones to heal and renew. Information more equally accessible encourages a more learned response to unexpected events. Medical advances bring hope and healing where only a short time ago there was little choice but to let illness run its course. In the face of senseless bloodshed, the Amish community of Nickle Mines, Pennsylvania, transfigured violence through forgiveness, reconciliation, and rebuilding. Like theirs, other grace-filled responses to the epidemic of violence can inspire hope for the future. Refrains of agony and ecstasy play continually throughout the world.

In an effort to meet such challenges, a group of Episcopal leaders came together after the 2012 school shooting at Sandy Hook Elementary School in Connecticut. These leaders offered an initial response to the growing awareness that society suffers from an epidemic of violence.

> *Reclaiming the Gospel of Peace: An Episcopal Gathering to Challenge the Epidemic of Violence* was held April 9–11, 2014 at the Reed Convention Center in Midwest City, Oklahoma. Episcopalians came together to renew their commitment to the Gospel call to make peace in a world of violence. Through deep conversation, prayer, and skill-building the event empowered our Church to address violence and reclaim our role in society as workers for nonviolence and peace.
>
> Reclaiming the Gospel of Peace was focused around four pillars: advocacy, education, liturgy, and pastoral care. These four areas are key avenues that our Church can use to address the culture of violence within and outside of the Church and were woven throughout all aspects of the event including plenary time, workshops, small group conversations, and worship.[27]

At the conference Archbishop of Canterbury Justin Welby, along with Bishop Edward Konieczny, Bishop Eugene Sutton, and Presiding Bishop Katharine Jefferts Schori of the Episcopal Church, offered support and guidance as they addressed the culture of fear formed by unsettling global acts of violence.

Presiding Bishop Jefferts Schori's sermon at the conference situates violence, more than simply physical harm, in the context of spirituality.

> Violence is anything that seeks to diminish life–especially another person's integrity or dignity or life possibilities. The word comes from the same root as *vital*, but it moves in the opposite direction, away from what God has created and called good and blessed. Violence misuses the gift of life, trading it for some dull or brassy idol that promises control, predictability, or certainty. That brassy idol is simply a dressed up and tricked out phantasm of death. The life God has created is free to choose–and it can choose life or death. Violence seeks to steal that freedom or end it. Violence can be an instinctive reaction to preserve life when other violence threatens–like attacking a charging animal likely to maim vulnerable children. Violence can also be a more or less conscious choice that seeks to augment life at the cost of others–the assassination of a political opponent, or the crazed mayhem of an unstable shooter.[28]

Drawing out the theological implications, she continues,

> Countering violence requires custody of the heart. Violence begins in the heart, especially in hearts that have been wounded and scarred by the violence

27. http://www.episcopaloklahoma.org/reclaiming-the-gospel-info.html
28. http://www.episcopalchurch.org/pb/reclaiming-gospel-peace

of others, and then react and respond aggressively, in overly defended ways. Violence begins in the heart that cannot countenance vulnerability–rooted in fear that its own vitality will be extinguished. As the counterforce to abundant life, violence is intrinsically kin to evil. The ultimate counterforce to fear is perfect love, the ability to share life to the full, with radical vulnerability, in the face of those who would destroy it. The undefended Jesus shows us the way. He does not go about with armies or weapons, he does not protest the words of his captors, he does not defend himself or attack others with violent words or actions, and it is ultimately his ability to set his life-force and spirit free, fully free, that deprives the evil around him of any ultimate power.[29]

Violence and vitality grow from the same spiritual soil.

Countering violence begins in our hearts–with the words we choose, the judgments we make, and the vulnerability we're willing to assume. Choices affect what or who has custody of the heart. . . . Custody of the heart is a spiritual discipline that unleashes the power of love and abundant life.[30]

With these words, Presiding Bishop Jefferts Schori names the challenge Christians face.

Brother James Dowd, a member of the Order of the Holy Cross, during a panel discussion at the same conference, asserted that in order "to move more deeply into non-violent discipleship of Christ, the contemplative life is essential." The contemplative life makes way for God to have "custody of the heart."

What God needs is people on the street and people in the parish and people in their homes and people in the workplace who are contemplatives. There's all kinds of ways to do that in terms of your prayer life; there's all kinds of prayer techniques. Whatever it is that you were to develop; it is a prayer life that helps you to love more deeply.[31]

An enduring and faithful life as a maturing Christian, as one who "loves more deeply," requires spirituality that draws on the Christian tradition in a way that encourages, strengthens, enlivens, and nourishes. The Christian tradition of spirituality, of course, offers many ways to practice a life of loving more deeply. Faced with a myriad of choices, how does one choose? It is akin to the old joke:

Question: How do you eat an elephant?

Answer: One bite at a time.

Spiritual practices can be tried on, one at a time, until one that fits best is found. During this year in EfM we will focus on contemplative living as a

29. Ibid.

30. Ibid.

31. http://episcopaldigitalnetwork.com/ens/2014/04/14/reclaiming-gospel-of-peace-wraps-up-in-oklahoma-city/

pattern of spiritual practices that can draw a person more fully into Christian maturity in the world.

Contemplative Living as Habitus

What is the contemplative life? When a person is described as a contemplative, images of a cloistered monastic may come to mind. Pictures of a person robed in monastic garb kneeling quietly in a chapel filled with light filtered by stained glass windows in an ambience of profound silence may flood the imagination. Such images are frequently stereotypes associated with the word contemplation, and like all stereotypes may prevent us from seeing the whole picture. Contemplative persons do not withdraw from the dangers of human cruelty but instead enter the fray emboldened by the Spirit of God. Their courage grows from a life nurtured through prayer, worship, and compassionate service.

The contemplative life can be described by three commitments found in the Rule of St Benedict: listening with the ear of the heart; commitment to place; and continual conversion. Although the rule was written for contemplatives who did live as cloistered monastics, these commitments are just as applicable to contemplative living in the world.

St. Benedict's guiding image for living a contemplative life, "listen with the ear of the heart," calls Christians into an attitude of openness. A focus on the heart as the place where humans encounter and receive God was a staple image for the fourth century desert monastics echoing the prophets' call to transform stony hearts. Episcopal Presiding Bishop Frank Griswold opened his remarks at the 1998 Trinity Institute by drawing on this image:

> "Acquire a heart and you shall be saved." These are the words of Abba Pambo, a desert father of the fourth century. According to the desert tradition, the focus of ascetical practice and prayer was ordered to the acquiring of a heart, achieving purity of heart. Finding one's heart rendered one permeable and available to God's mystery. Historically there is a tension between the mind and the heart, which calls to mind an Orthodox phrase: we must learn to stand before God with "the mind in the heart." It suggests the profound unity that we are called to express in our lives as Christian persons.
>
> The heart is not simply a physical organ or seat of emotions; it is the core and center of our personhood as well. According to Jewish tradition, the heart is the throne of God's glory, which is the place where the *shekinah*, the presence of God, most deeply is to be found. Therefore, when Paul in the letter to the Romans speaks about the love of God being poured into our hearts through the Holy Spirit that has been given to us, he is speaking of God's reality breaking through to the inmost chamber of our own reality. We experience it then as a unified and transfiguring and transforming love.[32]

32. Frank Griswold, *Cross Currents*, Winter 1998–99, Vol. 49 Issue 1, http://www.crosscurrents.org/griswold.htm

Listening with the ear of the heart and allowing ourselves to become permeable to the mystery of God are essential to the work of building a sustaining spirituality. Attentive listening with the whole person is the first characteristic practice of the contemplative life. Deep listening opens a person to the experience of knowing God as a unified and transfiguring love.

A common poster from the latter half of the last century said, "bloom where you are planted." Commitment to place, the second characteristic of contemplative living, means attending to the present situation as it is rather than to how it once was or how one might wish it would be. It is a radical orientation to the present. Living in the present moment requires laying aside pining for the past along with turning from a preoccupation with the future. A mature spirituality receives the present situation. The reality of now is where one meets God.

Conversion, the third characteristic of a contemplative life, does not mean simply a once-in-a-lifetime event that is seen as the sole mark of becoming a Christian. While such born-again experiences are important life-changing events, they are not what conversion means in the contemplative life. Another word for this characteristic is *metanoia*, the ongoing process of transformation. Like the Apollo spacecraft's onboard gyroscope navigation system that continually corrected its course, and without which the mission would not have been successful, *metanoia* (conversion) is a state of being where recurring adjustment of attitude, understanding, and relationships moves a person more fully into knowing and loving God.

Listening with the ear of the heart; accepting and committing to the present; and participating in continuous *metanoia* fashion a contemplative life in the world. Yet even as one embraces a vision of living as a contemplative on the way to Christian maturity, practical issues arise. How does a person develop the capacity to listen with the ear of the heart? How does a person practice commitment to place? What daily activities does a person engage to make *metanoia* a way of life? In short, the answer involves finding, developing, and using practices that enhance listening with one's whole being, enable being attentive to the present moment, and create a willingness to be transformed by repeated conversions. These practices contribute to forming a *habitus.*

A *habitus* encompasses the totality of a person. *Habitus* refers to the foundational attitude of the person. It is the person's way of being-in-the-world; the constitutional characteristics; the integration of mind, body, soul into a whole. A *habitus* of prayer, worship, and service involves the entire person—the core and center of the person.

Similar to Van der Ven's micro, meso, and macro levels of human behavior, a person also has an individual spirituality, a corporate spirituality, and a cosmic spirituality. Each individual has unique and distinctive qualities that constitute that person's identity. Individual spirituality consists of the particularities of the person that shape his or her relationship to God. Part of a group greater than the individual self is the social self shaped by language, clothing, food, customs, stories, myths, organizations, and institutions.

These elements of social identity shape corporate spirituality with nuances and tacit apprehensions that impact one's relationship with God. At the same time, the individual and social selves live within the larger context of the universe. How one understands the universe, whether as "the vast expanse of interstellar space"[33] or dark energy and matter, profoundly forms a person's cosmic spirituality. In building a spirituality, a mature Christian moves beyond a focus on the individual to embrace commonality with other people, then transcends those social interconnections by recognizing connections with all of creation.

Living into the full stature of Christ means developing as fully as possible our individual, corporate, and cosmic relationships. The Letter to the Romans describes a struggle with multiple dimensions of spirituality: "We know that the whole creation has been groaning in labor pains until now; and not only the creation, but we ourselves, who have the first fruits of the Spirit, groan inwardly while we wait for adoption, the redemption of our bodies." (Romans 8:22–23)

To create a spirituality that becomes a person's *habitus* requires spiritual practices that engage life as fully as possible. In a holistic approach the intellect finds ways to know and love God; the emotions are engaged in the God-person relationship; and the body too forms a relationship with God. A sustaining spirituality is an embodied spirituality formed over time through numerous spiritual practices, including prayer, worship, study, and service. EfM helps develop a *habitus* of contemplative living through the normative individual and group practices of prayer, worship, study, and theological reflection (which points us to implications for service) over four years. These practices continually form us for Christian ministry.

Worship and Liturgical Practice

A focus on worship, in particular on liturgical practices, can provide rich ways to attend to the process of becoming a spiritually mature Christian seeking wisdom, wholeness, and integration. In particular, corporate liturgical practice can move us beyond individual interests into a deepening relationship with others in social organizations and institutions and eventually into environmental and even cosmic veracities.

Liturgy works simultaneously on the micro, meso, and macro levels of human behavior. As an individual participates in the Eucharist, individual fears, concerns, hopes, loves, and dreams are intertwined with the drama of the liturgy. The context of the liturgical action also draws worshipers into collective concerns within society and culture. The imperatives of the Baptismal Covenant in the Episcopal Book of Common Prayer direct attention to collective concerns such as "striv[ing] for justice and peace among all people, and respect[ing] the dignity of every human being."[34] Theological imagery and symbols invite the imagination into creation's

33. *The Book of Common Prayer* (New York: Church Hymnal Corporation, 1979), 370.
34. Ibid., 305.

cosmic context. The words of the rite, along with ceremonial actions within its architectural setting, move the worshiper into the divine drama of salvation and wholeness.

Liturgy involves all the senses and faculties of a person. Reason and intellect are fed through the words of the liturgy. Liturgical colors, symbols, and music stimulate the imagination. Ceremony and vestments engage the body in worship as participants stand, kneel, bow, gesture, and move about. Engaging our physical senses of sight, smell, touch, and sound, the performance of the liturgy draws the worshiper into God's sacred drama. According to Anglican theologian Sarah Coakley, participation in the divine drama inaugurates a distinctive knowing.

> What is distinctive to liturgical "knowing" I have argued, is the way that bodily movement, sensual acuity, affective longing, and noetic or intellectual response, are intricately entwined and mutually implicated in what is occurring, and indeed are being trained over time to intensify and deepen their capacity for response to the risen Christ. . . . [T]here is a goal, and the goal is nothing less than divine truth itself. [35]

Liturgical practices such as praying the Daily Offices and celebrating the Holy Eucharist within a faith community disclose "divine truth itself." Coakley gives primacy to prayer and liturgy as means through which a person knows God. Out of direct experience within worship and prayer, she asserts that "liturgy does not merely rehearse, or inculcate, the propositional beliefs of Christian faith that may have already been acknowledged rationally sometime previously, but that *liturgy in and of itself purveys a particular kind of "truth"*[36] (emphasis added).

Worshipers attend to the words that engage reason; worshipers also "think" through their bodies and "see" through their imagination as they "listen with the ears of their hearts." Rite, ceremony, and space, in concert with one another, invite the whole person (mind, body, emotion, imagination, and spirit) into relationship with God.

David Ford expands this idea of theological knowing to include propositional commitments (creedal and doctrinal affirmations); commandments (ethical imperatives); questions (honest inquiries); experimentations (trying out ways of thinking, being, praying, worshiping); and desiring (deep yearnings that are responsive to God's desiring). Ford views wisdom as the meeting of the cries of humankind with God's grace and glory. A well-performed liturgy engages all five modes of knowing.

David Brown, Anglican scholar and priest, has written extensively about how religious experience is mediated through the arts and culture. Tucked

---

35. Sarah Coakley, "Beyond Belief: Liturgy and the Cognitive Apprehension of God," in *The Vocation of Theology Today: A Festschrift for David Ford*, Tom Greggs, Rachel Muers, Simeon Zahl ed. (Eugene, OR: Cascade Books, 2013), 143–144.

36. Ibid., 132.

within an analysis of enchantment, he writes, "Worship has therefore to be seen as more than just a matter of strengthening the community for mission and service. At its heart lies the adoration of God, basking in his presence in and for its own sake."[37] Adoration, often mistakenly conflated with praise and thanksgiving, is foundational to worship and prayer. The nature of adoration is distinct from forms of praying like confession, petition, intercession, praise, oblation, and thanksgiving.

An incident from the Action source illustrates the meaning of adoration.

> I had watched and watched that bird nest for days. Four perfect eggs inside. At last came the day I saw three baby birds hatch, and the fourth on the way. They were beautiful! I gasped, then the words flew out: "Oh! Thank you, Lord."

Adoration occurs in that moment, however fleeting, between awareness of something that causes us to draw our breath deeply and our release of that held breath. In that moment, one can experience the essence of adoration: an intensified and active awareness of God's presence and work.

In adoration one breathes in God, as lungs fill with air, and exhales prayers of penitence, intercession, petition, thanksgiving, or praise. To become breathtakingly attentive to the presence of God is to become keenly conscious of one's own need for repentance; of the needs of others; of our own need; of thanksgiving for all that God gives us; or of the desire to praise God. Adoration is foundational prayer. No other prayers are uttered without active awareness of God (adoration) just as no breath is exhaled without first taking in air.[38]

Sarah Coakley points to the insight of Evagrius, fourth-century monk and ascetic, who wrote, "If you are a theologian, you will pray truly. And if you pray truly, you are a theologian."[39] In an essay in the *Christian Century* Coakley describes how her work as a theologian changed when she began a regular regimen of meditation.

> This is not the story of a classic conversion experience, let alone of a pietistic revulsion against the intellect. On the contrary, it is an account of how prayer–especially the simple prayer of relative silence or stillness–has the power to change one's perception of the theological task. What started as an adventure in personal prayer–which drew me in much faster and more disconcertingly than I was ready for–has ended in a program for systematic theology (and its handmaid, philosophy of religion) which is as much implicated in the corpo-

37. David Brown, *God and the Enchantment of Place* (New York: Oxford University Press, 2004), 20.

38. Angela Hock and Richard Brewer, "Continuing the Community's Teaching: Come Let us Adore God," *Practically Christian: A Guide for Practical Christian Action, Reflection, and Prayer* (Sewanee, TN: The University of the South, 1995), 6.

39. Evagrius, "On Prayer," 61, in http://desertfathers.blogspot.com/2011/06/works-of-evagrius-ponticuson-prayer.html.

rate and the social as it is in the personal. For that is where prayer inexorably leads us.[40]

Developing a *habitus* of contemplative living that includes regular prayer and worship in the form of liturgical practice can orient the maturing Christian toward attention to all three levels of spirituality and support growth toward the full stature of Christ. Maturity grows as one integrates disparate voices that play within an individual. Listening with the heart, living in the present, and committing to *metanoia* nurture the desire for wholeness that guides the convergence of incongruent individual, social, and cosmic realities toward congruence–toward dwelling with God. Wisdom (God's light) enlightens actions, guiding choices so that they more nearly contribute to the Vision of God.

Looking ahead: For Week Seventeen there will be substantial reading for those in Year One. Try not to worry about all the details, but allow yourself to read for the sweep of the biblical story. Still, you may need to plan ahead to allow sufficient time to accomplish the assignment.

Focus

The Education for Ministry program encourages developing a *habitus* that comprises prayer, worship, study, and services. Identify ways in which participation in EfM is supporting you in those practices.

Respond

How would you describe your relationship with God? What image of your relationship comes to mind?

Of the categories of prayer, worship, study, and service, which challenges you the most? Identify the factors that contribute to that challenge.

How might you rise to the challenge?

What concerns in your home, your work, your community, or the world claim your heart and mind at the present time?

Practice

During the week before the next EfM seminar session, make a chart of the amount of time you worship, pray, study, and engage in service.

If you named one or more concerns in the **Respond** section, apply worship, prayer, study or service consciously to that area this week. Note how that affected your heart and mind regarding that concern.

Decide on one spiritual practice to build during the six weeks of this unit.

---

40. Sarah Coakley, "Prayer as Crucible," *Christian Century*, March 9, 2011, in http://www.christiancentury.org/article/2011-03/prayer-crucible.

Week Seventeen

YEAR ONE

Read

1 Samuel
2 Samuel
Collins, Chapter 11, "1 Samuel," and Chapter 12, "2 Samuel," pages 139–158

Looking ahead: There will be substantial reading for Week Eighteen. Again, read for the sweep of the story and try not to feel overwhelmed by the details.

Focus

First and Second Samuel paint a sweeping picture of the formation of the Jewish faith. Identify ideas, images, and actions that expressed knowledge of God, of human nature, and of the world for the people of the time.

Create a chart listing concerns and interests at the time of Samuel on the micro, meso, and macro levels of human interaction. That is, what was going on for Samuel on a personal/interpersonal level, a community level, and a social/intellectual level?

Describe Samuel's relationship to or with God.

YEAR TWO

Read

Powell, Chapter 10, "New Testament Letters," and Chapter 11, "Paul," pages 215–253
Hyperlinks 10.1–10.4 at www.IntroducingNT.com

Focus

Define: Pastoral Epistles; Prison Letters; Catholic Epistles; *cuneiform*; *ostraca*; *papyrus*; *amanuensis*; structure of epistles; Gamaliel; *chiasm*; pseudepigraphy; Muratorian fragment; gospel (*euangelion*); Jesus' death, resurrection, and ascension; life after death; being made right with God (justification); new age of God; nature of Jesus

Powell, Chapter 11, "Paul," pages 231–253

Using the material in Powell's eleventh chapter, construct a spiritual autobiography of Paul's life. For example, identify ten to twelve events that cover his entire life: born and raised as a member of the people of Israel within the tribe of Benjamin; lived as a Pharisee observing the Jewish law; studied at the feet of Gamaliel. Read through the events of Paul's life to get a sense of his life as a whole.

Note the various experiences Paul has that shape his spirituality–how he prays and worships; revelations and/or visions he reports; encounters with others; and other experiences that form his relationship with God.

How does the story of Paul provide a voice of wisdom for you?

YEAR THREE

Read

MacCulloch, Chapter 11, "The West: Universal Emperor or Universal Pope?" pages 363–395

Focus

Define: Monastic revival in England; Cluny Abby's legacy, especially noting the agrarian economy, pilgrimage piety, origin of purgatory, and the Peace of God movement; universal monarchy; marriage as sacrament; rise of papacy–from Vicar of Peter to Vicar of Christ; clerical celibacy; dividing lay and clergy

Describe the growth struggles of the Church in the West during this historical period.

What were the costs and promises of dividing lay and clergy?

YEAR FOUR

Read

Allen, Chapter 11, "The Temptation in the Wilderness," pages 107–116

Focus

Define: Biblical use of the number 40; Jesus' three temptations for ministry in daily life; misguided theology based on premise: faith in God means being protected from harm; felicity and joy in God's presence; self-limitation of Jesus; hiddenness of God

What theological questions does the Temptation in the Wilderness raise?

ALL YEARS

Respond

Name those you studied this week who listened with the ear of the heart, demonstrated commitment to place, and/or revealed continual conversion.

How does their witness deepen your sense of compassion, justice, and human flourishing?

Practice

A suggestion in Week Sixteen was to decide on one spiritual practice to build during this unit. Describe what you are doing and how that is going.

In a brief video titled "Goodness," available on the Internet at The Work of the People site, Jonathan Wilson-Hartgrove states that goodness is rooted in scripture, prayer, and the pursuit of God.[41] Quoting the Galatians 5 passage about the fruits of the Spirit, he describes the pursuit of God as the process of drawing closer to the heart of God. Further, he brings confession into the action as a key part of that pursuit–confession that has no pretense, that is honest.

How is your journey towards the heart of God going?

THEOLOGICAL REFLECTION BEGINNING WITH A PERSONAL EXPERIENCE

Identify a focus.

Write about your journey of spiritual maturity in the last five years.

Review your writing. If you described any aspect of your experience in image language, try to draw that image and use that as the focus for the Explore phase. If not, select one key point in your journey and create a picture that expresses that point. Just using a phrase that conveys a metaphorical or image idea works well, too.

Explore the focus.

Sit quietly with your image or statement and then identify which theological perspective(s) the metaphorical expression contains.

Describe how the image reveals something of compassion, justice, or human flourishing.

Add consideration of anything in the image that reveals damage or brokenness.

How does God fit into the image?

41. www.theworkofthepeople.com

Connect

Consider what other sources may contribute meaning to the reflection.

Return to the writing you did at the beginning of this reflection. Mark any of the following that you may have mentioned:

Culture/Society–Did you refer to any books or stories you have read, movies you have seen, social environment that supports or challenges you, social norms that help or hinder you?

Christian Tradition–Did you recall any stories of the Bible, or hymns, or prayers of the Church?

Personal Beliefs/Position–Did you make any statements of conviction, hope or doubt in your writing?

How have those areas helped you recognize God's presence in your image?

Apply

Relate this learning to ministry in your daily life. What do you see in a new way? Is there any area of your life that the reflection draws you toward in ministry?

How does this reflection contribute to listening with the ear of your heart, your commitment to place, or your continual conversion?

Week Eighteen

YEAR ONE

Read

1 Kings
2 Kings
Collins, Chapter 13, "1 Kings 1–16: Solomon and the Divided Monarchy," and Chapter 14, "1 Kings 17–2 Kings 25: Tales of Prophets and the End of the Kingdoms of Israel and Judah," pages 159–184

Focus

Prophets speak God's truth and frequently have the most to lose. Difficulties arise when prophetic voices do not agree on what the truth is. Possible responses to the uncertainty are to wait to see which leads to the most life-giving outcome, to decide in the midst of the uncertainty which is correct for you and act accordingly, or to view the variations as each addressing something of truth.

How do you discern in the midst of uncertainty?

Reflect on the place of uncertainty in spiritual maturity.

YEAR TWO

Read

The Letter to the Romans

Focus

The Letter to the Romans likely contains familiar quotations. Be sure to place any you notice in the context of the letter.

How is the letter structured?

How does Paul build his case?

How does the letter to the Romans reflect Paul's spiritual growth?

YEAR THREE

Read

MacCulloch, Chapter 12, "A Church for All People?" pages 396–423

Focus

Define: Waldensians; *scholae* educational method; Peter Abelard's *Theologia Christiana*; Dominic and Dominicans (Blackfriars); Francis, Franciscans, and

Francis's *Testament*; Carmelites; Fourth Lateran Council; transubstantiation (Real Presence); Thomas Aquinas; *Summa Theologiae* (Sum Total of Theology); Anselm, Abelard, Hildegard of Bingen; *The Cloud of Unknowing*; Meister Eckhart; Bridget of Sweden; Catherine of Siena

In this week's study, what persons or events interest you and how do they support your spiritual growth?

YEAR FOUR

Read

Allen, Chapter 12, "The Sacrifice of the Cross," pages 117–127

Focus

Define: ransom; satisfaction/substitutionary; theories of Atonement posed by Paul, Anselm, and Abelard; distance; Suffering Servant; self-limitation of God; ancient meaning of passion; sin as life apart from God; biblical view of God's power, wisdom, and goodness; atonement as the restoration of the human capacity to know, love, and obey God

The chapter discussed teachings on atonement–the only doctrine that has no established consensus. Describe the various atonement theories you studied.

Describe any changes over time for you in your understanding of Jesus' act on the Cross.

ALL YEARS

Respond

Study this week included both books of Kings in the Old Testament, Paul's letter to the Romans in the New Testament, Western Christianity in 1100–1300 CE for Year Three, and developing an understanding of the meaning of Jesus' act that led to the Cross for Year Four.

How did your study this week address the matter of sacrifice as part of a relationship to God?

Practice

Read through the entire reflection outline first. Let your mind and heart receive images and memories naturally. Keep clear for yourself what the overall movement of reflection is: Identifying a focus, Exploring the focus theologically, Connecting other "voices" that confirm or challenge the focus, and Applying the results to ministry in daily life.

THEOLOGICAL REFLECTION BEGINNING WITH A PERSONAL EXPERIENCE

Identify a focus.

When did you sacrifice for the sake of someone or something?

Write a paragraph describing that experience. Locate it in time and place.

Circle the point of most energy in the experience–the heart of the experience.

Name two or three key thoughts and two or three key feelings you had at that focused instant.

Create an image in picture or words to capture the essence of that moment.

Explore the focus theologically.

Try exploring the image you created above by using the aspects of spiritual growth introduced earlier in this *Guide*: striving for wholeness, acting wisely, assuming responsibility, and living authentically.

How does your image reflect any or all of those aspects?

Are any of the aspects not represented?

Connect

Connect the image with the voices of Christian tradition, personal beliefs, and the culture in which you live.

How do those voices guide you in a moment like the image?

What voices speak against the image?

Apply

The next time life is like the image you created, what can this reflection contribute to your action?

How do you relate ministry and sacrifice?

Week Nineteen

YEAR ONE

Read

Amos
Hosea
Collins, Chapter 15, "Amos and Hosea," pages 185–202

Focus

Define: prophecy; royal archives of Mari; the essence of prophecy; focus of Amos's prophecy; Amos's themes of social justice and of condemnation of the cult; the day of the Lord; metaphor of marriage to a promiscuous woman; Gomer; two crucial differences between Amos and Hosea's messages; Hosea's basic critique

What contemporary prophetic statements like those of Amos or Hosea can you identify?

YEAR TWO

Read

Powell, Chapter 12, "Romans," pages 255–271

Focus

Define: justification

For Western Christianity, the Pauline teaching on justification is highly influential and formative. On page 263, Powell presents "Models for Understanding Justification." Which model or combination of models best clarify the "justification issue" for you?

YEAR THREE

Read

MacCulloch, Chapter 13, "Faith in the New Rome," pages 427–465

Focus

Describe three or four characteristics of Orthodoxy.

Identify distinctive qualities of Byzantine spirituality.

What concerns motivate both sides of the iconoclastic controversy?

Name one or two reasons that understanding the controversy is important in today's world.

Summarize Photios's missionary strategy and the significance for Christianity in the twenty-first century.

YEAR FOUR

Read

Allen, Chapter 13, "The Resurrection of Jesus and Eternal Life," pages 131–146

Focus

Everlasting life or eternal life issues turn on the understanding one holds of life. *Bios* and *zoe* distinctions frame thinking about the nature and purpose of life. Think about how those distinctions affect your theology of ministry.

Allen uses a painting analogy to support understanding the Good News found in the Gospels. Which of the resurrection "pictures" painted in the Gospels appeal to you?

What difference might a person's view of life after death have on daily ministry?

ALL YEARS

Respond

Name elements of spiritual or Christian maturity recognizable in the period you studied this week.

How did those in the period you studied this week engage in advocacy, education, liturgy, or pastoral care to address the issues of their time?

Practice

Regular deliberate theological reflection is a meaningful asset for building a *habitus* of prayer, worship, study and service.

THEOLOGICAL REFLECTION BEGINNING WITH A PERSONAL EXPERIENCE

Identify a focus for reflection.

Write a paragraph describing a moment in the last two weeks when you personally were challenged by something or someone. Describe the circumstance as fully as possible for yourself.

Highlight your thoughts and feelings.

Highlight any image language, often preceded by a phrase such as "it was like . . ."

Select the key moment. Use any image you wrote or create an image and identify the thoughts and feelings that go with the image of that key moment.

Explore the image.

How does your image reflect or relate to any of these themes from this week's study: social justice or "cult" critiques; faithfulness; justification; faith; resurrection; spirituality; life?

Describe how compassion, justice, and human flourishing are represented in your image.

Connect

Bring other sources or voices into the conversation.

Christian Tradition: In the Bible, stories of the saints, or stories of the Church, where do you find someone in the same circumstance as your image described? List all examples that you can recall. Select one example and read carefully the Bible story, or story of the saint, or story of the Church.

What does that connection help you see about your image?

What did you learn as you read that story?

Compare and contrast the world of the Christian Tradition you reviewed and the world of the image you explored, particularly in relation to compassion, justice, and human flourishing.

In terms of the natural sciences or humanities, how does our Culture support or challenge the image you explored?

What is at stake in this reflection?

What personal Position are you prepared to state about what is at stake?

Apply

Name one area where you have opportunities for ministry in your life.

What ministry commitment does this reflection help you make in that area?

Write a prayer that conveys your intentions, petitions, and hopes as a result of this reflection.

Week Twenty

YEAR ONE

Read

Micah
Isaiah 1–39
Excerpt on Micah from Collins's longer volume on the Hebrew Bible, reprinted on pages 192–195 in Part II of the *Reading and Reflection Guide*
Collins, Chapter 16, "Isaiah," pages 203–212

Focus

Micah and First Isaiah contain familiar and often-quoted passages. Identify key verses from both prophets that speak to knowing and being in relationship with God.

YEAR TWO

Read

Hebrews
Powell, Chapter 23, "Hebrews," pages 427–443

Focus

Powell noted that "persistent Christians have found real substance in this [Hebrews] letter: teaching that not only reveals who Christ is but also discloses who they are (and can be) in relation to him."

What significance does knowing who Christ is and who people are in relation to him have for sustaining one's spirituality?

Notice especially the role faith plays in fostering spirituality.

YEAR THREE

Read

MacCulloch, Chapter 14, "Orthodoxy: More Than an Empire," pages 466–502

Focus

MacCulloch covers eight centuries of history to show how Orthodoxy became more than an empire's religion. Describe the profile of Orthodoxy that comes through to you from the chapter.

What key figures, ideas, and events contribute to what Orthodoxy becomes?

YEAR FOUR

Read

Allen, Chapter 14, "Jesus as Lord and Jesus as Servant," pages 147–168

Focus

Allen outlined a theology of Jesus as Servant-Lord that defines a Christian's relationship with God and others. Describe the essence of the doctrine of discipleship described by Allen and the importance for ministry in daily life.

ALL YEARS

Respond

How is your participation in EfM helping you live a life of striving for wholeness, acting wisely, assuming responsibility, and living authentically?

What spiritual practices help you live that kind of life?

How is your relationship with God going?

Practice

Theological reflection brings us into an awareness of God's presence in our life. It is a process that deliberately places us in an open stance before God with a willingness to hear and respond to God. Theological reflection can deepen and sustain our spirituality in a continually maturing Christian life.

Read through the entire outline first to get a sense of its movement and to begin noticing responses and connections you make. If the mentor decides to use the outline or a variation, your work will feed into that.

THEOLOGICAL REFLECTION BEGINNING WITH A PERSONAL EXPERIENCE

(With notes on group reflection process)

Identify a focus.

Reflect theologically on a recent incident in your life. Begin by writing a paragraph or two describing a recent incident that had some impact on you. Write as though you are watching the event through a camera, leaving out for now any comments about thoughts or feelings or any interpretation. Those aspects will fold in later. Simply write the action of the event.

Locate the moment when you experienced the most energy in yourself, when the feelings were strongest. Mark that in some way. List two or three thoughts and the attendant feelings you had at that single moment.

If you were reflecting on this moment with a group, all would now join you in this moment from their own life. Each would recall and recount a time when those specific thoughts and feelings were present.

Leave the rest of the incident aside and focus on the identified thoughts and feelings. Recall them. Notice their general tone, color, temperature, and location in your body.

In a group reflection, all would contribute ideas to identify an image that reflects the thoughts and feelings. The group would agree on one image they are interested in exploring further.

Draw an image or make a statement about what it's like inside those thoughts and feelings. The image universalizes the moment as we move from the specific to the eternal.

This image is your focus for theological reflection.

Explore the focus.

Sit quietly with the image or statement you created from your thoughts and feelings. Allow yourself to be present to the world represented in the image.

Clarify your perspective. You are inside the image. The image represents a particular world at a particular moment. For instance, if the thoughts are "I can't handle this!" and "What just happened??!" and the feelings are anger, relief, and uncertainty, one image might be of the moment of releasing restricted pressure from a hose. The image should capture that set of thoughts and feelings and so the perspective is that of the pressure being released, not of the cause of releasing the pressure. Do you recognize the difference in perspective?

Identify the perspectives in the image and focus on the one that represents the initial thoughts and feelings.

Consider the theological perspective questions all together and respond where a theme fits with the image. What do you want to know about the world in your image? What might those in that world want to know or believe? How might they act? For instance, if the world is one of restricted pressure suddenly released, what are the dynamics of existence? What are the challenges and hopes? What might be needed of grace or forgiveness or repentance?

Connect other wisdom to the focus.

As you consider the theological perspectives of the image-world, what else comes to mind for you? Where have you read an account of someone in our Christian story who experienced a similar dynamic? Look up that story. Compare the challenges and hopes, the grace, forgiveness or repentance in that account with the world of the image.

Have you read an account in the local news, or a book or magazine, or seen a movie or play about someone faced with a similar dynamic? What in that account helps you to understand about such a moment as it is captured in your image?

State your beliefs about living in a world like the image.

Apply insight.

Read all of the questions at once and respond as is fitting for you.

What do you hear with your heart in a new or deeper way that you can apply to your life?

What commitment to place can you make?

How does the reflection and action on the reflection contribute to your own continued conversion?

What might you do to sustain your spiritual life in the moments when daily life is as your image describes?

What will support you in building a spiritual life for sustaining you at those moments?

Write to God about this.

Week Twenty-one

YEAR ONE

Read

Jeremiah
Lamentations
Collins, Chapter 17, "The Babylonian Era," pages 213–224

Focus

The prophetic writings that Collins considers this week are full of poetic imagery. Describe how that imagery has contributed to Christian theology and worship.

What are the books of Jeremiah and Lamentations addressing on a micro, meso, and macro level of human interaction?

YEAR TWO

Read

1 Peter
2 Peter
Powell, Chapter 25, "1 Peter," and Chapter 26, "2 Peter," pages 463–491

Focus

As you read First and Second Peter notice what Powell has to say about the letters and what each contributes to developing one's spirituality.

Which aspects of spiritual maturity–striving for wholeness, acting wisely, assuming responsibility, and living authentically– do you recognize in the letters?

YEAR THREE

Read

MacCulloch, Chapter 15, "Russia: The Third Rome," pages 503–547

Focus

Using MacCulloch's discussion of the advent of Christianity to Russia, describe how he understands the view of God, society, and human nature in that time and place.

YEAR FOUR

Read

Allen, Chapter 15, "Revelation and Faith," pages 155–168

Focus

Allen uses the metaphor of a flashlight to point to how theology functions. Theology illuminates our view of important questions and issues. How does the theology that Allen presents shed light on understanding humanity, the world, and God?

ALL YEARS: PREPARING FOR THE SEMINAR

Respond

Which issues in today's world do you believe require the most spiritual maturity for responding? Write your response.

Practice

Look on the web for other ideas in the area of spiritual practices. What appeals to you?

If you have access to a Book of Common Prayer, look through that for ideas in the area of spiritual practices. What appeals to you?

Describe your "ideal" spiritual practice.

How could that practice enable you to listen with the ear of your heart, commit to place, and engage in continual conversion?

How could that practice increase compassion, justice, and human flourishing?

UNIT FOUR

Integrating Belief, Behavior, and Doctrine

Week Twenty-two

ALL YEARS

Read

Toward Wholeness in Knowing God

What Is Systematic Theology and Why Is It Important?

Systematic theology, says Sarah Coakley, "is an *integrated* presentation of Christian truth"; the goal is "a coherent, and alluring, vision of the Christian faith."[42] Developing a systematic vision of "knowing God" as God has been revealed in the Christian tradition and in our own lives offers important contributions to the process of ministry formation.

Ministry formation is dynamic, developing from the interplay of increasing knowledge and skill that impact identity and attitude. In EfM knowledge grows through learning the narratives, concepts, and images that constitute the content of the Christian tradition. As the ability to work with the content of the Christian heritage develops through reflection on that learning, there is a change in personal identity that simultaneously shapes one's attitude, that is, how one approaches life.

Human beings have a capacity for self-awareness that may be likened to a stream in which ebb and flow form currents and eddies that continually change. Through intentional practice in reflection a person gains a more heightened awareness of and access to similar movements and currents in life. Such reflection often results in forming concepts that can act as receptacles that give shape to the illusive quality of consciousness.

Water has been used as a metaphor for human consciousness. What shape is water? The answer can only be found contextually, through the form provided by containers. Access to life's water can be given shape through the containers of ideas and images. As concepts become more distinctive, awareness increases. The increase gives rise to greater understanding of the mystery that life holds.

Life often seems fragmented. Assistance in bringing the pieces together into a whole–or at least in moving toward wholeness–can be found within the academic discipline of systematic theology. Like most disciplines, the use and abuse has created mixed responses to the work of systematic theologians, but Coakley advocates an approach that avoids some pitfalls that have befallen of the past and provides a descriptive definition of the systematic task as one of practice and integration.

---

42. Sarah Coakley, *God, Sexuality, and the Self: An Essay 'On the Trinity'* (Cambridge, UK: Cambridge University Press, 2013), 41.

> The central theme (and this is vital to the understanding of systematic theology. . . .) is that the task of theology is always, if implicitly, a *recommendation for life*. The vision it sets before one invites ongoing–and sometimes disorienting–response and change, both personal and political, in relation to God. One may rightly call theology from this perspective an ascetical exercise–one that demands bodily practice and transformation, both individual and social. And to admit this is also to acknowledge that the task of theology is always in motion (*in via*), always undoing and redoing itself, not only in response to shifting current events, but because of the deepening of vision that may–and should–emerge from such ascetical demand and execution. Such deepening of vision will eventually also involve at some point a profound sense of the mind's *darkening*, and of a disconcerting reorientation of the senses–these being inescapable fallouts from the commitment to prayer that sustains such a view of the theological enterprise.
>
> . . .
>
> In short, it is an *integrated* presentation of Christian truth, however perceived, that 'system' connotes here: *wherever one choses to start has implications for the whole, and the parts must fit together*. However briefly, or lengthily, it is explicated (and sometimes . . . the shorter versions have been at least as elegant, effective, and enduring as the longer ones), 'systematic theology' must attempt to provide a coherent, and alluring, vision of the Christian faith.[43]

Finding ways into an integrated system of beliefs about fundamental human questions within the context of the Christian faith has always been challenging. Given the unprecedented forces at work in the twenty-first century, the call to "attempt to provide a coherent, and alluring, vision of the Christian faith" can be overwhelming. However, the time frame for developing such a vision covers a lifetime. Once again,

Question: How do you eat that elephant?

Answer: One bite at a time.

As with building a *habitus* in spirituality, so too, with building a coherent, alluring vision of Christian living. It is done within community, one day at a time, and one doctrine at a time.

Theology understood as "knowing God" opens the horizon of "doing theology" beyond intellectual affirmations of propositions. Christian living deals with the whole person on a journey toward an ongoing, holistic approach that brings all the processes of human consciousness into play. A balanced theology includes affirming statements and advocating imperatives, but also honest inquiries, authentic explorations, and deep yearnings, five frames of consciousness that when held in balance help individuals and their communities move toward wholeness and health. David Ford describes the dangers of imbalance:

43. Coakley, *God, Sexuality, and the Self*, 18–19, 41.

The importance of a wise balance of questions, explorations, affirmations, commands, and desires goes far beyond the writing of theology. Whole communities and traditions can be characterized according to their habitual balances between them. What in our time is often rightly labeled "bad religion" or "dangerous religion" tends to be based on packaged theologies with a heavy investment in telling members exactly what to believe and what to do, and in limiting any scope for questioning and exploring. Such packages have enormous attraction, especially in times of insecurity, pluralism, and rapid change. They appear in all the religions today and also in secular forms of dogmatism. Within many Christian denominations and local congregations there are ongoing battles over the soul and spirit of the faith, and over the boundaries of the community, in which packaged certainties fight it out with more balanced ecologies. Unwise theology has serious practical effects.

There is an opposite pole: forms of religion that are so wide open, fluid, vague, or fragmented that they seem to lack the capacity to make definite affirmations or give any clear guidance for living. "Mix-and-match" temporary blends of experimental beliefs and practices, satisfying the desire for self-fulfillment, would be an extreme version of this, but the mindset represented by these is common in consumer societies and therefore within many religious communities. Often these are not much concerned with theology, but the tendencies contribute to a caricature of theology that is common among those whose own theology is more packaged.

This is the caricature of "liberal" theologies as endlessly interrogative and experimental without ever being able to come to conclusions or to offer nourishing theological food for ordinary people. They are so alert to the array of possibilities, to the suspicions and critiques that can undermine all positions, and to the dangers of exercising authority by supporting doctrinal and ethical instruction (think of all those fundamentalist extremists!), that they cannot say anything definite at all. So there is a dissipation of intellectual energy, and despair at finding a habitable faith. . . . There are very high stakes here, both for the church internally and for its ways of relating to other religions and to the rest of society. To advocate a balance of moods that constantly tries to discern what the right blend is for a particular topic, situation, or genre is not only to require continual debate and deliberation but also to invite attack from those many positions that want to eliminate or minimize one or more of the moods. This means that the balanced position must be theologically supported–mostly in the indicative mood![44]

The "indicative mood" asserts what is held to be true and trustworthy. Since the Enlightenment, Western theology has been captivated, if not captured, by the idea that the way into faith is through carefully constructed statements of beliefs. The unexamined assumption has been that if a Christian gives intellectual assent to "right beliefs" (orthodoxy) they are "saved."

44. David F. Ford, *The Future of Christian Theology* (West Sussex, UK: Wiley-Blackwell, 2011), 70.

The beliefs, in turn, were translated into prescribed ethical behaviors that describe what one is to do or not do: no work on Sunday; attend church every Sunday; dress properly (especially in church); behave according to the norms laid out by authorities, especially church leaders. Commandments, especially the Ten Commandments, are taken to heart–literally memorized. Children nearing adulthood are required to commit to memory the catechism or some "confession of faith." The intent is to order lives so that self and society live according to God's Laws in order that all will be well. Belief and commandment contain all that is "necessary for salvation."

Overemphasis of confessional beliefs and prescribed behavior causes an atrophy of other vitally important features of a complete person. Much of a person is left behind when wonder (curiosity), exploration (experimenting), and heartfelt yearnings are devalued. Curiosity gives rise to questions and wondering, which in turn give rise to searching and exploration. Recall that the Hebrew understanding of heart meant the whole person–mind, body, emotion, and imagination. A theology that neglects emotion, imagination, searching, and deep desires is a truncated theology. Balance is necessary for growth into Christian maturity.

Coakley recasts her work as a theologian under the descriptive term *théologie totale*–a way of knowing God that is grounded in contemplation (listening prayer); in honest consideration of issues raised by gender, sexuality, and race; and incorporates insights from art, science, literature, and music. Above all, *théologie totale* is an ongoing process (*in via*.)[45]

Systematic theology is important because it affords an opportunity to carefully and thoroughly view knowledge of and about God from a holistic standpoint. Systematic theology provides categories such as creation, sin, judgment, repentance, redemption, and so forth as avenues that lead to knowing God. A person undertakes the systematic task when he or she considers how belief, attitude, action, and behavior form a coherent whole. Such methodological workings hold the potential and promise to guide a Christian into wisdom. Systematic theology, when done with humility and courage, brings the whole of human experience into play that results in a "recommendation for life" and provides "a coherent, and alluring, vision of the Christian faith."

Doctrines and Dogmas

Patterns of beliefs over centuries have formed the subject areas of theology. Traditionally, the basic affirmations contained in the creeds outline the general areas of belief. Creation, human nature (theological anthropology), the nature of Christ (Christology), church (ecclesiology), and Heaven/Hell/Judgment/Death (eschatology) are the usual topics for building a theological system. How the answers to these fundamental theological questions fit together is the concern of the systematic theologian.

45. Coakely, *God, Sexuality, and the Self*, 88ff.

To answer the question of whether some pieces of the theological system are more important than others, church teachings are sometimes grouped into two categories: doctrine and dogma. Theologian Robert Hughes carefully draws distinctions between the two for Episcopalians.

> Doctrines are more or less official teachings of particular faith communities. However fun it may be to inquire into their general, philosophical truth, they are always linked to particular faith communities and their conversation. They are not simply free-floating propositions with no context and no history. The Episcopal Church has never been shy about the teaching office, though it has often been lax about it. Our doctrine is rooted in Scripture, and expressed in the Book of Common Prayer, in both liturgies and historical documents. The authorized hymnals are a further source of teaching. Where further questions arise, General Convention, with the initiative in the House of Bishops in this case, clarifies. That is our polity.[46]

Among the numerous doctrines of the church some are held with significant authority, sometimes described as "core doctrines," yet Hughes admonishes the reader to treat this term with care:

> "Core doctrine" is a very loose and slippery term. We have no clear sense of how big that bag is or might become. That leaves us open in the current mess to debates about whether or not ethical norms and rules for their application are or could be "core doctrine."
>
> Dogma, by contrast, is a very precise word. A doctrine becomes a dogma when an ecumenical council of the universal church declares that such and such a doctrine has become dogma because all the known alternatives can be shown clearly to damage and subvert the gospel. This council then must be received by the consent of the faithful as indeed truly ecumenical.[47]

Doctrines of the church are categorized using three Latin terms: *esse*, *bene esse*, and *plene esse*.

> *Esse* indicates that which is of the essence of the very existence of the life of the church. *Bene esse* indicates that which is of benefit for the life of the church. *Plene esse* indicates that which is of the fullness of the Church's life.[48]

Dogmas are *esse*, those teachings that speak "of the essence of the very existence of the life of the church." According to Hughes:

> From an Anglican point of view, indeed from the point of view of any non-Roman Christian body which accepts any role for tradition, there are precisely and exactly two dogmas: the doctrine of the Holy Triadic Unity as the proper doctrine of God, and the doctrine of two natures in one hypostasis of our Lord Jesus Christ.[49]

---

46. Robert D. Hughes, III, "Dogma and Freedom," *Anglican Theological Review* Vol. 86, No. 4 (Fall, 2004), 585.
47. Ibid.
48. *Glossary of Terms*, http://archive.episcopalchurch.org/109399_14308_ENG_HTM.htm
49. Hughes, "Dogma and Freedom," 585.

Trinity and Incarnation become the dual foci around which a theological ellipse forms. Individual beliefs and behaviors, especially about human nature and God's self-revelation, implicate one's understanding of the doctrines of Christology and Trinity. Likewise, these two doctrines open the horizon to new vistas of humanity, nature, mystery, and holiness.

Knowing God Through the Micro, Meso, and Macro Levels of Human Behavior

Imagine walking down a giant spiral stair (shaped something like a bedspring) that circles while moving progressively deeper. Creating a mature theology means passing through the formation areas of identity, attitude, knowledge, and skill. Beliefs (positions) and behavior (actions) mark the journey. Each Christian person is challenged to find in any moment, what she or he believes about the nature of Christ (Christology) and how those beliefs are supported within the Christian tradition. How a Christian sees God must also be held in dialogue with views of the Trinity. Questions regarding beliefs about the Incarnation and Trinity impact the formation of identity and attitude as lived within daily life.

The particularities of individual beliefs (usually introduced with "for me") every so often expose a universal "truth." Step by step the individual's specific beliefs expressed either verbally or behaviorally, move into the communal level, morphing from "for me-isms" into "we-isms." The corporate, shared positions woven through institutions fashion a society.

James K. A. Smith describes the influence of institutions.

> For a boy growing up in Ontario, it was never a question: you're going to play hockey. Though Embro was a village of only 600 people at the time, we had a new arena, a robust minor hockey system, and a long legacy of the sport encoded in our civic DNA. So at four years old, we all moved from the pond to the ice pad, donning the purple hockey sweaters that many of us wore until we were twenty.
>
> This was also part of something bigger. You could count on neighbouring villages like Drumbo and Plattesville and St. George having minor hockey systems, all webbed together by the OMHA.
>
> When you're ten years old, you think this is just part of the furniture of the cosmos; something given, natural, and taken for granted–that Saturday morning clinics and Tuesday night practices are just part of the rhythm of the universe, as if when God said, "Let there be light," the big klieg lights in the rafters of the arena also came on. You never really think about what sustains all this, and if you do, you just imagine some anonymous "them" holds it all together, a vague, distant "they" who are responsible for all of this.
>
> But when you're an adult you realize: this doesn't just happen. That something as mundane and yet enduring as Embro minor hockey is not a given; it is an institution. It is only because it is sustained by communities. It is bigger than the people who inhabit it, but it also depends on the people who embody it. The "they" you never saw in your youth turn out to just be people like you who have taken the reins and taken ownership. We could only take minor

hockey for granted because, in fact, each generation received it anew, owning it, tending it, reforming it, and passing it on to the next generation.[50]

Individuals become socialized through the institutions that surround them. Basic human questions and concerns are "answered" by participating in such social assumptions. The institutional church communicates often explicitly, but more powerfully implicitly, the fundamentals of Christianity, and there is a direct relationship between the health of the institutional church and a life-giving theology. Smith points to the importance and power of institutions. He also notes that ministry happens in and through them.

> In a cynical age that tends to glorify "startups" and celebrate anti-institutional suspicion, faith in institutions will sound dated, stodgy, old-fashioned, even (gasp) "conservative." So Christians who are eager to be progressive, hip, relevant, and creative tend to buy into such anti-institutionalism, thus mirroring and mimicking wider cultural trends (which, ironically, are often parasitic upon institutions!).
>
> And yet those same Christians are rightly concerned about "the common good." They are newly convinced that the Gospel has implications for all of life and that being a Christian should mean something for *this* world. Jesus calls us not only to ensure our own salvation in some privatized religious ghetto; he calls us to seek the welfare of the city and its inhabitants all around us. We love God by loving our neighbours; we glorify God by caring for the poor; we exhibit the goodness of God by promoting the common good.
>
> But here's the thing: if you're really passionate about fostering the common good, then you should resist anti-institutionalism. Because institutions are ways to love our neighbours. Institutions are durable, concrete structures that–when functioning well–cultivate all of creation's potential toward what God desires: *shalom*, peace, goodness, justice, flourishing, delight. Institutions are the way we get a handle on concrete realities and address different aspects of creaturely existence. Institutions will sometimes be scaffolds to support the weak; sometimes they function as fences to protect the vulnerable; in other cases, institutions are the springboards that enable us to pursue new innovation. Even though they can become corrupt and stand in need of reform, institutions themselves are not the enemy.[51]

Communal living as carried on through institutions occurs within an even greater context. From time to time it is prudent to take a look at the macrocosm in which individuals and institutions are installed. Teilhard de Chardin, paleontologist and Jesuit theologian, wrote extensively about the larger context in which humanity lives.

---

50. James K. A. Smith, "Editorial: We Believe in Institutions," *Comment: public theology for the common good,* http://www.cardus.ca/comment/article/4039/editorial-we-believe-in-institutions/

51. Ibid.

> We know, theologically, that Christ, the Divine Word, was with God in the beginning and during the entire creation process. "All things came into being through him, and without him not one thing came into being. What has come into being in him was life" (John 1:1–4). Everything that exists is imbued with this life and is inescapably part of the cosmos that God loves passionately (see John 3:16). So why should God want to discard any part of it?
>
> We now know, scientifically, that our planet itself cannot be seen as something independent of our neighboring planets and the sun, but in reality the Earth is totally dependent of the balance and makeup of our solar system. If the planets Mars and Venus, for example, weren't in precisely their orbits relative to the Earth and all the planets relative to the Sun, then our atmosphere would not be able to sustain life as we know it. We are, in fact, one with our solar system. So our entire solar system must also be a part of the great Christ Body.[52]

Teilhard folds the entire universe into his theology: "Through the Divine Word at the Big Bang all things came into being. Whatever came to be had its existence founded in him. So for its truest fulfillment, the Total Christ must be at least as large as the universe."[53]

Christian theology speaks to Christian maturity at the micro, meso, and macro levels of existence. On the micro level living well (*eudemonia*) is the goal (*telos*); on the meso level, human flourishing (*pleroma*). On the macro level, the consummation of all things (*eschaton*) becomes that toward which all are moving. Attending to each level is necessary as one constructs a personal systematic theology that moves toward coherence and consistence of doctrine, belief, and behavior.

The journey into Christian maturity requires maneuvering through the swamps and gardens found in individuals and institutions. Embedded within individuals and expressed through institutional living we find affirmations of "truth"; commandments to "do this"; questions being permitted or even cheered; encouragement (or not) to explore and search; and support to follow desires and yearnings. In addition, one's view of the universe (cosmology) shapes what is expected or considered even possible. What are the affirmations, commands, inquiries, explorations, and desires that you hold? And how do these expressions inform your understanding of the Incarnation and the Trinity? How do the doctrines of Trinity and Incarnation inform and shape your own expressions, institutional realities, and cosmic awareness? All of this becomes part of how you shape a comprehensive and coherent theology that systematically considers all possible dimensions. The task is daunting, to say the least. Yet, reflecting on the whole picture from time to time is part of the process of a maturing faith lived out among the chances and challenges of this transitory life.

---

52. Louis M. Savary, *Teilhard de Chardin–The Divine Milieu Explained: a Spirituality of the 21st Century* (New York, NY: Paulist Press, 2007), 24–25.

53. Ibid., 25.

Focus

Describe some of the aspects of systematic theology, according to Sarah Coakley.

Distinguish between doctrine and dogma.

Respond

How do the ongoing development of knowledge, attitude, identity, and skill contribute to forming a personal systematic theology?

How does a personal system of theology shape ministry and how is such a system shaped by ministry?

Practice

Theology, especially within the Anglican tradition, is both an individual and a communal project. Each individual, congregation, denomination, and world-wide communion acts out of a theological system. EfM participants are asked to participate in the reconstructing process of Christian theology by constructing their own theological system in collaboration with other seminar members in light of increasing knowledge of the Christian traditions. It begins as each participant constructs her or his theological questions and answers within a systematic structure.

The theological reflection model used in EfM provides a careful and unique way to apply a theological system to a personal experience; a circumstance in our society; a personal belief; or a writing, hymn, or image from our Christian tradition. In theological reflection we look through the lenses of theological categories. We can use the traditional theological names for these categories, like Creation, Sin, Judgment, Repentance, and Redemption, or we can frame them in more contemporary terms, such as Wholeness, Separation, Recognition, Reorientation, and Restoration. Whichever language we choose, these categories generally help us see the dynamic relationship of God and humankind. A systematic approach reveals the panorama of its goodness or creative presence, our sin or separation from God's vision of wholeness, how we recognize our separation, what we need to do to reorient and turn back towards the wholeness God holds out to us, and what that restoration to wholeness or redeemed creation looks like.

This systematic approach is not a simple chart of all the answers, to be filled out completely and finally. Each question when answered in turn leads to another, perhaps better question. Throughout history, Christians have deployed a variety of systems to envision the whole of Christian theology. That visioning process is the work of constructing a systematic theology. The building of a theological system has taken different forms. For example, a catechism (which is a systematic theology) proceeds in a question and answer format, often structured around the Apostles' Creed. For example, see the Catechism on pages 845–862 of the Book of Common Prayer. Each answer can lead to further questions such as "How do we understand the 'image of God'?"; "What does it mean to be part of God's creation?" or "Who is this creator God?" Questions of belief lead to questions of behavior and vice versa. Through the 20th Century in the United States it was common for theological books to have chapters employing the same creedal organization.

Some academic theologians construct their theology in numerous volumes, such as Karl Barth's thirteen volume *Church Dogmatics (Kirchliche Dogmatik)*. These approaches tend to work from common theological interests: God and God's self-expression; human nature; creation (goodness and wholeness); sin as brokenness, separation, and alienation; events that bring recognition (judgment); decisions to change (repent); restoration to wholeness (redemption).

A grid may serve as a map to illuminate our own view of theological relationships.

Make five columns across a sheet of paper, labeling them "Goodness or Wholeness," "Brokenness or Separation," "Recognition," "Reorientation," and "Restoration to Wholeness."

At the side of the page, create three rows labeled "Micro: Individual," "Meso: Institutions," and "Macro: Global."

	Goodness or Wholeness	**Brokenness or Separation**	**Recognition**	**Reorientation**	**Restoration**
Micro: Individual					
Meso: Institutions					
Macro: Global					

Work through the map created by this set of theological perspectives (wholeness, and so forth) and the terrain of our life and world at each level. Each intersecting spot provides a location for constructing questions. For example, in the Goodness/Wholeness column one might frame a series of questions modified by the different levels: "How do I recognize goodness/ wholeness in my individual experience?"(micro level) ; "How is goodness/ wholeness shown in the institutional church or in any other institution?" (meso level); "How is goodness/wholeness manifested globally?" (macro level). Frame a few questions in several of the intersecting spots to get a sense of applying the map or system to any matter, that is, a personal experience (micro level), an institution's life (meso level) or global realities (macro). Write you how presently answer the questions posed by the map. How might your answer lead to a better question?

A theological system can help us use a vision of the kingdom of God to explore any variety of circumstances in daily life. It can be a diagnostic/ identifying tool for utilizing Coakley's way to flesh out an interrelated theology, a *théologie totale*. In what way does this work (and it is ongoing work) contribute to forming your knowledge of Christian theology, your personal attitudes about God and creation, your personal identity as one who serves in Christ's name, or your skills of ministry?

Week Twenty-three

YEAR ONE

Read

Ezekiel
Collins, Chapter 18, "Ezekiel," pages 225–238

Focus

State some noteworthy elements that distinguish the Book of Ezekiel.

Identify the two traditions that combine in Ezekiel's opening vision.

How does symbolic action figure into Ezekiel's prophetic work?

Describe the impact of Ezekiel's prophetic work on your personal beliefs.

YEAR TWO

Read

Philemon
Jude
Powell, Chapter 22, "Philemon" and Chapter 28, "Jude," pages 415–425

Focus

Use the online resource for this textbook at bakerpublishinggroup.com/books/introducing-the-new-testament/264690/esources to respond to the objectives stated there for Chapters 22 and 28.

Describe how the Christian (as seen in Paul's letters) and Roman cultures viewed slavery.

YEAR THREE

Read

MacCulloch, Chapter 16, "Perspectives on the True Church (1300–1517)," pages 551–603

Focus

Define: Erasmus; translation of Matthew 3:2; some key views of Erasmus

With this chapter, MacCulloch returned to Western Christianity. Events, especially tragic ones, impact how people think about and know God. Describe how the Black Death influenced behavior and belief. Notice especially how multicultural realities contributed to the perspectives described in the chapter.

YEAR FOUR

Read

Allen, Chapter 16, "The Holy Spirit, the Church, and the Sacraments," pages 171–182

Focus

Define: apostle; Pentecost; "colony of heaven"; eschatological community

Describe how the nature of the New Testament church broke down barriers between people.

ALL YEARS

Respond

What barriers does religion create or eliminate?

Practice

THEOLOGICAL REFLECTION BEGINNING WITH A PERSONAL EXPERIENCE

This variation of theological reflection has sometimes been referred to as the "microscope method" because it describes the refining process that helps focus intently on a beginning point for theological reflection. Typically, the method begins in someone's experience and systematically focuses the circumstance to one fleeting moment in which to open the self or group to the eternal. In this form of theological reflection, we move into the particular to discover the eternal.

Identify a focus from which to reflect:

Recall and recount a time when you were confronted with a barrier of some sort. Describe the circumstance in as much detail as possible.

Notice when there were significant shifts in energy in the event and identify the one moment of greatest energy for you. Let all else fall away and mentally stand just in that discrete instant.

List two or three primary feelings and two or three key thoughts you had *at that tiny moment.* Decline any internal mental invitation to explain, justify, or interpret. Just let yourself accept your key thoughts and feelings of the moment.

Let yourself feel the feelings and notice where in your body they are. What is that like? Do they create a sensation of heat or cold? What color do they have? Settle into those thoughts and feelings and create a picture of what it's like for you when you experience that combination. For instance, is it like a tea kettle whistling because pressure has built up, or like walking barefoot on rocks, or like hanging from a limb high off the ground?

Write or draw a picture of what it's like when those feelings and thoughts are present. From this point forward, the reflection is on the image or picture-world that represents your thoughts and feelings, not on the original incident.

Theologically explore the world represented in your picture.

Stay inside the picture-world for this exploration. How does that world reveal something about wholeness or goodness, or about brokenness?

What does someone in that picture-world have to recognize in order to know there is brokenness? What would that person have to change in order to move towards wholeness?

What would it take to restore wholeness?

Connect by letting your mind freely move through and around the image.

What does your image-world call to mind for you? Are there events in the world around you that relate to the image and help you make sense of those kinds of moments?

If you've been thinking of some scripture passages or a hymn or prayer, stop and look those up. This is a very important part of theological reflection. How do any of those connections help make sense of this kind of moment?

What do you believe about living in a world such as the image captured? What helped to form that belief? Do you sense any other possible beliefs?

Apply to daily life. Theological reflection provides support for living a life of maturity in faith and action.

In what ways might this reflection inform your behavior when you again have an experience that raises these thoughts and feelings? Make notes about how reflecting theologically on this moment helps you integrate belief and behavior and raises any kind of possibilities for you in ministry and maturity.

There may be opportunity during the group's seminar time to explore the theological reflections of various group members. There may be time to do a group reflection around a central theme of the group's choosing. If so, what do you notice about the difference(s) between reflecting alone and reflecting in a group?

Week Twenty-four

YEAR ONE

Read

Isaiah 40–66
Haggai, Zechariah, Malachi, Joel, and Jonah
Collins, Chapter 19, "The Additions to Isaiah," and Chapter 20, "Postexilic Prophecy," pages 239–268

Focus

What issues of belief and behavior do these prophets try to address?

How are the same issues present today?

YEAR TWO

Read

Philippians and Colossians
Powell, Chapter 17, "Philippians," and Chapter 18, "Colossians," pages 343–369

Focus

Review the online resources for these chapters at http://www.introducingNT.com. Take time to make notes relative to the chapter objectives Powell identifies.

What beliefs and practices are at stake in the letters to the Philippians and the Colossians?

How is Paul attempting to mentor spiritual maturity with those to whom he writes?

YEAR THREE

Read

MacCulloch, Chapter 17, "A House Divided," pages 604–654

Focus

Define: Luther's view of indulgences; Zwingli; importance of Romans 13:1 to Luther and the Reformation; Calvinist; Augsburg Confession; soteriology

Describe the values that drive the actions of reformers. Think about how those values shape doctrines of God, humanity, and creation.

How do those values relate to your personal experience and values?

How are those values reflected in our contemporary society?

What challenge or support is there for living faithfully with your values?

YEAR FOUR

Read

Allen, Chapter 17, "Sin, Evil, and Hope for the Future," and the Epilogue, pages 183–199

Focus

Allen presents several key ideas in these two essays: Julian of Norwich's comparison of knowledge of God to wounds; a "colony of heaven"; and "truth which is active in the soul [the whole person]" (Simone Weil), among others.

State key ideas you found in your reading.

What significance, if any, do these ideas have for tensions between belief and behavior?

How do any of the ideas contribute to developing Christian maturity?

ALL YEARS

Respond

State your understanding of how working on the connection between belief and behavior can contribute to maturing in faith and spirituality.

What are the resistances to that work?

Practice

THEOLOGICAL REFLECTION BEGINNING WITH A DILEMMA

First, read through this method a time or two before working with it and then try applying it to a dilemma from your past.

Identify

Describe a time when you faced a dilemma in decision and action. For the purposes of this reflection, the incident should be one that is already completed, with no decisions pending.

Ex.: When my son died suddenly I was given the option to view his body in the morgue before he was taken for cremation. I was so torn and so deeply in sorrow and pain and shock. I could barely absorb this loss. The thought of seeing him that way was horrifying. I wanted only to think of him as alive. I guess to deny the death. And yet, I wanted to see him one more time. I chose not to view.

Name the turning point in your incident once you have written about the experience.

What's the central moment of your incident? Where is the tension greatest? What was happening? What were you thinking and feeling at that moment?

Describe the central moment and your thoughts and feelings at that moment.

State the central dilemma at the moment of greatest tension. Often a simple statement of the dilemma works better than an image in this type of reflection. Dilemmas tend to get represented metaphorically as "walking a tightrope," or "between a rock and hard place," but these are metaphors for any dilemma and too generic to work well. The specific dilemma in an incident needs to be clarified and clearly stated in universal terms. Universalizing is a corrective for giving advice or overly focusing on one person.

To help get to the dilemma statement, list statements about what you wanted at the moment you felt the tension or what interests were at stake at that moment. You will likely have several "I wanted" statements.

Ex.: I wanted my son alive. I wanted to see him. I wanted to protect myself from the pain. I wanted to remember him as he had been. I wanted this to be a dream.

Select the pair of statements that best represents the central dilemma. Record the dilemma statement as "I wanted _____ **and** I wanted _______."

Note: A dilemma is a tension between two things a person wants, not between an "I want" and "I don't want." It is a challenge to get to two "I want" statements that clearly reflect the dilemma. The dilemma is between two goods, but a choice has to be made.

Most important step: Record the *universal* dilemma. For instance, if my dilemma is between using recently received birthday money for myself and bailing out an indigent friend's child who is in jail for the first time, the universal nature could perhaps be stated as "the dilemma is between taking care of self and helping others." Universalizing is especially necessary when reflecting in a group in order to avoid advice-giving and problem-solving.

Note: If this were a group reflection, each person would identify a moment when they, too, experienced the same universal dilemma. In a group, this is another way in which a tendency to continue to focus on the presenter can be redirected.

Explore the universal dilemma by considering what it is like to live in that dilemma/tension.

Use Cost/Promise (Risk/Hope) or Theological Perspectives as a tool to explore the universal dilemma.

COST/PROMISE

Name the costs (risks) and promises (hopes) of each side of the dilemma. For instance, what is the cost of taking care of oneself and what is the promise of doing that? Likewise, what are the costs and promises of helping others?

OR

THEOLOGICAL PERSPECTIVES

Questions exploring theological concepts can be used either with an image or a dilemma statement. For instance, in the universal dilemma between taking care of self and helping others, it would be possible to consider what that dilemma reveals about justice, compassion, and human flourishing.

Use only one or two of the following question examples when exploring:

What are the power dimensions of the dilemma or image? Who has power? What has to be yielded?

What sacrifice(s) might be called for? What are the temptations of the cross, of powerlessness? To whom or what is power yielded?

How is power transmitted to the powerless party? What is required in order to enter the cycle that leads to empowerment? What builds endurance?

What tomb is left in the image or dilemma?

How does resurrection or hope occur in the image or dilemma?

Connect to other ways this universalized dilemma has been engaged in our Christian story or the culture around you or in your personal beliefs. *Remember, these connections can come in any order. This is not a rote exercise, but a reflection. The purpose of laying out the sources is only to help remind you of these areas if one or more do not come to mind on their own.*

CHRISTIAN TRADITION

Identify some stories from scripture or church history that relate to the dilemma. In the stories of the people of God, who has been in the same dilemma? Or perhaps some prayers or hymns come to mind that relate to this reflection. Look up what you recall and spend time with the story or account or prayer or hymn. How does the connection help or challenge you in this dilemma?

Compare and contrast what our Christian Tradition and the initial experience have to say about the universal dilemma. What choices would the Tradition support? Not support? Why?

CULTURE/SOCIETY

How is the universal dilemma you identified experienced in our culture? Have there been news stories about it? Have you read a book or seen a movie that dealt with that dilemma? Is there a political dimension to that dilemma?

POSITION

What do you believe about the issues raised by the dilemma? How were your beliefs in conflict in the dilemma? What do you hope for regarding the dilemma? What formed your beliefs about this matter?

Apply

INSIGHTS AND QUESTIONS

What do you see in a new way now? What have you learned about facing this dilemma? What questions remain for you in this kind of dilemma?

IMPLICATIONS

Identify how the reflection has helped you to listen with the ear of your heart, bolstered commitment to place, and/or contributed to continual conversion for you.

What do you want or need to do? Do you feel a call or a tug to do something specific? Consider social implications, actions you could take, what else you could or need to learn, support that would help in the midst of such a dilemma, and where you could find that support.

There may be opportunity during the group's seminar time to explore these individual theological reflections, and/or to do a reflection around a dilemma of the group's choosing.

Week Twenty-five

YEAR ONE

Read

Ezra
Nehemiah
Collins, Chapter 21, "Ezra and Nehemiah," pages 269–282

Focus

The authors of Ezra and Nehemiah place a high value on identity, security, and justice. Identify how these values shape Israel's understanding of God's promises.

What role do identity, security, and justice play in maturing spiritually?

YEAR TWO

Read

1 Timothy
2 Timothy
Titus
Powell, Chapter 21, "Pastoral Letters," pages 397–413

Focus

Define "pastoral letters"; Titus; Timothy; major themes in the pastoral letters; Arius

Describe Paul's struggle against "false teachings" and advocacy of "sound doctrines."

Compare Paul's struggles with similar issues in the church today.

Use the chapter's hyperlinks to deepen your understanding.

YEAR THREE

Read

MacCulloch, Chapter 18, "Rome's Renewal," pages 655–688

Focus

Define: Valdensians; Jesuits; importance of the oratory movement; Regensburg; Council of Trent; Tridentine liturgy; counter-reformation; role of Queen Mary; King Sigismund III; significant effects of the Reformation and Catholic Reformation on Latin Christianity

Make a list of several belief and behavior issues that were part of Rome's renewal.

YEAR FOUR

Read

Sedgwick, *The Christian Moral Life: Practices in Piety*: "Introduction," Chapter 1, "Describing the Christian Life," and Chapter 2, "An Anglican Perspective," pages ix–51

Focus

Given Sedgwick's presentation, reflect on how the study of ethics contributes to the formation of theology. What are the creative aspects of Sedgwick's views? What choices do his views present to you? Reflect on how his views of ethics relate to what you see in the culture in which you live.

Note what you believe about the study and practice of ethics. What do you view in a new way after reading this week's assignment? State any implications of that awareness for what you might do differently in the future.

ALL YEARS

Respond

News reports may often expose gaps between how individuals or groups seem to believe and how they act. Gather some examples to share at the seminar session.

Practice

Notice how you feel and what you think as you come across examples in the news of behavior-belief gaps. Write a paragraph or two about your response to one of the news items.

Review what you have written and highlight any elements of reflection you can identify.

What implications did you arrive at in your writing?

How do the implications relate to Coakley's "recommendation for life . . . ongoing–and sometimes disorienting–response and change, both personal and political, in relation to God"?

Week Twenty-six

YEAR ONE

Read

1 Chronicles
2 Chronicles
Collins, Chapter 22, "The Books of Chronicles," pages 283–292

Focus

Define: the overall theme of 1 Chronicles and that of 2 Chronicles; organization of priests and Levites in 1 Chronicles; Hezekiah; Josiah

What view of God is evident in these texts?

YEAR TWO

Read

1 Thessalonians
2 Thessalonians
Powell, Chapter 19, "1 Thessalonians," and Chapter 20, "2 Thessalonians," pages 371–385

Focus

Define: *parousia*; eschatology; value of 1 Thessalonians; primary differences between 1 and 2 Thessalonians

Notice doctrines that are either implicitly or explicitly mentioned in the two letters to the Thessalonians. What light does Powell shed on the doctrines?

YEAR THREE

Read

MacCulloch, Chapter 19, "A Worldwide Faith," pages 689–715

Focus

Define: Bartolomé de las Casas; Francisco de Vitoria; pattern of settlements in New Spain; João de Cruz and the Paravas; Robert de Nobili; Mvemba Nzinga; *Santeria*

Well-crafted histories aid in understanding the social and intellectual period in which contemporary theology has developed. Name the primary factors that influence the building of theology for today's world.

YEAR FOUR

Read

Sedgwick, Chapter 3, "Incarnate Love," and Chapter 4, "Love and Justice," pages 53–101

Focus

In Chapter 3 Sedgwick uses sexuality, idolatry, and hospitality as elements to sketch a picture of incarnate love. Chapter 4 brings an important discussion of love and justice to the table. How does either of those themes contribute most to the theology you are building?

ALL YEARS

Respond

The people of the biblical testament affirm God's relationship with them in history. As a result of your EfM study, what sense do you have of God's acting in history and into the present?

What examples can you give to show how people of faith have struggled to make belief and behavior congruent?

Practice

THEOLOGICAL REFLECTION BEGINNING WITH A PERSONAL EXPERIENCE

Recall a recent experience on which you would like to reflect. The incident could have been one with either "good" feelings or with the opposite.

Identify a focus in that experience. What was the incident about? Identify the moment when you felt the greatest amount of internal energy.

Name the two or three key thoughts and feelings you had at that moment of highest energy. What was at stake?

Recall that specific moment. Sit quietly in that moment. Feel the feelings. Put your moment's thoughts and feelings into picture or statement form–"when I had/have those feelings, it was like . . . "

Explore the focus. Exploration is the practice of considering the focus from several angles, such as what kind of world is pictured, how the image reveals something about brokenness, what would require repentance, how new life might result for those in the image.

Other perspectives could be ones of power–who has power, or is powerless, or is empowered, what has to be relinquished to give up power.

What part do love, grace, or forgiveness play in the image?

Connect with other sources of understanding. You began the reflection in personal experience. What beliefs do your actions convey in that experience? Where do those beliefs come from? Where does the Christian tradition speak in the image; that is, does anything in the image remind you of someone or something in the Christian story? If so, look up the passage or teaching that relates to that connection. What books or movies or wisdom figures of our culture have dealt with the situation depicted in the image?

How do those connections shed light on the incident with which you began?

Apply

How did the experience connect belief and behavior for you?

What might this connection between belief and behavior help you do in the future?

Week Twenty-seven

YEAR ONE

Read

Psalms 1–150
Song of Songs
Collins, Chapter 23, "Psalms and Song of Songs," pages 293–306

Focus

Notice how the Psalms are grouped and reflect on the purpose.

Identify one psalm that illustrates each of the following categories:

- Complaints
- Hymns of praise
- Royal psalms
- Thanksgiving

YEAR TWO

Read

James
Powell, Chapter 24, "James," pages 445–461

Focus

Define: wisdom literature; dispersion; purpose of the Letter of James

What view of God and of Christian community does James promote?

YEAR THREE

Read

MacCulloch, Chapter 20, "Protestant Awakenings," pages 716–765

Focus

Define: covenant in the establishment of the church in North America; John Winthrop; congregational; Anne Hutchinson; Roger Williams; Quakers; John Eliot; John Locke; William Penn; Non-Jurors; pietism; Moravians; August Hermann Francke; place of hymnody and music; Count Nikolaus Ludwig von Zinzendorf; Methodism; John Wesley; evangelicals; George Whitefield; Gilbert Tennent; Great Awakenings

What aspects of North American Christianity's growth are most evident in your religious heritage?

YEAR FOUR

Read

Sedgwick, Chapter 5, "The Practices of Faith," Chapter 6, "The Call of God," and "Appendix," pages 103–158

Focus

Define: *kataphatic*; sacramental acts; sacrifice

Record your answers to Sedgwick's questions, "What has been most significant in your experience of worship, and what has been most difficult?" (p. 103)

ALL YEARS

Respond

Spiritual disciplines described by Timothy Sedgwick in the reading for Year Four are meditation and contemplation; examination of our lives; denial and simplification of life; and action. Which of these have you engaged the most?

How do spiritual disciplines contribute to the formation of coherence in belief and behavior?

Practice

Of the four disciplines/practices described in the Respond section, identify the one you have engaged the least. If so desired, make a plan for how you could incorporate that practice in your life more regularly.

What will it take to move from plan to practice?

The letter to the Romans names specific practices for the followers of Christ: "Do not lag in zeal, be ardent in spirit, serve the Lord. Rejoice in hope, be patient in suffering, persevere in prayer. Contribute to the needs of the saints, extend hospitality to strangers." (Romans 12:11–13). What are the costs and promises of living that life?

What happens when you regularly engage spiritual practices?

SECOND INTERLUDE

Knowing Who We Are

Week Twenty-eight

ALL YEARS

Read

Thompsett, *We Are Theologians: Strengthening the People of God,* Preface and pages 1–54

Focus

How is memory essential to liberation?"

What is the Bible's overall message about the Church?

In what ways can knowing our history help us look back in order to think ahead?

What are the primary legacies of our Protestant inheritance as Anglicans?

Identify some of the ways Christian laypersons led the way in nineteenth-century social reforms.

ALL YEARS

Respond

A comprehensive systematic theology includes ecclesiology, a theology of the church. "Whether implicit or explicit, our theology of the church, our ecclesiology, shapes expectations for the church's work in the world."[54]

54. Fredrica Harris Thompsett, *We Are Theologians: Strengthening the People of God* (New York: Church Publishing, 2004), 2.

Practice

"Our theology of church needs to shape our definitions of 'ministry.'"[55]
In what way does your own definition of ministry incorporate Thompsett's assertion that ministers are

- Created?
- Chosen?
- Pursued?
- Sent?
- Trusted?

Think back to the spiritual autobiographies offered this year. What examples of members of your seminar group being created, chosen, pursued, sent, and trusted come to mind?

At what point in your own life (Personal Experience/Action source) were you aware of being

- Created?
- Chosen?
- Pursued?
- Sent?
- Trusted?

What patterns do you see, if any? How might this awareness affect your own identity as a minister? What implications for your ministry in the world can you identify?

55. Thompsett, 8.

Week Twenty-nine

ALL YEARS

Read

Thompsett, *We Are Theologians,* pages 55–136

Focus

How does knowledge of the development of Anglican theology during the Reformation support the assertion that the laity are theologians?

What do liberation theologies contribute to a conversation about the ministry of all?

How can the Church live into the future?

ALL YEARS

Respond

Coakley cites Evagrius, fourth-century monk and ascetic, who wrote, "If you are a theologian, you will pray truly. And if you pray truly, you are a theologian" (page 79). Compare this with Thompsett's reference to Erasmus of Rotterdam: "All can be Christian, all can be devout, and I shall boldly add–all can be theologians."[56]

Practice

Identify your position in response to Thompsett's statement, "One cannot function in isolation from others and still be a Christian."[57] Do you agree or disagree? Try to write your position in one concise statement.

Explore your position statement.

- What constitutes wholeness/goodness?
- What is evidence of brokenness/separation from God?
- What brings recognition of that brokenness?
- What might make reorientation possible?
- What would be evidence of restoration to wholeness?

56. Thompsett, 65.
57. Thompsett, 93.

Connect to other sources. What does the Christian tradition have to say in response to your position? What does your culture/society say about this? What has been your personal experience on this subject?

Bring the theological perspective questions above into the conversation with at least one of these sources. Compare and contrast with the theological perspectives of your position statement.

Apply to your own current situation. What implications do you find for your own identity as a minister? Is there an action you can or wish to take? Is there something you are called to do or change–at the micro, meso, or macro levels? Are there implications for your work in ministry going forward?

UNIT FIVE

Vocation: A Way to Love in Permanent White Water

Week Thirty

ALL YEARS

Read

A Mature Theology of Vocation

What should I do with my life? How can I know? Will I find something that gives my life a sense of purpose or meaning? Even though the context in which we ask such questions has grown ever more complex, the Christian tradition still provides us with a wide range of resources for thinking about how to answer them.[58]

Over the course of this year in EfM we have been weaving the threads of Christian maturity with its multiple dimensions of physical, emotional, social, and spiritual habits of being into a complex, yet brilliant, vocational tapestry. Attending to physical, emotional, social, and spiritual realities can reveal possibilities that expand, deepen, and even mature an individual's current understanding of vocation and ministry.

As William Placher indicates above, the Christian tradition provides "a wide range of resources" to support the development of a maturing Christian theology of vocation and ministry. The stories, images, concepts, and categories that each participant in EfM encounters, whether they are found in the Bible, Christian history, or theology and ethics, provide essential touchstones for creating meaning out of the "stuff" of experience.

As the year closes we bring our study and reflection into focus around vocational questions. What is the meaning and purpose of my life? In what direction is my life going? And is that the direction I desire or hope for? What is meaningful to me? What should I do with my life? What is the deepest hope I hold for the world, my neighborhood, my family, my own life? How is God acting today and how am I related to that action? What do I value and hold dear?

Throughout the EfM year, participants have mined Christian scripture, history, theology, and ethics for wisdom while considering what it means to be an adult Christian in today's world. During the remaining few weeks you are encouraged to set aside time to reflect on what has been gleaned from your work together this year and its importance for discerning your vocation and ministry.

58. William C. Placher, *Callings: Twenty Centuries of Christian Wisdom on Vocation* (Grand Rapids, MI.: William B. Eerdmans Publishing Company, 2005), 332.

Defining "Vocation"

Vocation, as understood from a United States cultural perspective, is a word that often refers to individual decisions that determine what income-producing activity a person wants to pursue. Young persons frequently are asked, "What do you want to be when you grow up?" Children recite rhymes that playfully indicate what the future may hold: "Rich man, poor man, beggar man, thief." These mirror cultural expectations that one day the child must hold a job, taking on his or her vocation as an adult. On the other hand, the question, "Do you have a vocation?" is sometimes understood as decidedly religious. For much of history in the Christian tradition "having a vocation" meant becoming ordained or entering a religious order. From this perspective, those who "have" a vocation are said to be "called" to become clergy, monks, or nuns.

Both meanings of "vocation" direct attention to how a person participates in society's institutional life. Sociologists name five institutions, each needing people to lead, maintain, and develop them: religion, education, government, family, and economy. Religious institutions in North America are generally understood to mean congregations, but may include related institutions such as outreach centers and denominational offices (diocese or district). Non-Christians may use different terms, but all religious institutions need people to lead and maintain them. Government institutions that order society by providing laws and regulations need people to lead, maintain, and develop them as well; so, too, with economic, educational, and family institutions. Participation in any of the basic institutions can be designated a vocation.

In the context of Culture/Society, one's vocation may be understood simply as one's job. In the context of a spiritual or religious tradition, it may have a different, perhaps deeper meaning.

"What are you called to do with your life?" "Do you have a vocation?" Put like that, these may seem strange questions, not the sort of thing we would ordinarily ask. We may not even be sure what they mean. Yet many of us worry about finding a direction or purpose or meaning for our lives. *We wonder if the bits and pieces of our struggles, disappointments, and successes will add up to a significant whole.* "Call" and "vocation" are categories the Christian tradition has long used to address such issues.[59] [emphasis added]

A full definition of vocation includes more than simply naming one's role and function in society, what one *does*. It also can be understood as a way of *being* in daily life that forges meaning out of the mundane and ordinary. Speaking of vocation from this perspective requires facing questions raised from "the bits and pieces of our struggles, disappointments, and successes." Framing the concern within Christian vocation begins with an assumption that the "bits and pieces" will be part of a whole. Immediate existential questions evoke vocational concerns.

---

59. Ibid., 1.

Vocation as a theological category includes more than a job or career. In the context of theological disciplines vocation refers to a call from God. The word comes from the Latin *vocare* which literally means "to call." "Call" is a metaphorical way of speaking about a strongly held inclination to a course of action. The action may be a sweeping change of course in life that results in a career change or may be short lived, such as extending aid to someone in present need where the exchange is immediate and has no further involvement beyond the moment. Both inclinations fall theologically under a vocational rubric that understands the action as a response to God's call.

Creating a Theological Understanding of Vocation

Determining if a compelling sense of call is from God begins with a process of discernment that draws on one's theological system. It may begin with wondering "if the bits and pieces of our struggles, disappointments, and successes will add up to a significant whole." Like Placher, we may ask, "How will I know?" Discerning a call involves the answers given (consciously or unconsciously) to basic and interconnected theological questions about God, human nature, and the world, as well as sin, judgment, and redemption. In a systematic view, how human beings are understood is connected to how God is seen, and what one believes about the physical world is shaped by doctrines concerning God and human nature. Beliefs exist in an intertwined matrix of positions that have a symbiotic relationship with one another. A shift in one impacts the others.

Revisiting the work of Sarah Coakley offers a way to construct a theology of vocation. In a video from St John's University, Nottingham, U.K., she speaks of several themes that systematically guide her theology in *God, Sexuality, and Self*, referenced in Unit Four.[60] Most important, Coakley places prayer in a privileged position all through her work as a systematic theologian. Naming it essential for theological study and understanding, she contends that prayer is an activity without which speaking about God has an inauthenticity. Prayer, especially prayer of the contemplative sort, stops our human agendas and interrupts our human monologue so that an attitude of active waiting and listening becomes central to the creating process.

A key passage to understanding what Coakley asserts is found in the Letter to the Romans.

> We know that the whole creation has been groaning in labor pains until now; and not only the creation, but we ourselves, who have the first fruits of the Spirit, groan inwardly while we wait for adoption, the redemption of our bodies. For in hope we were saved. Now hope that is seen is not hope. For who hopes for what is seen? But if we hope for what we do not see, we wait for it with patience. Likewise the Spirit helps us in our weakness; for we do not

---

60. St John's University, Nottingham, UK, https://www.youtube.com/watch?v=Y0gxtpmlgBg

know how to pray as we ought, but that very Spirit intercedes with sighs too deep for words.

Romans 8:22–26

Here Paul places prayer within a cosmic context. Among other things, prayer is a lifelong process that "groans" toward completion, especially as we recognize that human language is inadequate to the task of expressing our deepest desires. The connection is forged when the one praying is able to adopt an attitude of patient listening while turning over the process to the Source of our being. The approach might be described as developing an attitude of contemplative attention.

In Coakley's approach theology is *in via*, that is, on route to "transformative union with the divine." Doing theology this way is a bit like sailing a ship while still building it. Speaking about God has a provisional quality in that the positions one takes are open to frequent if not constant revision as a result of revelation. To some this may seem disconcertingly directionless, yet Coakley rightly asserts that the dynamic, transitory quality of theology is not rudderless, but is stabilized and guided by the primary authority of scripture and the secondary authority of tradition, both evaluated through and in conversation with reason.[61]

Thus, while continuing study and reflection on scripture and Christian tradition map the theological journey, engaging the voices of the sciences, the arts, and philosophy is also important to theological discourse, even when those voices are disturbingly challenging. Coakley holds to this fundamental openness because of her conviction that, flowing where it will, the Spirit experienced in prayer is the same Spirit moving through science and art. For some, engagement with these cultural voices will be accomplished through focused study in the academic disciplines of science, the fine arts, and philosophy. For others these voices may be heard through visiting cultural centers such as museums and planetariums, or attending concerts and the theater. Engaging in discourse with voices outside the church is an essential part of contemplative attention.

Located within a heritage of orthodoxy, contemplative attentiveness, understanding theological thinking as a work in progress, and being open and receptive to voices from science and art together support the construction of a full theology of vocation. Orthodoxy in this sense is not understood as a container filled with "correct" theology, but as context in which the goal (*telos*) is developing wisdom and grace as God's people move toward transformative union. The work is also done contextually, within the specific particularities that frame the person doing theology. All theology is created within particular cultural realities such as language, mores, customs, gender, and technology.

61. Ibid.

Creating a Systematic Framework for Vocational Discernment

As noted in Week Two, David Ford's writing on human discourse may provide a structure to express a balanced theology, in this case a theology of vocation.[62]

- **Desires**–interests that an individual holds
  *What do you **long or yearn** for?*
- **Questions**–inquiries that are raised and that motivate and guide increased learning
  *What do you **wonder about or doubt**?*
- **Explorations**–experiments available for "hands on" practical experience
  *What **possibilities** do you **want to explore or test**?*
- **Affirmations**–positions held as true and that are valued
  What are you coming to **believe or affirm**?
- **Imperatives**–commands that call for action
  What **should, ought, or must you do**?

Desire is a key to discerning vocational interests since much of an individual's identity is intertwined with desire in the form of interests, longings, and yearnings. Desires get expressed in a number of ways. One yearns for intimacy, to be loved and known by another and to love and know another, to have and be a "significant other." Another form of desire is the need to belong, to be part of a family or group, as in "these are my people." Desire also finds expression in the need to contribute, as when someone says, "I want my life to have made a difference, a contribution, no matter how small." Yearning for intimacy, belonging, and contributing all may lead to the desire for transcendence, for meaning that endures.

Questions often arise from desire. The need for more information and additional experience leads to inquiry. As one asks questions in order to flesh out an interest, answers will lead to exploring and experimenting. "I would like to give it a try to see how it feels," one might say. After sufficient exploration, one might then be ready to commit to a position that affirms a course of action. As the commitment grows, it becomes imperative to take action. At this point the discernment process becomes ongoing as one reflects on the action taken, noticing how the action itself may have affected the original interest or desire.

Ford's five "moods" work together to form what he calls a "dynamic ecology of theological thinking."[63] A well-constructed balance of Ford's five elements of theological expression with the "contemplative attention" stance drawn from Coakley's theological method move one's theological understanding of vocation toward maturity, wholeness, and wisdom. Interweaving Coakley's theological method with Ford's theological ecology

62. Ford, *The Future of Christian Theology*, 68.
63. Ford, ibid.

provides a framework for systematic discernment within a coherent theology of vocation.

Expressing Vocation in Ministry

An individual exists within givens that create a fabric of life in which interests, yearnings, desires and abilities weave together to form a pattern of vocational possibilities. These constitute the micro dimension of one's vocation. At the same time the individual lives within a network of institutional givens that shape and are shaped by the persons who participate in them. Family patterns that form the person, educational systems that create and convey knowledge, businesses that convey the economy, government that orders society, and religious institutions that give shape to the tradition work together at the meso level. All are contained in global and cosmic realities that make up the macro level. Either explicitly or implicitly these three levels of reality shape any expression of a theological vocation.

Vocation and ministry operate in concert with one another. In its most practical sense, vocation is expressed in ministry. Vocational discernment thus is focused not only on whether one has a call but also on what one is being called to do. Further, a person's response to the discerned call draws on four formative factors. Shaping a ministry involves a view of self (identity). An individual ministers in a particular style or way of being in the situation that reflects an orientation to daily life (attitude). Basic concepts, narratives, images, and information contribute to understanding (knowledge). As one takes action, the ability to act effectively and efficiently comes into play (skill). The identity, attitude, knowledge, and skill of the minister contribute to any expression of vocation in ministry.

A ministry is fashioned through a dynamic process of decision, commitment, discipline, experience, and reflection. Decisions made contribute to commitment. Discipline in carrying out the commitment in action with skill and grace develops patterns of experience. Cumulative experience enriches action as one reflects on learning in the dynamic process. The process continues with each compelling sense to take action, in other words, with each discernment of vocation. A coherent theology of vocation expressed in ministry understood as contributing to God's purpose and vision provides motivating energy and animates ministry within individuals and institutions.

Finally, as the expression of vocation through ministry is identified and takes shape, the question of sustainability should be part of the discourse. Because we live in a dynamic, fluid world in which change is a constant reality, vocational decisions may be formed with a sense of impermanence. The image of maneuvering in permanent white water aptly describes present realities, whether viewed from individual, institutional, or global levels, raising questions of sustainability, relevance, and flourishing. "Can the direction of my life be sustained and for how long?" "What relevance do my individual life and the institutions in which I work have for the big picture?" "What keeps my ministry fresh and vibrant?" Questions concerning sustaining and flourishing are central to theological positioning and need to be considered in creating a mature and comprehensive vocational theology.

Focus

Describe a connection and a distinction between vocation and ministry.

Define the four categories of yearning named in the essay.

Respond

Identify one to three issues concerning vocation and/or ministry that concern you at this time.

Practice

A caveat regarding charts or outlines: Sometimes blank spaces can seem to demand filling. Go where interest and energy take you and let God's Spirit work in you, as always.

Using the issues you named in the Respond section, place each in the interaction level it reflects; that is, is your concern a personal matter, an institutional matter, or a global/cosmic matter.

Micro level: individual interests and abilities

Meso level: societal and institutional relations (there are five basic institutions: religious, economic, governmental, educational, and family)

Macro level: global experience

Week Thirty-one

YEAR ONE

Read

Proverbs

Collins, Chapter 24, "Proverbs," pages 307–316

Focus

Define: wisdom literature; Solomon; Hezekiah; collections in Proverbs; Lady Wisdom

Spend some time reading and reflecting on Wisdom 8.

YEAR TWO

Read

Galatians

Powell, Chapter 15, "Galatians," pages 307–321

Focus

Define: purpose of the letter to the Galatians; the issue of Christ and the Law; paradoxical portrait of liberty

What is your response to Powell's two questions on page 320 about God's universal favor?

YEAR THREE

Read

MacCulloch, Chapter 21, "Enlightenment: Ally or Enemy?" pages 769–816

Focus

The Enlightenment produced a sea change in Western Christianity that continues well into the contemporary social and intellectual context. In what ways has the Enlightenment revolutionized the understanding of human nature?

Think about the positive and negative impact the altered views of humanity have had on understanding vocational development.

YEAR FOUR

Read

Peace, Rose & Mobley, "Forward," "Introduction," and "Part I: Encountering the Neighbor," pages xi–44

Focus

In the Forward to *My Neighbor's Faith* Joan Chittister aptly describes the book's intention and rationale: "In this book all the languages of God are spoken–Hindu, Buddhist, Jewish, Christian and Muslim–so that we can learn from one another."[64]

What specific ideas, images, or stories foster vocational development?

ALL YEARS

Respond

Identify the views of human nature described in your study this week.

Practice

THEOLOGICAL REFLECTION BEGINNING WITH A SOCIAL CONCERN

(Culture/Society Source)

Identify a global/cosmic concern you have right now.
Example: water distribution

Explore how that concern is expressed or responded to at an institutional and personal level.

What institutions are causing problems or helping to solve them? Pick one institution, such as national government, religious, family, educational, or economic.

Connect
Use at least one of the following baptismal vows familiar to The Episcopal Church to connect to your concern at any of the three interaction levels. Note: Other churches, both Anglican and other denominations, may have vows. Use the following or any that work for you.

---

64. Jennifer Howe Peace, Or N. Rose, and Gregory Mobley, eds., *My Neighbor's Faith* (Maryknoll, NY: Orbis Books, 2012), xii.

Continue in the apostles' teaching and fellowship, in the breaking of bread and in the prayers.
Persevere in resisting evil and whenever you fall into sin, repent and return to the Lord.
Proclaim by word and example the Good News of God in Christ.
Seek and serve Christ in all persons, loving your neighbor as yourself.
Strive for justice and peace and respect the dignity of every human being.

Use the chart below to connect the global issue of water distribution with one or more of the Baptismal promises:

CHRISTIAN VOCATION AND ACTION MATRIX

Level of human interaction	Issue or concern	Baptismal vow: Continue in the apostles' teaching . . .	Vow: Persevere in resisting evil . . .	Vow: Proclaim by word and example . . .	Vow: Seek and serve Christ . . .	Vow: Strive for justice . . .
Personal level	How am I affected by or affecting the concern of water distribution?					What personal actions contribute to justice in water distribution?
Institution level	Who is helping or hurting in this matter of water distribution?			What is my church or school doing?		
Global/ cosmic level	***Water distribution***					

Apply

What does your consideration of a global concern suggest for your ministry?

Week Thirty-two

YEAR ONE

Read

Job
Ecclesiastes (Qoheleth)
Collins, Chapter 25, "Job and Qoheleth," pages 317–328

Focus

Define: character of God; role of Satan; conclusion reached in Qoheleth (Ecclesiastes)

How do Job and Qoheleth challenge the view in Proverbs?

Job and Qoheleth (Ecclesiastes) provide literary classics from the Hebrew Bible, exposing human agony and glory. How do those men and women speak to us today?

YEAR TWO

Read

1 Corinthians
2 Corinthians
Powell, Chapter 13, "1 Corinthians," and Chapter 14, "2 Corinthians," pages 273–305

Focus

Define: Macedonia and Achaia; location of Corinth; major themes in each letter to the Corinthians; glossolalia; purpose of the Lord's Supper; the issue of authority; apostolic authority; the Erastus Inscription

Identify how passages in the letters to the Corinthians developed a theology of vocation.

YEAR THREE

Read

MacCulloch, Chapter 22, "Europe Re-Enchanted or Disenchanted?" pages 817–865

Focus

This chapter described components necessary for setting the context of contemporary Anglo-American and European theology. Note the people or ideas that particularly interested you.

What theology of mission, ministry, or vocation was forming during the period you studied?

YEAR FOUR

Read

Peace, Rose & Mobley, "Part II: Viewing Home Anew," and "Part III: Redrawing Our Maps," pages 45–124

Focus

What implications for mission and ministry did your study suggest?

How do the stories affect your sense of self?

ALL YEARS

Respond

How do events shape spirituality?

What yearning was most prominent in the people you studied this week: yearning for intimacy, belonging, contributing, or transcendence?

Practice

THEOLOGICAL REFLECTION BEGINNING WITH A PERSONAL POSITION

Identify a personal yearning you have experienced. Describe the circumstances and dynamics.

Create an image or statement that captures the energy of that yearning.

Explore by identifying the level of human interaction that is most represented in your image or statement of yearning.

What theology does that image or statement express: a theology of wholeness, of brokenness, of recognizing something is off-track, of reorienting towards wholeness, or of restoration of wholeness?

Another way to ask the theological perspective questions would be to reflect on how the image or statement expresses a theology of how the world is, which includes what is broken in the world, how we are called into awareness that things are broken, what needs repenting, or of how redemption occurs.

Connect with the other areas of human interaction by considering how the yearning image or statement speaks to those levels. For instance, if the yearning is to contribute and you placed it in the institution level (for instance, government), how does the yearning relate to the personal and global levels?

Apply by first stating any insight or awareness you reached during your reflection. Then, carry that insight into statements of commitment, using baptismal promises or other such vows.

An example might be that you have become aware of some ways you can contribute in your community by supporting a local campaign for fair wages, connecting to the promise to strive for justice and peace for all people.

Week Thirty-three

YEAR ONE

Read

Ruth
Esther
Collins, Chapter 26, "The Hebrew Short Story: Ruth, Esther," pages 329–338

Focus

Describe how either Ruth or Esther saw herself (identity), her orientation to daily life (attitude), her basic images or narratives (knowledge), and her ability to act effectively (skill).

YEAR TWO

Read

Ephesians
Powell, Chapter 16, "Ephesians," pages 323–341

Focus

Locate Ephesus and state its significance in Paul's journeys.

Describe the decisions, commitment, discipline, experience, and reflection that are present in Paul's letter to the Ephesians.

YEAR THREE

Read

MacCulloch, Chapter 23, "To Make the World Protestant," pages 866–914

Focus

Identify and describe a thread that runs through the chapter.

Examine the thread using theological standpoints: human nature; creation, sin, judgment, repentance, and redemption; the way God is disclosed; the kind of future desired.

YEAR FOUR

Read

Peace, Rose & Mobley, "Part IV: Unpacking Our Belongings," and "Part V: Stepping Across the Line," pages 127–206

Focus

How are the dynamics of human interaction present in the two sections you studied this week?

What categories of yearning can you identify in this week's reading: intimacy, belonging, contributing, or transcendence?

ALL YEARS

Respond

What most contributed to spiritual maturity (Christian or otherwise) for those you studied this week?

Maturing in Christian spirituality sometimes has been approached in checklist fashion. Today, many Christians ask, "How can I be more Christ-like?" rather than, "How can I be a better Christian?" Identifying what "Christ-like" means for each of us is essential.

Describe what you would mean by "Christ-like."

What helps you most in your journey of becoming more Christ-like?

Practice

The essay described five dynamics that fashion ministry. What would you add or remove?

Which of the five dynamics offered in the essay would you most want to apply next week?

Take one step towards applying that dynamic.

Week Thirty-four

YEAR ONE

Read

Daniel
1 and 2 Maccabees
Collins, Chapter 27, "Daniel, 1–2 Maccabees," pages 339–354

Focus

Define: apocalypse; apocalyptic literature; Maccabee; pseudonymity as a literary device; martyrdom and militancy

What messages come across in Daniel and in the Maccabees books?

YEAR TWO

Read

1 John, 2 John, and 3 John
Powell, Chapter 27, "The Johannine Letters: 1 John, 2 John, 3 John," pages 493–507

Focus

Define: purpose of the three Johannine letters; authorship of the Johannine letters; major themes of the Johannine letters.

What issues of growth in Christ existed for those to whom these letters were written?

YEAR THREE

Read

MacCulloch, Chapter 24, "Not Peace but a Sword," pages 915–966

Focus

Define: the major events for the Church from 1914–1960; key aspects leading to both World Wars; the four Christian emperors at the beginning of the first world war; Bolshevik; Pius the IX and Christ the King feast day; Benedict XV; *Cristeros*; Bernardino Nogara; Charles Brent and Nathan Söderblom; Josiah Olulowo Ositelu

How do your view of the Church's change and MacCulloch's view connect?

YEAR FOUR

Read

Peace, Rose & Mobley "Part VI: Finding Fellow Travelers," pages 207–242

Focus

Define: *ru'ah hakodesh*; William Sloane Coffin

ALL YEARS

Respond

A statement in the Year Four reading this week asserted that a problem in Judaism and Western Christianity is that they have become over-verbalized and under-experienced. How do you respond?

Practice

One of the Year Four readings this week describes spiritual practices that Dean Howard Thurman directed for his students at Union Theological Seminary. One practice was to read a psalm several times and then listen to a piece by Bach in order to hear the psalm's meaning in music.[65]

Try that practice once or twice before the seminar meeting if you have the time.

What stood out for you as you practiced this spiritual exercise?

What did you see or hear that spoke of goodness, brokenness, repentance, reorientation, or redemption?

What connections to other experiences or events in the world around you came to you?

Identify decisions, commitments, disciplines, experiences, or reflections that this practice leads you to.

65. Ibid., 210.

Week Thirty-five

YEAR ONE

Read

Collins, Chapter 28, "The Deuterocanonical Wisdom Books," and Chapter 29, "From Tradition to Canon," pages 355–369

Focus

Define: tradition, canon, deuterocanonical

YEAR TWO

Read

The Revelation to John
Powell, Chapter 29, "Revelation," pages 519–537
At least one of the hyperlinks

Focus

Define: Patmos; apocalyptic literature; three approaches to understanding Revelation; gematria; date of Revelation; forms of millennialism and tribulationism; major themes in Revelation

What attitudes about the Book of the Revelation to John have you entertained or encountered?

YEAR THREE

Read

MacCulloch, Chapter 25, "Culture Wars," pages 967–1016

Focus

Reflect on how MacCulloch's context as an Oxford-trained British citizen shapes his understanding of history. How does his understanding compare with yours and the context out of which you read history?

YEAR FOUR

Read

Peace, Rose & Mobley, "Part VII: Repairing Our Shared World," pages 241–266

Focus

Describe the sense of God's call evident in the essays you studied this week.

ALL YEARS

Respond

How were the existential questions relating to call dealt with in this week's study? These questions were introduced in the unit's beginning essay:

Purpose

Meaning

Acting

Hope

What God is doing and how one is connected to that

What one values

Practice

List the white water concerns in your life now, e.g. violence in your community, personal finances, climate change, and so forth.

Select one that you want to explore now.

Explore your concern using the Christian Vocation and Action Matrix (levels of human interaction and faith commitment statements) in Week Thirty-one, or the questions above relating to call.

What would you most want to do in response to the concern and what would you least want to do?

Once you have spent at least a bit of time with this consideration, sit quietly with God for any amount of time you can give. Just sit and listen. Don't talk. Listen.

Week Thirty-six: Closure

There likely will be opportunity at the group's meeting to share responses to the material in the following Read, Focus, Respond, and Practice sections. The mentor and group will decide how they want to incorporate this work and the sharing into any celebration of the year they might want to create.

ALL YEARS

Read

Closure is a time to acknowledge what has been, to celebrate what now is, and to anticipate what will come. The time given to this depends on the length of time the group has been together and the personal styles of group members and the mentor. EfM provides an opportunity to form a close and supportive community that cannot be easily replaced. It is important for participants to acknowledge the blessing of the group's time together, while also helping each other shift to new forms of emotional, spiritual, and intellectual support for their ministry.

Closure includes telling stories about significant events in the life of the group and the ways the group has affected each person. Name any regrets or frustrations people have, look ahead to what steps seem to be in view, and help one another plan for alternative forms of support for future life and ministry. The following design combines closure with a focus on ministry going forward.[66]

Focus

Review notes you made during the year, material you studied, and your spiritual autobiography.

Recall your original motives, intentions, and expectations in committing to EFM.

Respond

This year's theme is Living as Spiritually Mature Christians. With that theme in mind and your review of your EfM work, respond to the following.

1. This year in EFM has helped me:
   - let go of . . .
   - adopt . . .
   - affirm . . .
   - focus on . . .

---

66. Adapted from EfM *Common Lessons and Supporting Materials*. 6-16-1 to 6-16-2. June, 2005.

2. Complete the affirmation, "On this day I am a point of God's loving presence in this world and my purpose is to. . ."

Practice

Begin with prayer in whatever manner you choose, allowing yourself to become present to your experience and to the Spirit of God.

When you are ready, continue with the following, adapted and edited from a design created by EFM trainer Bill Coolidge. This drawing can be made with an upward turn rather than a downward turn if that fits better for someone. This movement captures a bit of what discernment of ministry can be like. *Notice that at the right side, the line begins down again, indicating that the process repeats and that discernment is ongoing.*

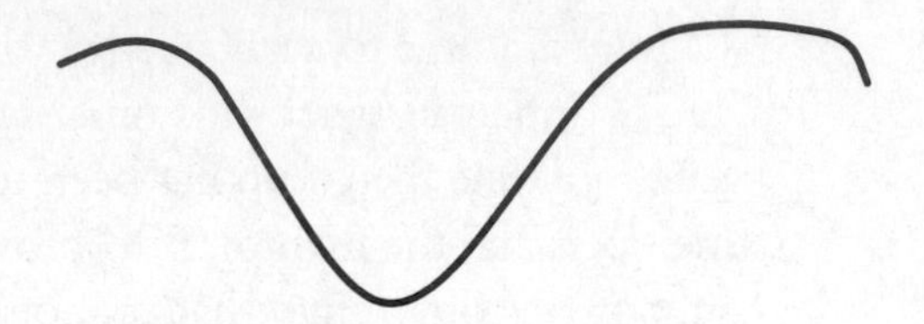

Label the design: CALL on the left top

DISCERNMENT on both the downward and upward arcs

VOCATION at the bottom

MINISTRY at the top right

Return to quiet as you let yourself connect to times in your life when you experienced this movement of ministry discernment. Perhaps you are in such a cycle right now.

Call–Record what God may be calling you towards, or recall a time when you experienced a sense of call. A call can be like Moses just doing the daily task of tending his flock and suddenly having an awareness of God asking him to do something. It may be just a persistent kind of inner urging or idea about something you could do. Just try to get hold of such an experience and make a note about it.

Proceed through the movement.

Discernment–Think of factors you have to consider in relation to the sense of call. Perhaps leave your job in order to pursue another path; what plans will you have to make; what preparation will you need?

Vocation–Consider what the call is about; is it about teaching, or serving the poor, or serving in medicine, or having a family, and so on?

Discernment–Further discern how and where you would act on that call. Will you need training, where might you have to go, who needs to be informed, will you need credentials?

Ministry–What do you believe you can do with the call and vocation as a result of discernment?

Remembering that for Christians any ministry is Christ's ministry through and with us, identify valuable support for your ministry in the future.

My personal ministry goals:

- For the next three months
- For the next year
- For the next five years

What spiritual practices will help you continue forward from this point?

PART II

Resources

Overview of the Year: Reading Assignments for Volume C

Notes

1. Common readings at the beginning of each unit are read by all years.
2. Assignments for Years One and Two marked with an asterisk are readings in the Bible. Chapters in the survey texts are numbered. Please note that chapters are sometimes read out of sequence. When both are assigned, it is suggested that the Bible be read before the survey text chapters.
3. Readings in each of the three texts for Year Four are indicated by name of the author(s).

WEEK	UNIT	YEAR ONE	YEAR TWO	YEAR THREE	YEAR FOUR
		Collins	Powell	MacCulloch	Allen, Sedgwick, Peace
1	**Introductory Meeting**	Orientation and Organization	Orientation and Organization	Orientation and Organization	Orientation and Organization
2	**Unit One** Spiritual Autobiography and Listening	Common Reading: Spiritual Maturity	Common Reading: Spiritual Maturity	Common Reading: Spiritual Maturity	Common Reading: Spiritual Maturity
3		Preface, Introduction 1 The Near Eastern Context 2 The Nature of the Pentateuchal Narrative	Preface 1 The New Testament World 2 The New Testament Writings	Acknowledgements, Introduction 1 Greece and Rome	Allen: Preface Introduction: What is Theology?
4		* Genesis 1–11 3 The Primeval History	3 Jesus 4 Gospels	2 Israel	Allen: 1 The Holy One of Israel
5		The Priestly Creation Story RRG Pt II 166–183	* Matthew	3 A Crucified Messiah	Allen 2 Holiness for Today
6		* Genesis 12–50 4 The Patriarchs	5 Matthew	4 Boundaries Defined	Allen: 3 The Maker of Heaven and Earth 4 Limits of Science
7		* Exodus 1–15 5 The Exodus from Egypt	* Mark 6 Mark	5 The Prince: Ally or Enemy?	Allen 5 What Is Meant by "God"

WEEK	UNIT	YEAR ONE	YEAR TWO	YEAR THREE	YEAR FOUR
8	**Unit Two** Theological Reflection as a Life Skill	Common Reading: Seeking Meaning	Common Reading: Seeking Meaning	Common Reading: Seeking Meaning	Common Reading: Seeking Meaning
9		* Exodus 16–40 6 Revelation at Sinai	* Luke	6 The Imperial Church	Allen: 6 Nature as Witness and Innocent Suffering
10		* Leviticus * Numbers 7 Priestly Theology: Exodus 25–40, Leviticus and Numbers	7 Luke	7 Defying Chalcedon: Asia and Africa	Allen: 7 Innocent Suffering and Life beyond Death
11		* Deuteronomy 8 Deuteronomy	* John	8 Islam: The Great Realignment	Allen: 8 Suffering from Nature and Extreme Human Cruelty
12		* Joshua * Judges	8 John	9 The Making of Latin Christianity	Allen: 9 The Sacrifice in Creation DuBose Essay: The Trinity, RRG Pt II 184–191
13		9 Joshua 10 Judges	* Acts of the Apostles 9 Acts	10 Latin Christendom: New Frontiers	Allen: 10 The Incarnation as Sacrifice
14	**Interlude 1** A Spirituality of Liberation	Common Reading: Thurman, vii–47	Common Reading: Thurman, vii–47	Common Reading: Thurman, vii–47	Common Reading: Thurman, vii–47
15	**Interlude 1** A Spirituality of Liberation	Common Reading: Thurman, 48–102	Common Reading: Thurman, 48–102	Common Reading: Thurman, 48–102	Common Reading: Thurman, 48–102
16	**Unit Three** Developing a Sustaining Spirituality	Common Reading: Prayer and Worship	Common Reading: Prayer and Worship	Common Reading: Prayer and Worship	Common Reading: Prayer and Worship
17		* 1 Samuel * 2 Samuel 11 First Samuel 12 Second Samuel	10 New Testament Letters 11 Paul	11 The West: Universal Emperor or Universal Pope?	Allen: 11 The Temptation in the Wilderness
18		* 1 Kings * 2 Kings 13 First Kings 1–16 14 First Kings 17– 2 Kings 25	* Romans	12 A Church for All People?	Allen: 12 The Sacrifice of the Cross
19		* Amos * Hosea 15 Amos and Hosea	12 Romans	13 Faith in a New Rome	Allen: 13 The Resurrection of Jesus and Eternal Life
20		* Micah * Isaiah 1–39 Micah, Pt II 192–195 16 Isaiah	* Hebrews 23 Hebrews	14 Orthodoxy: More Than an Empire	Allen: 14 Jesus as Lord and Jesus as Servant

WEEK	UNIT	YEAR ONE	YEAR TWO	YEAR THREE	YEAR FOUR
21		* Jeremiah * Lamentations 17 The Babylonian Era	* 1 Peter * 2 Peter 25 1 Peter 26 2 Peter	15 Russia: The Third Rome	Allen: 15 Revelation and Faith
22	**Unit Four** Integrating Belief, Behavior, and Doctrine	Common Reading: Toward Wholeness in Knowing God	Common Reading: Toward Wholeness in Knowing God	Common Reading: Toward Wholeness in Knowing God	Common Reading: Toward Wholeness in Knowing God
23		* Ezekiel 18 Ezekiel	* Philemon * Jude 22 Philemon 28 Jude	16 Perspectives on the True Church	Allen: 16 The Holy Spirit, the Church, and the Sacraments
24		* Isaiah 40–66 * Haggai * Zechariah * Malachi * Joel * Jonah 19 Additions to the Book of Isaiah 20 Postexilic Prophecy	* Philippians * Colossians 17 Philippians 18 Colossians	17 A House Divided	Allen: 17 Sin, Evil, and Hope for the Future Epilogue
25		* Ezra * Nehemiah 21 Ezra and Nehemiah	* 1 Timothy * 2 Timothy * Titus 21 The Pastoral Letters	18 Rome's Renewal	Sedgwick: Preface, Introduction 1 Describing the Christian Life 2 An Anglican Perspective
26		* 1 Chronicles * 2 Chronicles 22 The Books of Chronicles	* 1 Thessalonians * 2 Thessalonians 19 1 Thessalonians 20 2 Thessalonians	19 A Worldwide Faith	Sedgwick: 3 Incarnate Love 4 Love and Justice
27		* Psalms * Song of Songs 23 Psalms and Song of Songs	* James 24 James	20 Protestant Awakenings	Sedgwick: 5 The Practices of Faith 6 The Call of God Appendix
28	**Interlude 2** Knowing Who We Are	Common Reading: Thompsett, Preface and 1–54	Common Reading: Thompsett, Preface and 1–54	Common Reading: Thompsett, Preface and 1–54	Common Reading: Thompsett, Preface and 1–54
29	**Interlude 2** Knowing Who We Are	Common Reading: Thompsett, 55–136	Common Reading: Thompsett, 55–136	Common Reading: Thompsett, 55–136	Common Reading: Thompsett, 55–136
30	**Unit Five** Vocation: A Way to Love in Permanent White Water	Common Reading: A Mature Theology of Vocation	Common Reading: A Mature Theology of Vocation	Common Reading: A Mature Theology of Vocation	Common Reading: A Mature Theology of Vocation
31		* Proverbs 24 Proverbs Collins on Micah 16 Isaiah	* Galatians 15 Galatians	21 Enlightenment: Ally or Enemy?	Peace, Rose, Mobley: Foreword Introduction 1 Encountering the Neighbor

WEEK	UNIT	YEAR ONE	YEAR TWO	YEAR THREE	YEAR FOUR
32		* Job * Ecclesiastes (Qoheleth) 25 Job and Qoheleth	* 1 Corinthians * 2 Corinthians 13 1 Corinthians 14 2 Corinthians	22 Europe Re-enchanted or Disenchanted?	Peace, Rose, Mobley: 2 Viewing Home Anew 3 Redrawing Our Maps
33		* Ruth * Esther 26 The Hebrew Short Story	* Ephesians 16 Ephesians	23 To Make the World Protestant	Peace, Rose, Mobley: 4 Unpacking Our Belongings 5 Stepping Across the Line
34		* Daniel 27 Daniel, 1–2 Maccabees	* 1 John * 2 John * 3 John 27 Johannine Letters	24 Not Peace but a Sword	Peace, Rose, Mobley: 6 Finding Fellow Travelers
35		28 The Deuterocanonical Wisdom Books 29 From Tradition to Canon	* The Revelation to John 29 Revelation	25 Culture Wars	Peace, Rose, Mobley: 7 Repairing Our Shared World
36	**Final Meeting**	Closure	Closure	Closure	Closure

Terms in the New EfM Curriculum

Common Reading	A common reading is assigned to all year levels. Each unit begins with an introductory essay read by all participants. Interlude texts are also assigned for common reading.
Identify, Explore, Connect, Apply	Theological reflection is described in four movements: *Identify, Explore, Connect, Apply.* This pattern also underlies the *Read, Focus, Respond, Practice* pattern of the Reading and Reflection Guide.
Interlude	An interlude is a two-week session in which all participants in a group read and respond to a common text chosen in relation to the theme of the Reading and Reflection Guide. There are two interludes in each program year.
Interlude Text	The text assigned to an interlude session is called an interlude text or interlude book. Two interlude books are read each year. The books address special topics that reinforce the theme of the Reading and Reflection Guide for that program year.
Participants	Those enrolled in a seminar group are generally referred to as participants or group members.
Program Year	The approximately nine-month period (thirty-six sessions) during which the group seminar meets is its program year. An EfM group can begin its program year in any month *except June, July, or August.*
Read, Focus, Respond, Practice	The guide for each session follows the sequence of *Read* (assigned reading), *Focus* (questions or terms specific to the assigned reading), *Respond* (connects the reading to the unit theme), and *Practice* (suggested application for individual and/or group work). This sequence provides a four-fold discipline for the practice of ministry.

Reading and Reflection Guides These guides outline what is needed for participants to prepare for each of the thirty-six seminar meetings in a program year, including individual reading assignments and suggested ways to focus, respond, and practice what is being learned. There will be four volumes, A–D, used in a cycle. All groups will use the same Reading and Reflection Guide volume in a program year.

Readings in the Christian Tradition The textbooks that replace previous chapters in the red notebooks provide participants with their weekly readings in the Christian tradition: the Hebrew Bible in Year One; the New Testament in Year Two; church history in Year Three; and theology, ethics, and interfaith encounters in Year Four.

Theme Each volume of the Reading and Reflection Guide has a central theme that is carried through each of the units and interludes. Volume A's theme is ministry in your own particular context. Themes for the subsequent volumes are (B) ministry in an intercultural and interfaith context, (C) growth into spiritual maturity, and (D) the journey into a deepening relationship with God.

Expectations and Purpose

The Participants

You, the participants in an EfM seminar group, are all adults. You set your own learning goals and need the latitude to learn as each individual does best. This requires a certain commitment to the program, but every participant does not need to work in the same way or with the same intensity. EfM has the flexibility for each of you to work in his or her own way.

There are some basic expectations of each participant:

- Attend the seminar sessions or at least maintain the community by letting others know when you will be absent.
- Read the materials and complete the work assigned to the best of your ability.
- Participate in the discussions, reflections, and worship of your seminar group.

The Mentor

The role of the mentor is crucial to the life of the group. The term "mentor" originates in Greek mythology. Mentor was a friend of Odysseus who remained in charge of his household while he was away. "Wisdom" in the form of Athena took shape in Mentor to be the guide and teacher of Telemachus. A teacher who guides is a description of an EfM mentor.

The EfM mentor brings skills in working effectively with small groups of people. The responsibility for the life of the group belongs to everyone, but the mentor is the initial convener. The mentor works to allow everyone an opportunity to learn, to share, to discover. At the same time, the mentor is also a member of the group. The mentor is also there to learn, to share, and to discover. The mentor has a second role, that of administrator for the group. The mentor handles registrations, receives and distributes materials, files reports, and is accountable to the administrative staff in Sewanee.

The mentor serves the group neither as a teacher whose most important task is to provide information nor as a therapist. The mentor is a guide in a journey of discovery. Some groups have co-mentors who work together as a team. This can be very helpful to the process since it can be very difficult to lead and participate simultaneously.

Mentor training and accreditation by an EfM trainer is required. It is an important component of the EfM program. Mentors must renew their accreditation every eighteen months.

The Seminar Group

The EfM seminar group is the crucible for learning in the EfM program. A seminar group usually contains no fewer than six and no more than twelve participants and a mentor (or two co-mentors). The group provides an environment that supports the exploration and expression of ideas so that discovery and learning occur. It is a place of trust and confidentiality as participants in the seminar reflect upon ways to pursue a life of faith on a daily basis.

Seminars usually meet for two-and-a-half to three hours once a week over a period of thirty-six weeks during the academic cycle. For many of us this cycle begins in September and ends in June, but the group may decide to meet more frequently for shorter periods of time or less frequently for longer periods of time. Less frequent meetings can be very helpful when participants are scattered or they live in a region where bad weather can make travel difficult for extended periods. Some seminar groups meet online.

EfM seminars regularly engage in three different aspects of learning. These may not all be done in any one session, but attention needs to be given to all three aspects.

- There is time for social and spiritual needs to be addressed. This is a way to build trust, friendship, and community. It is an opportunity to support each other and maintain the freedom we all need to express our thoughts and feelings.
- There is time to discuss the materials which participants read in the texts. It is not a time for classroom presentations, rather an occasion to raise questions, wrestle with the materials, obtain clarifications, and generally share impressions about what has been read.
- There is an opportunity to engage in reflective activity. This may come in the form of a spiritual autobiography, one of many forms of theological reflections, studying and following a spiritual discipline, or exploring the meaning of the ministries we have.

The Program

The EfM Program expects participants, mentors, and trainers to remain faithful to the program. EfM is a program for adults and one expectation of the program is that adults take responsibility for their lives, set their own goals, and seek the support necessary to move forward. The program asks participants and mentors to provide an arena in which learning can take place on a mature adult level.

The relationship of EfM and The University of the South to the local church and to the judicatory/diocese is one of collaboration. Together we join to provide a program of theological education for the laity that carries a number of benefits.

- Portability–Participants can begin in one location and continue their work in another one.
- Accreditation–EfM grants Continuing Education Units to indicate completion of the work.
- Access to an international network
- A training opportunity for the laity
- Connection with The University of the South and its School of Theology
- Basic theological education to support the laity in responding to the call to ministry in daily life. For some the theological groundwork in EfM may be supplemented with additional opportunities to prepare for ecclesial roles such as that of lay reader, vocational deacon, or educator.

Providing the program is something in which various agencies participate. The local church provides a setting and may offer some financial assistance to participants. The diocese may contract with EfM, which lowers the tuition for participants. When there is a contract with the local jurisdiction, a function of that contract is the appointment of a coordinator who maintains a liaison with the EfM program in Sewanee, arranges for mentor training locally, acts as a communicator for EfM, and promotes the program.

What EfM Is NOT

- *EfM is not only Bible study.*

  EfM participants study what the Bible says, but they also learn how to understand the Bible within its historical context and literary setting. Biblical studies form the primary work of the first two years. EfM is more than a Bible study in which one reads the Bible, seeks to understand it, and then applies it to daily life. EfM takes seriously God's revelation through all of Christian tradition, from the earliest biblical messages, through the development of liturgy and theology, and even in the context of the challenges we face in our own times.

- *EfM is not a program in personal therapy or problem solving.*

  While EfM groups develop a close community in order to delve deeply into matters of faith and theology, the group does not exist as a problem-solving agency or as a setting for analyzing or addressing personal and social problems. In an EfM group, members may wish to share various aspects of their lives, but EfM is not a place to probe or press individuals to talk about those things they would prefer to leave unexamined.

- *EfM is not a closed community.*

  The content of EfM materials and the processes we use for reflection are not secrets. A group may invite a guest such as someone who brings some special information or someone who would like to participate for a session in order to decide if he or she might like to join. On the other hand, we do respect one another's privacy. This means that we expect the group to maintain confidentiality about personal matters. The rule of thumb is: secrets–no; privacy–yes. Participants may share with others what they have learned and how that was learned, but they are expected to retain in confidence specific personal aspects of their colleagues' lives which may have been shared during the course of the program.

- *EfM is not an academic program leading to a degree or an ordination program.*

  Local arrangements may permit EfM to become part of the work leading to a degree or to ordination, but the School of Theology of The University of the South makes no recommendations about ordination nor does it grant course credit for completing the Education for Ministry program.

Purpose Statements for the Five Units

Unit One, Spiritual Autobiography and Listening: to develop the theme of ministry in personal context through creating a spiritual autobiography using contextual lenses and to approach listening as a fundamental skill for ministry.

Unit Two, Theological Reflection as a Life Skill: to learn how to use theological reflection models and methods as a means for integrating experience and content and to develop the discipline of theological reflection as a life skill for ministry in daily life.

Unit Three, Developing a Sustaining Spirituality: to guide the work of developing a personal spirituality through prayer and worship which, when combined with study and theological reflection, offer a four-fold spiritual discipline that can help sustain us in the practice of ministry.

Unit Four, Integrating Belief, Behavior, and Doctrine: to provide means by which a person can examine and build a personal theology through the integration of belief, behavior, and doctrine.

Unit Five, Vocation: A Way to Love in Permanent White Water: to offer perspectives on discerning and responding to God's call; and, second, to provide a framework for reviewing the year's work.

Supplemental Readings in the Christian Tradition

Week Five, Reading Assignment for Year One

The Priestly Creation Story[67]

The Priestly creation story in Genesis 1–2:4a is one of the shortest and yet most tightly packed theological statements in the Bible. In its present form it dates from the time of the Restoration in the fifth century BCE. It had developed, however, over a much longer period and had been polished smooth by the time P gave it its final working. We must study it line by line in order to unpack the many levels of meaning in it.

Let us go over the main points.

First read **Genesis 1–2:4a.**

Then read again the biblical reference for each point in conjunction with the discussion.

1. God alone is the creator of all, with no divine helpers. The world is not simply shaped by God. (1:1)
2. God creates by speaking; God simply says, "Let there be . . . ," and what is spoken comes to be. (1:3, 6, 9, etc.)
3. God creates light; it is not the gift of the sun, which shines only with the light God has given it. (1:3)
4. God keeps the waters of chaos in their place by calling for a firm dome to keep out the waters that are above and by gathering the waters below into the seas so that the dry land appears. (1:6–10)
5. The heavenly bodies–sun, moon, planets, and stars–which were thought to be gods by many cultures in the ancient Near East, are only creatures of God. (1:14–18)
6. The earth shares in the task of creation, though only at God's command: the earth brings forth vegetation. The waters also bring forth sea creatures and the earth, animal life, but not in the same way as the earth brings forth vegetation. God creates the higher forms of life. (1:11, 20–21, 24–25)
7. God creates humankind in God's own image and gives it dominion over all the creation. (1:26)
8. God creates humankind male and female, and this fact is connected closely with humankind's creation in the divine image. (1:27)

67. *Education for Ministry–Year One: Old Testament,* 4th edition, ed. Patricia Bays (Sewanee, Tennessee: The University of the South, 2006), 29–46.

9. God blesses humankind with sexuality and the gift of children. (1:28)
10. The final work of creation is God's rest on the seventh day. (2:2)

The First Words

Even from this brief outline we can see some of the things that were on the mind of the author. First, one important aspect of this story cannot be seen in most English translations. Grammatically, the Hebrew begins in the middle of a sentence. What could this mean? Is it a mistake? Was the first corner of a manuscript lost? No, there is a theological meaning. Beginning a sentence in the middle is a way of saying, "We do not know what God was doing before our world came into being. Our knowledge cannot pry before the beginning of our world; God's beginning is unknowable to us."

God and Creation

Next, it is important to say, above all else, that God is completely different from everything else. Other religions may have said that there were all sorts of divine beings: animal monsters, heavenly bodies, the seas, storms–anything that seemed powerful or mysterious. For the P writer, nothing in the world is divine. Rather, the whole universe is God's creation. Some religions may have thought of at least part of the universe as being made out of the substance of the divine, flowing forth out of the god. For P, nothing of God flows into the universe; God is God, and all else that exists is not God and is not divine.

Third, there is no need to look to lesser gods for the fertility of the earth. Vegetable crops and animals are included in God's design for the world, and the earth brings forth her increase at God's command. The worship of Baals (fertility gods), with all the gross practices that went with it, is not necessary; indeed to worship them would be to deny the power of the one Creator.

Fourth, the whole creation leads up to the creation of humanity. Life has not been created in order to provide playthings for the gods nor to act as slave-servants to the gods. Humanity, man and woman, is created to be God's representative in governing creation. It is a position of great dignity and worth.

Israel, the Chosen People

Each of these points was important in the life of Israel. She had been chosen to be God's people; God had made a covenant with her and had promised that, through Israel, all the nations of the earth would be blessed. The covenant was the basis for all of Israel's religious faith. After the Israelites had settled in Canaan, they were tempted and led away from God to the worship of the Baals and the *astral deities*–the sun, moon, planets, and stars–which the other nations worshiped. The prophets constantly tried to overcome the worship of these false gods so that Israel would be faithful to the covenant. When the northern kingdom was destroyed and the leaders of Judah (the southern kingdom) were carried into exile, the warnings of the prophets were shown to have been correct. Thus we can see the P writer–in the circumstance of exile–expressing in this story the true dignity of humankind and the complete sovereignty of God as these facts had been learned in Israel's life and taught by the prophets. All of what Israel stood for was expressed by the covenant. This was how Israel knew God; God was the God who had made the covenant with Abraham, Isaac, and Jacob and who had sealed it at Sinai through Moses. This God, and this God alone, had created the nation of Israel, and this God alone had created the heavens and the earth and all things.

The creation story expresses the faith of Israel learned by her experience as the people of God's covenant. Just as God had made Israel God's people at Sinai, so also God had made all of humanity in God's own image at creation. Both the covenant story and the creation story say the same thing: God has given humanity dignity and worth and dominion; therefore, the creation story reaches its climax in the creation of humankind.

The Sabbath

The P author does not end the story with the creation of humanity. The final day of creation is not the sixth, on which human beings are created, but the seventh, on which God rests. This rest does not mean only a mere recuperation from the exhaustion of creation. Rather it is a cessation of regular work in order to enjoy the fruits of that labor. God rests in order to enjoy creation. The P author, with special interest in the *cult*–the practices of worship–leads us to the practice of the Sabbath. This is not, however, a contradiction of what we have just said about the creation of humanity as the climax. The covenant, the basis of Israel's faith in the dignity of all people, is what the Sabbath is all about. The Sabbath is the celebration of the covenant. Therefore, the story leads to two ends, both of which refer to the same central point of Israel's faith: (1) God's gift of life and authority–a people under God–and (2) the Sabbath, which is the celebration of this people under God through the covenant.

You are not expected at this point in your studies to be able to feel all that is involved in the covenant. The point you should be able to grasp at this stage is that the P creation story sums up the experience of Israel and is not a simple childish story. You will come back to this story again and again, and the more you become familiar with the rest of the Old Testament, the more you will feel the power of it. Now look back again to the beginning of the story, and we will go over it more closely.

The Priestly Creation Story

This verse, which looks so simple in the English translation, is very strange in the Hebrew because it begins mid-sentence. The text can be translated, carrying it on through verse three, in several ways. (1) "In the beginning God created the heavens and the earth. The earth was without form and void, and darkness. . . ." (2) "When God began to create the heavens and the earth, the earth was without form and void, and darkness. . . ." (3) "In the beginning of God's creating of the heavens and the earth–(when) the earth was without form and void, and darkness was upon the face of the deep, and the wind of God was moving over the face of the waters–God said, 'Let there be. . . .'" None of these translations really fits the text as we have it, but each one is possible. Somewhat closer might be to start with an ellipsis ". . . " and then use the wording of option 3 above.

What difference would it make which translation we pick? Some people have argued that if we use the first one, there is nothing before God creates. God creates the heavens and the earth, and they are formless and empty until God then shapes and fills them. While it is fine theology to believe God created from nothing–*ex nihilo* is the Latin phrase that is used–Genesis 1 does not make such a claim. If we take the second or third translation, there is already a formless empty abyss and God begins to create; God shapes and fills a chaos that already existed.

Dualism

Later theology, especially Christian theology, has insisted that God created out of nothing not simply as a way of choosing one of these translations over the other. Theologians have been trying to oppose a point of view which was very common in the world of the first few centuries of the Christian era and is still very much with us. This point of view is called *dualism.* It says that there are two aspects of the world: the material and the nonmaterial, sometimes called the "spiritual." The material is usually regarded as less good, sometimes evil. Theologians have not wanted to say that there was something, anything, already existing when God began creation, because this already existing something, chaos, could be used by the dualists to refer to matter, the material stuff, which God shaped. They could then say that this matter is the source of evil. So the theologians said that God created *ex nihilo,* out of nothing; anything and everything that is, matter included, is created by God and is good. You can begin to see here that many beliefs, many truths, are not stated explicitly by every biblical passage on a similar theme.

Dualism had a great effect on the thinking of the early church. It came from eastern roots. In Persia the religion of Zoroastrianism taught that there were two gods, one evil and one good. The good god was the god of light; the evil god, the god of darkness. (The name of the god of light, Mazda, is known to many people although they may not know where it originated.)

A man named Mani, who was greatly influenced by Zoroastrianism, developed a religion, dualistic in nature, that prescribed ways of combating the power of the material world and escaping into the world of spirit and light. His religion, usually called *Manichaeism,* flourished in the third and fourth centuries, especially in North Africa, and influenced many Christians. St. Augustine, one of the greatest theologians of the church, was a Manichee before he converted to Christianity.

Plato

The teachings of the great pre-Christian philosopher Plato have also led to dualistic conclusions. Plato taught that, although individual things in this world come and go–they are born and they die, they come into being and they decay–there lie behind the individual things the *ideas* of them. There are many individual trees, each different to some degree from the others and each destined to die and decay, but each is a partial representation of the idea Tree. The idea contains all that it is possible for a tree to be; it is complete and single, not needing many separate examples of itself to express its completeness; it lasts forever, eternally existing while the individual representations of it come and go. Why Plato said this, what problems he was trying to understand, we shall look at later. The fact that he said it, however, allowed people of a later time–during the third through the fifth centuries CE–to develop a religion that was dualistic in a much more subtle and sophisticated way than was Manichaeism. The Neo-Platonists taught that the ultimate One lies beyond all things, and it is impossible to speak of that One at all. The *via negativa* is all that is possible. From the One all the rest of the universe emanates as light emanates, flows, or shines from a light bulb or a candle. The farther away from the source, the less like the One a thing becomes, until finally, at the farthest remove, there is matter. A human being, according to Neo-Platonism, is really spirit, akin to the One, but the spirit is trapped in a material body. Below humanity there is no spirit; all is merely material. Only by mystical exercises can humankind rise above the material body and reach union with the One. This point of view has influenced much of Christian piety. Augustine was also a Neo-Platonist before becoming a Christian.

Whatever the correct translation of this verse may be, theologians were right in thinking that the Old Testament opposed dualism. The Hebrews did *not* make a distinction between matter and "spirit." As we shall see in the JE (Yahwist-Elohist) creation story, the first human being is made from the dust of the earth and has life breathed into him so that he becomes "a living being." The entire creature, without division into body and spirit, is a living being. When the Christian church said that Jesus is the word of God made flesh, it also spoke against any kind of dualism.

This is why many theologians prefer the reading of verse one that says, "In the beginning God created the heavens and the earth." But there is no way to decide on the basis of the text itself. The P writer has other ways of dealing with the problem of dualism.

Genesis 1:2

Whichever way you translate the first verse, when the earth appears it is without form and void–that is, it is chaotic, empty of all form, design, or meaning–and darkness is upon the face of "the deep." "The deep" is a translation of the Hebrew word *tehom.* Behind this word there lies a whole mythic tradition. In the ancient world of the Mesopotamian basin there existed a story of the creation of the world by means of a great battle between a warrior god and a dragon, a sea-monster, who represented watery *chaos.* To many peoples who lived in desert lands far from the sea, the sea was fearsome. Its great storms were powerful and destroyed ships and houses built close to the shores. Stories of sea monsters were told by returning sailors. So "the deep," the waters of the sea with its monsters, was a symbol of chaos to the ancient people.

The Babylonian creation myth is a long story about the birth of various gods and about the eventual conflict between the god Marduk and the goddess Tiamat. In the course of the conflict, Tiamat is slain, and it is from her body that the firmament, the great dome of heaven, is made. It is worth noting here that the name Tiamat is closely related linguistically to *tehom.* By slaying Tiamat, the chaos monster, the monster of the deep, Marduk makes it possible for order to reign.

Much has been made of the common background out of which the Babylonian and the Hebrew creation stories come. The differences between the stories are more important–and more instructive–than their similarities. The Babylonian myth is an involved story of the birth of the gods and of the struggles among them for supremacy. Human beings are created almost as an afterthought, to serve as slaves for the gods, tending the earth so that the gods might have leisure. In the P story, the reference to "the deep" is virtually the sole remnant of this older myth. There is no birth of God; God is there before the story begins. Only by taking a broad meaning of myth as we have done can the P story be called a myth at all. P has stripped the narrative of all features of a "story about the gods" and has reduced it to a statement of doctrine, using the older myth as a framework only. By using an older framework with which people were familiar, the writer is also able to "start where they are" and show them greater truth.

The capriciousness of the gods and the denigration of humanity in the Babylonian myth stand in complete contrast to the picture of the sovereign and loving God of the Hebrew story. Nothing is told of God except God's acts toward the world he is creating. No questions of God's origins are raised; no relationship to any other god is assumed (until we get to the plural pronouns in verse 26); and the dignity of humankind toward which the whole story moves is a contradiction of the Babylonian estimate of human worth.

Still, the symbol of chaos, tehom, the deep, like Tiamat–the monster of the deep–is important. Chaos, or the threat of chaos, is always present in life. We know that we are insecure in the world we live in. We feel the threat of destruction. The world itself is not secure. The ancients felt this, too, in the dark, a storm at sea, a tornado, wild forces of any kind. As the P story of creation unfolds, by bringing order to chaos, God takes possession of it and subdues it. In Hebrew thought, it is God alone who keeps chaos under control. In the story of Jonah, a man who refuses to obey the word of God finds himself thrown back into chaos where he is swallowed up by the very monster of the deep herself. Jonah returns to dry land when he promises to obey God.

There is an additional level of meaning in the use of tehom/Tiamat. Since the Priestly account comes to us through the experience of exile, using the term may be a subtle way for the Israelites to remember that ultimately the Lord and not the Babylonian gods is the source of all creation. (We see another example of this with the creation of the sun and moon.)

The wind or storm of God was moving over the chaos. The word that the English Bible translates "spirit" is *ruach* (pronounced ROO-ahk). This word can mean "spirit," but also means "wind, breath, or storm." In this verse, the picture is that of the great divine wind blowing storm-like over the sea, or "hovering" over the deep like a great bird about to light on its nest, especially one incubating its eggs. The "spirit" of God here should not be thought of as acting to create; it is simply there, a storm, almost part of the chaos itself in wildness, yet showing forth the presence of God about to create, to bring order into the chaos. The image of the "hovering" of the spirit is one of almost-life, of the care and tending immediately before birth.

Genesis 1:3

Light is created. It is not some god-like stuff that flows from God into the darkness. Some religions have thought of light itself as a god. With the fear of darkness that most people have, it is understandable that light should be thought of as divine, as saving in some way and giving safety. In Genesis light is from God. God alone is the source of the safety that light brings. Notice also that light is created before the sun, stars, and moon. Light does not come from them, according to this story, but directly from God.

The form of words in verse 3 is important: "God said . . . ." God creates by his word. In the P account God creates by speech alone. This shows God separated from his creation and speaking to it. It portrays God with such immense power that it takes only a word for there to be a creative response. Later philosophers and theologians speak of both the transcendence of God and immanence of God. Transcendence refers to the separateness of God from God's creation; immanence refers to God's nearness. The creation-by-speech here in Genesis 1 shows God's transcendence. In Genesis 2 the immanence of God is evident in the manner of creation, for God shapes the clay.

Thought about God swings between these two poles. On the one hand, if God is not transcendent, God tends to become confused with the rest of the world. Pantheism is a form of religion that overemphasizes the immanence of God at the expense of transcendence. The term means literally "all is God." Stoicism is an ancient religion, prominent in the world of the first few centuries of the Christian era, which is pantheistic. Much modern thought tends also toward pantheism, confusing nature with God. Unless God is not the world, God loses the dimension of divinity.

On the other hand, if God is not immanent, near to us, then God is irrelevant. A merely transcendent god who was not accessible to his people could not even be known, let alone worshiped. In the eighteenth century, when people were supremely confident in the power of human reason to know and understand all things, a view of the world developed that did not allow God to have any significant relationships with the world. The universe was thought to be like a huge machine, operating according to the laws inherent in it. A theological school of thought called deism pictured God as a clockmaker. God designed the universe and made it as a clockmaker makes a clock, in such a way that it could continue to run on its own. Then God withdrew from it, allowing it to run in accordance with its inherent laws, never intervening again. This is a doctrine of God that overemphasizes the divine transcendence. If it be true, there is no point in praying to God or expecting any relationship with God other than adoration for the work that the almighty has done in time long past.

By saying that God creates both by the word and by handling the stuff of creation, the biblical writers express both the transcendence and the immanence of God. God is the one who stands over against us, completely different from us, and speaks the divine word to us; God is also the one who is immersed deeply in the world with the stuff of it clinging to God's hands. God is not the world, but God is deeply involved in it.

There is one further point that P wants to make: the world is "good." It is like a refrain in a song. Here, God declares the light to be good. This does not simply mean that it is pleasant or beautiful. God also creates the great sea monsters and creeping things and calls them good. When God calls them all good, the meaning is that they fit in with the great overall purpose of creation. They have their place in the grand design. The goodness of creation is based on God's purpose, not on our sense of beauty.

Genesis 1:4–5

Notice that although God creates the light, darkness is not created. God separates the light from the darkness, but darkness continues. Primitive people, like many of us moderns, feared the darkness, especially when there was no moon or when it was cloudy so that there were no stars. Evil spirits–and evil people–can work their wills in the darkness.

Notice also that, even though God does not create darkness, God calls the light "day" and the darkness "night." In naming the darkness God takes possession of it. Throughout our study of the Old Testament we become aware of the power that ancient people ascribed to the act of naming. If you were able to name something, you had power over it. Even today we see something of this. A parent gives a newborn child her or his name; the child has nothing to say about it. When children grow up, they can legally change their names, but while they are children, it is the parents who decide what they shall be called. It may be that the custom that teenage children have of taking a nickname by which their friends know them is an unconscious attempt to break loose from the bonds of parental control. A remnant of this control-by-naming can also be seen in the care with which some people try to ensure that coworkers never discover that childhood nickname. To know someone's embarrassing nickname would be tantamount to having a certain degree of control over the person.

In the Old Testament we see events in which God changes a person's name: Abram is changed to Abraham, Jacob to Israel. The meaning of the name is not as important as the fact that God has changed it and has thereby claimed the person. When God names the darkness "night," God claims it, takes possession of it, and thereby restrains it by his power. We said earlier, in discussing the first verse, that P had ways of combating dualism: This is one of them. The possibility of chaos taking control of God's creation is overcome because God takes possession of darkness and is Lord of the night as well as of the day.

The final sentence in verse 5 shows the Hebrew system for counting the days: A day goes from evening to evening, not from morning to morning as ours does. In Jewish custom this is still so; the Sabbath, for example, does not begin on Saturday morning, but on Friday evening at sundown. In the Christian church holy days are first celebrated on the evening before. Christmas eve and Hallowe'en (which is "All Hallows' Eve," the eve of All Saints' Day) are well-known examples, but the rule applies in all cases. Worship services held on such "eves" characteristically contain prayers and scripture readings concerned with the theme of the holy day itself.

Genesis 1:6–8

The word translated "firmament" means a hammered metal bowl; the firmament is like a great upside-down metal bowl that separates the waters. In this imagery we have the ancient view of a three-tiered universe, which was held, with modifications, until the sixteenth century CE when Copernicus put forth his theory of the motion of the planets around the sun. In the Genesis picture, the earth is a disk with waters beneath it and the firmament above it holding back the waters. So the three tiers are the waters under the earth, the earth, and the waters above the firmament. We see this cosmology (picture of the earth) again in the second of the Ten Commandments, when we read, "You shall not make for yourself an idol, whether in anything that is in heaven above, or that is on the earth beneath, or that is in the water under the earth. . . ." The reason for this commandment is that all the things in this three-tiered universe are creatures, not God.

Notice that heaven is not the sacred dwelling-place of God; it is simply the firmament. God dwells above heaven. The important point about this is not that it tells us where God is, but that it says God is not to be localized in any point within creation.

The creation of the firmament to keep the waters in their proper place reflects the ancient fear of water in large quantities; a deluge of water symbolizes chaos. Once again, the P writer deals with chaos and dualism. Chaos is held in check by the firmament, which God has made. Humankind is dependent only on the good God for safety. In the P account of the story of Noah and the flood, God opens the windows of heaven and the springs of the deep and releases the waters of chaos to destroy a large part of creation. As we see when we study that story, God makes a covenant with Noah promising never to do that again–God's creation shall stand and the watery chaos be held back forever.

Genesis 1:9–10

Again we see the fear of water, and God sets the proper limits of the seas so that the dry land appears. This is a different form of the creative act of God of withholding the power of chaos.

By having God name the dry land "Earth" and the waters that were gathered together "seas," the P writer is using the names of powerful gods in ancient religions. Because God both creates and names these, we are to see that they are merely creatures, not gods. The P writer thus combats the influence of polytheism (belief in many gods). Once again comes the refrain: "And God saw that it was good."

Notice that the refrain did not occur at the end of the second day when the firmament was constructed. This formula of approbation does not reappear until the seas and the dry land are created. This is because the creation of the firmament is only part of the complex work of creating the world of cosmos within which the rest of creation will take place. The formula of approbation designates the completion of an act. On the second day a creative act is left incomplete, and on the third day two acts occur. The fact that two days are spanned shows that P is using older traditional material, fitting it, sometimes awkwardly, into a seven-day scheme. The liturgical interest of P, the concern that the whole story leads up to the Sabbath, compels the use of a seven-day scheme and the fitting of material into that scheme as neatly as possible.

Genesis 1:11–13

In the ancient world, wherever the growing of crops took the place of hunting or herding as the chief means of life and livelihood, people became concerned about the fertility of the earth. Without the proper mixture of good soil, water, and sunlight, the crops would not grow. Almost all agricultural societies have religions that try to bring about the fertility of the earth. In the ancient Near East these religions often tried to do this by practicing sacred prostitution. By having sexual relations with a temple prostitute, one guaranteed that the land would be fertile. In these verses the P writer combats this kind of religion.

Plant life is created by God. But notice how this happens. Previously, God has created by his word. Here God speaks to the earth, commanding it to "put forth" vegetation. P does not try to deny the obvious fertility of the earth. The wonder of the seasonal rebirth of green things from the earth is too clear to be denied. But P has the earth act at God's command. The earth's fertility is God's gift.

The reference to "plants yielding seed and fruit trees of every kind on earth that bear fruit in it" is to grasses and herbs that yield seed directly, and those plants and trees that have their seed inside a fruit or nut. That is, all kinds of plants have within them the means of reproduction. The earth is fertile and plants have the power to reproduce, due to the command of the word of God. The self-contained powers of nature to bring forth life are not nature's own; nature is a creature. And it is good.

Agricultural fertility cults frequently have in their mythology a dying and rising god. When scholars of the history of religion noticed this, and especially when they saw the forms it took in the Near East, many of them suggested that this accounted for the Christian belief in the death and resurrection of Jesus. This, they thought, was simply a variant on the dying and rising god of the agricultural fertility cults. In fact there is much of the symbolism of the rebirth of nature in the proper celebrations of Easter. The lily, the rabbits, Easter eggs, all speak of the rebirth of natural life. (But for those of us who live in the northern hemisphere, it is too easy to drift into a belief that Jesus' resurrection was somehow part of the natural order, rather than a gracious act of a loving God.)

The ancient Hebrews were surrounded by these kinds of religions, particularly in the myths surrounding Baal, the Canaanite god of fertility, and Anath, his sister. The myth tells of the death of Baal. The god of death, Mot, holds Baal in the prison of death. Anath goes to Mot, slays him and cuts up his body, casting it about over the land, and Baal comes back to life. The prophets of Israel constantly fought against Baal worship. Israel had been created as a nation by God and must remain faithful to him. Still, the need for successful agriculture was obvious. In the P creation story the author maintains that the God of the deliverance from Egypt is also the one who gives fertility to the earth. Faithfulness to the covenant will suffice to ensure the fertility of the land.

The figure of Jesus comes out of this kind of background. There can be no possibility of adequately describing his death and resurrection in the terms of the fertility cults. His death was a once-for-all event and his resurrection has its meaning only in connection with the promises God made to Israel in the covenant. It speaks not of life coming naturally out of death, but of God being faithful to God's promises.

Genesis 1:14–19

On the fourth day the heavenly bodies are created. Worship of the astral deities–the sun, moon, stars, and planets–was widespread in the ancient world. Indeed, almost anywhere you go around the world you will find evidence of such worship. The stars and planets are one feature of nature that is there for all to see. Hunting tribes may not be concerned with growing crops; different animals that have been worshiped may not be known in places far from where they live; oceans may be unknown to inland dwellers, and deserts with their sandstorms may be unfamiliar to people who live along the coasts. But the lights of the heavens can be seen anywhere in the world.

One of the things about the stars that impresses people who pay close attention is that they move with such regularity. We are sometimes amazed that our astronomers can predict with accuracy where a particular planet will be at a specific time, but the ancient astronomers could do this, too. Ancient people were impressed with the fact that, although much in life was uncertain, the movement of the stars was always the same.

Because of the regularity of the heavenly bodies, many believed that the stars controlled everything else and determined what was to happen on earth. Even today astrology, the study of the stars to see what they tell of life, is popular. Some people really believe what their horoscopes say. Others may view astrology as mere superstition, but in ancient times it was a serious matter. All of life was thought to be governed by the astral deities. Men and women, in this view, simply live out lives that have already been determined at the time of their birth. They have no freedom and nothing much matters, since all is determined in advance.

For Israel, however, this could not be so. God had called the people Israel and made a covenant with them. God would be their God and bless them, and they were to keep God's commandments. Israel could be faithful to God or unfaithful. Israel was free–to obey or disobey. Therefore, Israel was responsible for what she did. To believe in the astral deities and their control over life was a denial both of the lordship of God and of human responsibility.

The P editor says that God created the lights in the firmament–they are not gods. Although P used the names of the gods Earth and Sea, "Sun" and "Moon" are not used. By using the clumsy expressions "greater light" and "lesser light," P makes it plain that these, too, are creatures of God. We may have here another example of the exiled Israelites being able to find a "safe" way to jeer at their captors. "You worship 'big light' and 'little light,'" they are saying, "while we worship the creator of all that is."

The heavenly bodies are creatures of God, and they have quite simple jobs to do. They do not control the lives of people: they are the means by which to tell time! They divide the day from the night and they mark off the seasons and the years. They also give light on the earth, but it is not their own light, but the light that God created first of all creatures. This, too, is good; another act of creation is completed. With this, the cosmos (the universe itself) is finished.

Genesis 1:20–23

On the fifth day living beings are created, beginning with those that are least like humans and moving, on the sixth day, to humankind, which is created in the image and likeness of God. Living creatures are treated in a special way in this story. The plants, which were brought forth from the earth, are not thought to be forms of life. They have their seed and reproduce, but they are not called living creatures. When we look at this first creation story, we see that humans were allowed to eat vegetables but not meat. The life given to God's creatures is sacred and is not to be taken away by any other creature.

There is a Hebrew word used in this chapter that is not translated into English in every instance. When used of human beings, the word *nephesh* is usually translated "soul." But when used of other members of the animal world, it is often left out. This is unfortunate, for the P writer's use of nephesh makes some important theological points. There is no simple English word or phrase to cover the two aspects of nephesh. It refers to the life force that separates animals from rocks, for instance, or stars, and also from plants. Nephesh also refers to the individuality of each creature. We are accustomed to recognizing each human being as unique; the P writer believes every animal–even the "creepy crawlies"–is unique to God.

Of the living creatures, first the sea monsters are created, then the rest of the sea creatures and the birds. The seas have been separated from the dry land and held in their place–chaos has been controlled. Now even the fearsome monsters of chaos are discovered to be creatures of God and are called good; they are nothing to fear. These living creatures are then given the gift of procreation as a blessing. Even for living creatures, fertility is not simply a power contained within them but is a special gift from God. Only God is the source of creativity.

Verse 21 uses the verb *bara*: create. This is a different verb from those used before, except in verse 1 when bara is used for the whole process of creation. This verb never has anyone or anything except God as subject. Both God and people can "make," "shape," "form," and so on; only God is said to bara.

Genesis 1:24–25

On the sixth day the earth brings forth living creatures: domestic animals (cattle), wild animals (beasts), and creeping things–all the forms of life on dry land. All are connected very closely with the earth, which acts as mediator of God's creation. There is no blessing or command to be fruitful; apparently, as with the plants, this is part of their nature. Perhaps the blessing was necessary for the creatures which came from the sea because the sea was not given the ability to give power to reproduce. This is the suggestion that Gerhard von Rad makes in his book on Genesis. He says, The absence here of divine blessing is intentional. Only indirectly do the animals receive the power of procreation from God; they receive it directly from the earth, the creative potency of which is acknowledged throughout. Water, by creation, stands lower in rank than the earth; it could not be summoned by God to creative participation. (p. 57)

Yet in verse 20 it seems that the same command is given to the waters as was given to the earth: "Let the waters bring forth. . . ." This is a case in which the English translation is somewhat misleading. In the Hebrew three different verbs are used in those places where the English reads "bring forth." In verse 11 the verb is *dasha*, "to yield tender grass," and it is in the causative form–"cause to yield tender grass." In verse 12, the verb is *yatsa*, "to go out," again in the causative–"cause to go out." Thus in the case of the earth's "bringing forth" vegetation, the verb is in the causative: the earth causes the grass to come forth. In verse 2 also the verb is yatsa in the causative, so the earth causes the living creatures to come forth. In verse 20, however, the verb is *sharats*, "to swarm," and it is in the simple form not indicating causation. Verse 20, therefore, means, "Let the waters swarm with living creatures. . . ." God created them directly, without the mediation of the waters, and gave them the power to reproduce.

The real significant contrast seems to be not so much between the creatures of the water, the birds of the air, and the animals of the dry land, but between the animals and human beings. The animals are closely tied to the earth, whereas humans are more intimately related to their creator.

Genesis 1:26–28

This is the climax of the story. In all the other acts of creation the form of words is very direct: "Let there be . . ."; "Let the earth put forth . . . ." Here, God takes counsel with God's self for a more deliberate and important act: "Let us make man in our image, after our likeness." This is a very strange expression. The name for God in this story is Elohim. When we discussed this before, noting that it is the name which the E writer uses and also the P writer at this point in the story, we mentioned that the word is in the plural: the gods. We also said that there was no doubt that both E and P believed in only one God. All through this story of creation the word Elohim has been translated "God," but now, in verse 26, the plural is used: "Let us . . . in our. . . ."

In the ancient world the idea of a heavenly court was common. The main god was surrounded by other heavenly beings the way a king or queen is attended by the members of an earthly court. In most of the old religions the court was made up of lesser gods. In the Old Testament there was only one God, but God was frequently pictured as being served by a court. In some present-day eucharistic liturgies this same imagery occurs: "Therefore with Angels and Archangels, and with all the company of heaven. . . ."

God is submerging God's self in the heavenly court. "Man" is made in God's image. "Man" is like God, but is also quite distinct from God. The P writer in this whole section seems to be saying these two things about humankind. On the one hand P uses the words "image" and "likeness": An "image" is a copy of the original, like a statue, and a "likeness" is an outline or silhouette. This would indicate a very close likeness to God, even in a physical sense. On the other hand, God is submerged into the heavenly court, so the likeness to God must be somewhat blurred.

In addition, the Hebrew word for man used here is *'adam* (the same word that later will be used as a proper name, Adam). This word is closely related to the word for earth, *'adamah*. Thus P also shows that though humankind differs from the animals, it remains tied to the earth and therefore to the animals and indeed the rest of creation.

The result of this very subtle use of words is to give a picture of humankind ("man," male and female: see below) as a being who is very much a creature, not to be confused with God, but one who stands in a very special relationship to God and is very much like God. It would seem that the point here is not so much to say that humanity, as the image of God, can give us an idea of what God is like, as it is to say that humanity is to act like God in the world: God gives human beings dominion over all the living things in the world. Their purpose is not to rule, but to act as God's agent or steward.

It was a common practice in the ancient world for statues of a king to be set up throughout his realm. These were not regarded simply as carved statues, but as the king's representatives, looking out for his interests in those places where the king himself could not always be. This seems to be the idea expressed here: Humankind is God's representative, looking after God's interests in the world. This authority, dominion over God's creation, is given in the creation.

'Adam is not a sexually specific word. There is another word for a male person: *'ish*. In spite of the male domination of ancient society, P means both "man" and "woman" when he uses 'adam. (Notice the change of pronouns in v. 27: "In the image of God he created them, male and female he created them.") In the P account, sexuality, male and female together making up 'adam, is a direct creation by God from the outset. (The JE story has woman made after man.) God blesses and commands humankind to procreate: "Be fruitful and multiply, and fill the earth and subdue it." Sexuality, then, is a gift of creation, a blessing, and a command.

Genesis 1:29–31

Notice that there is a limit to human dominion: Only vegetables may be eaten. Both humans and beasts are given vegetables for their food, though to humans both herbs and fruit are allowed while the animals have only herbs (green plants). The shedding of blood is not part of the divine plan for creation. In the Old Testament it is a basic belief that "in the blood is the life." God alone gives life, and it is not to be taken. Those who spill blood put an end to what cannot be revived. Later visions of the perfect time that will come when God brings in the kingdom show animals and humans living without shedding blood. The P writer, of course, knows that both animals and humans eat flesh, but a complete respect for life leads the writer to say that this is not part of God's plan. We shall see that P has God give animals to humans for food at the time of Noah. Even then the blood is not to be eaten. It is to be poured out to God as giver of life.

The final refrain is emphatic: ". . . indeed, it was very good." The world as it comes from the hand of God is perfect. This is the basic faith expressed in the Old Testament: whatever evil there is now in the world is not due to God. As God created the world there was no evil in it, and no dualistic power of evil. As the JE account will go on to show, evil comes when human beings overreach their assigned role. Not content to be God's representatives in the world, humans aspire to be as gods themselves.

Genesis 2:1–3

We would expect the P writer to say that creation ended on the sixth day, but this does not happen. God finished the work by resting on the seventh day. Rest is part of creation. To us rest sounds like doing nothing. To those who have to work until they are exhausted, to fight for the very possibility of life, leaving the old to die by themselves because there is no time to tend to them and still carry on the struggle for life, rest is an activity of sheer bliss. This is the kind of life that was usual for the ancient people, and is still true for most of the earth's people now. Rest, for them, is a necessary activity of life; without it, life is ground down into death. Thus the seventh day is not a day apart from creation, but the time of the creation of the act of rest. The Sabbath, in the Israelite calendar, is not a day of inactivity, but a day when work is not done so that rest may be done. As a celebration of the covenant, the Sabbath was especially seen as the day of recreation, of being restored to the very basis of life. God has hallowed, set apart, this day for this use. Verse 4a says that all this is a genealogy, the generations of the heavens and the earth. P usually puts this kind of verse first as a title. Here, since the creation story has its own introduction, it had to be put at the end.

Summary

1) *Dualism is rejected.* Light is created and comes from God. Though light is good and necessary, it is not to be worshiped. Darkness, though it is fearsome because it conceals evil action and makes it easier to commit evil, is not in itself to be feared; God claimed it and is Lord of it when God named it "night." The waters of chaos are set within their proper limits by God: the waters above are held out by the firmament and the other waters are gathered together as the seas and kept in their place by God's command. The monsters of the deep are like playthings to God, who created them and gave them the seas in which to roam. All this may sound very far from our way of thinking, but its message to us is clear. Biblical faith does not allow us to call anything that God has made evil or unclean, nor does it support our fears of the unknown. God is behind all that is, and we need fear nothing but God's absence.

2) *God is both transcendent and immanent.* God is the absolute Lord over creation. Nothing else is to be mistaken for God and worshiped. This means that we need not bow down before anything in the world! But God is also very near to everything in the world. God is involved in creation, so that we cannot treat anything that God has made as though it did not matter. The immanent side of God is presented more explicitly in the creation account of Genesis 2.

3) *There is freedom in the world.* Nature acts as God has created it to act, but it does so in respect to God's command to it. Human beings are given a role to play in God's design, but they must respond from their own freedom. The sun, moon, and stars do not control the things that happen. Nothing is decreed beforehand and sealed in fate. The astral bodies measure time, but they do not control it.

4) *Creation is fertile by the gift of God.* Ancient people thought that the powers of nature that gave or withheld fertility had to be worshiped. P says that fertility is from God, and God alone is to be worshiped. This belief, by assuring us that nature is not sacred, has allowed us to subdue it and bring it under our control. Much mischief has been done under the auspices of this word "subdue." The notion is one of responsible stewardship, not at all one of exploitation. We need now to remember that it belongs to God and brings its resources to us as a gift; ours to control, it is not ours to plunder.

5) *Humanity is in the image of God.* Humankind is shaped after the pattern of the elohim. This strange imagery both expresses the dignity of humankind and sets its limits. "Man," male and female, is like God, but is not to be confused with God.

6) *"Man" includes woman.* Sexuality is not simply a sign of our kinship with the animals and therefore a lower bestial function to be concealed and denied as unworthy of us. Humankind, 'adam, is not complete as male or female; neither is humankind originally a complete being, solitary and alone, who later "falls" into sexuality. From the outset God created humankind so that both sexes were needed for completeness. The modern notion of the self-sufficient individual is ruled out by this, as is the idea of male superiority. (This is quite remarkable since the place of women in ancient society, Hebrew included, was definitely lower than that of men. We can see this, and how it was made somewhat better, when we turn to the JE creation story.)

7) *Human beings are God's representatives.* Although the blessing of reproduction is given to humankind and animals alike, only human beings are commanded to fill the earth and subdue it. This has sometimes been taken to mean that we are given complete ownership of the world, but this is not the case. Humanity is God's steward. It is to fill the earth so that God may be

represented everywhere and to subdue the earth for the purposes of God. In spite of being made in God's image and being given the dominion, 'adam is still connected to 'adamah: that is, 'adam is of the earth and thus has limits set.

In these terms the P writer sees a perfection in humanity's original relationship to God and to the world. There is no downgrading of humanity as a mere puppet or slave to a tyrannical God; "man" (male and female) has great dignity and value. The terms of human dignity are clearly spelled out. The P writer was well aware of the fact that humankind had sunk to a level lower than that of the beasts, that we had denied our own dignity and taken it away from others, that we were such as to be worthy of complete condemnation before the righteousness of God. This merely points up the rightness of the terms of human life which humankind has violated. All, even the downfall of humankind, is set within the order which God has created.

Week Twelve, Reading Assignment for Year Four

The Trinity[68]

The truth takes its own forms and expresses itself in its own ways. Our efforts at defining, proving, or establishing it are all acts after the event. It is what it is, and not what we make it. Christianity prevails in the world in a fact which we have called Trinity, and which is Trinity, however inadequate and unsatisfactory our explanations of the term or our analyses of the thing may be. I would describe Christianity in its largest sense to be the fulfilment of God in the world through the fulfilment of the world in God. This assumes that the world is completed in man, in whom also God is completed in the world. And so, God, the world, and man are at once completed in Jesus Christ who, as He was the *logos* or thought of all in the divine foreknowledge of the past, so also is He the *telos* or end of all in the predestination of the future. That is to say, the perfect psychical, moral, and spiritual manhood of which Jesus Christ is to us the realization and the expression is the end of God in creation, or in evolution. I hold that neither science, philosophy, nor religion can come to any higher or other, either conjecture or conclusion, than that. But now, when we come to the actual terms or elements of God's self-realization in us and ours in Him, we cannot think or express the process otherwise than in the threefold form of the divine love, the divine grace, and the divine fellowship, in operation or action. Putting it into scriptural phrase, we speak as exactly as popularly in defining the matter of the Gospel to be, The love of the Father, the grace of the Son, and the fellowship of the Spirit. As our spiritual life is dependent upon each and all of these three constituents, so we can know God at all only as we know Him in the actual threefold relation to us of Father, Son, and Spirit.

The first element in the essential constitution of the Gospel is the fact in itself that God is love. That God is love means that He is so not only in Himself but in every activity that proceeds from Him. The very phrase the love of the Father expresses the whole principle of the universe. That God is Father means that it is His nature, or His essential activity, to reproduce Himself, to produce in all other that which He Himself is. That God in Himself is love carries with it the truth that from the beginning all things

68. This essay concludes *The Gospel in the Gospels* published in 1906 by William Porcher DuBose, the first dean of the School of Theology of The University of the South, Sewanee, Tennessee. You will find more information about him at http://liturgyandmusic.wordpress.com/2010/08/18/august-18-william-porcher-dubose-priest-1918/

else mean, and are destined to come to, love in the end. The mystery on the way that somehow light must come out of darkness, that love must needs conquer hate, and that in everything good seems to be only the final and far off goal of ill, may puzzle us but it does not disturb the principle itself. When we come to enter fairly upon the evolution of the future, the higher not merely psychical or social or moral but spiritual life and destiny of man, all the truth gradually dawns upon us in the following discoveries, which are already established facts of spiritual experience: The truth of all spirit is love; the matter of all law is goodness; God is not creator or cause only, nor lord or lawgiver only, but Father of all things, since all things through man are destined to share His spirit, to be partakers of His nature, and to reproduce Himself as Father in themselves as children. In order to be sons of God through actual participation in the divine nature there stands in the way indeed the need of a mighty redemption from sin and an as yet far off completion in holiness; but no matter how unredeemed or incomplete, we know beyond further question that all our salvation lies in redemption and completion, and that we shall be ourselves and the world will come to its meaning only when the self-realization of God as Father shall have accomplished itself in our self-realization as His children. If we knew the fact only that God in Himself is love, it would be to us a gospel indeed of great joy, because it would carry in it the assurance of the highest good, whatever that might be. But it would be but a partial gospel, and in fact only a gospel at all through its certainty of proceeding further.

The phrase Grace of the Son expresses that which perfectly complements and completes all that is meant by the Love of the Father. What is Fatherhood without a correlative Sonship? And what is all love even in God as its subject apart from its actuality and activity as grace in man as its object? The divine propriety of the terms Father and Son as applied to God cannot be too much magnified. The distinction between God as He is in Himself and God as He is in all possible expressions of Himself is one that we cannot think Him at all without making. The most perfect expression of love is contained in the statement, that Love loves love. Its nature is to produce, to reproduce, to multiply itself. Itself is forever the true object of itself, at the same time that it is ever a going forth from itself into that which is not itself. This essential principle of love or self-reproduction is what makes God eternally Father. But the eternal Fatherhood is actualized only in an eternal Sonship. Nothing proceeds from the Father which is not reproduction of the Father, and is not therefore Son. Man sees himself now in nature and destinature son of God. He feels his call and obligation to fulfil God in him as Father by realizing himself in God as son. His spiritual end and impulse is to know as also he is known, to love in return as he is first loved, to apprehend that for which he is apprehended of God in Christ. In proportion as he finds the meaning and truth of his own being in the reproduction of God, in being son of God, he finds the meaning and truth of the whole creation realized and expressed in his own sonship as heir of all and end of all. And in proportion again as he thus finds all things meaning and ending in sonship, he comes at last to see God Himself as realized in the universal sonship Himself therein realized as Eternal Father. So it is that in Jesus Christ we see everything expressed, because everything realized or fulfilled. He is all truth, because He is the truth of all things God, Creation, Man. And because He is thus truth and expression of all, He is Logos of all. What else could the Logos of all be but Son, or the Son but Logos? What could perfectly express God but that which is the perfect reproduction of Himself, or what is perfect sonship but perfect likeness?

The Grace of the Son is the divine gift of sonship. How could we have known God only in Himself? How could God have been actually our Father without the actuality of our sonship to Him? And could we have known, could we have wanted, could we have willed, could we have accomplished or attained our sonship without the gift or grace of sonship in Jesus Christ? God, we are told, predestinated us unto sonship through Jesus Christ unto himself. He predestinated us to be conformed to the image of His Son, that He might be the first born among many brethren. In bringing many sons to glory, He gave to us a Captain of our salvation, an Author and Finisher of the faith of sonship and so of the sonship of faith, who was Himself perfected as Son through the sufferings that are necessary to the perfecting of sonship in us. We see in Jesus Christ all that is meant, involved, or implied, in the fact that He is the divine Fatherhood realized and expressed in human sonship.

If that fact, viewed in its totality, signifies not only a human act, nor only a divine act, but a divine-human act, an act of God in man which is equally an act of man in God, then we say that Jesus Christ is not only as well the humanity as the divinity in that act, but He is the divinity as well as the humanity. He is not only the *gratia gratiata* in it but the *gratia gratians*–not only the manhood infinitely graced but the Godhead infinitely gracing.

Jesus Christ is therefore to us no mere sample or example of divine sonship. He is no mere one man who more successfully than others has grasped and expressed the ideal of a divine sonship. Neither is He a single individual of our race whom God has elected from among equally possible others, in whom as mere revelation or example to all others to manifest the truth of God in man and man in God. On the contrary, Jesus Christ is Himself the reality of all that is manifested or expressed in Him. He is as God the grace communicating and as man the grace communicated. He is both Generator and generated with reference to the life incarnate in Him both the sonship eternally in God to be begotten and the sonship actually begotten in man. As He was in the beginning with God and was God, so is He universally with man and is universal man.

When we have thus adequately conceived Christ as the universal truth and reality of ourselves, and in ourselves of all creation, and in creation and ourselves of God, then we are prepared for the conclusion that we know God at all, or are sons to Him as our Father, or are capable in that relation of partaking of His nature or entering into His Spirit or living His life, only in and through Jesus Christ; because Jesus Christ is the incarnation or human expression to us of the whole Logos of God that is to say, of God Himself as in any way whatever knowable or communicable. We cannot get at God to know or possess Him otherwise than as He reveals and imparts Himself; and He reveals Himself through His own Word and imparts Himself in His own Son. There and there alone is He to be known, and there He is all our own. The Logos who is the eternal Self-revelation of God manifests Himself as ideal principle, first and final cause, meaning and end, of creation; and the end of the whole creation which manifests God is realized through spiritual humanity in the imparted sonship of the Everlasting Son of the Father.

There is yet one other condition of truly knowing or really possessing God as wholly our God. As God is unknowable and incommunicable but through Christ, so is Christ, however perfectly He is in Himself the self-revelation and self-communication of God, not so to us but through the coequal action of the Holy Ghost. There is no knowledge of God in Himself only, there is no knowledge of God in creation only, or in others, or even in Christ only, without the answering knowledge of God in ourselves also. It is only like that answers to like. The deep that answers to deep must be the same deep. Jesus Christ expected in every son of man not only the answer of the man in him to Himself as eternal and universal Son of man, but the answer of the God in him to the perfect God head in Himself. Ye cannot see God in me, He says, because ye have not God in you. No man cometh unto me except the Father draw Him. I do not wish to urge the mere conventional language of Christianity, true as I believe it and helpful as I may find it to myself. I would if possible speak in the common language of common experience. When we speak of knowing God, and having God, it must mean knowing Him where He is to be known and having Him as He is to be had. Now, whatever God is in Himself, He is knowable to us only in Jesus Christ, and He can be our God only as He is conceived in us by the operation of the Spirit of God and born of the want which He implants and the faith which He generates.

The doctrine of the Trinity is ordinarily thought of as the very extreme of speculative reasoning upon the nature of God. But let us remember that practical faith in the Trinity antedated any speculative thought or doctrine of the Trinity. And behind that faith the fact itself of the Trinity is all that makes God knowable by us or us capable of knowing God. Before there was the word Trinity, the new world of Christianity had come to know God in Christ, and to know Christ in itself. The entire doctrine developed out of that actual experience was nothing but a positive affirmation and a determined defence of the fulness of the truth of God in Christ and Christ in us. We can do no better than conclude this entire exposition of the Gospel with an interpretation of it in the only terms in which it is expressible, viz.: in terms of the Trinity.

We have to do now with the Trinity, not as matter of doctrine nor as object of faith, but as fact in itself. But at the same time we neither forget nor minimize the essential Christian conviction that the fact of the Trinity through the actual operation of God's Word and Spirit has been so made matter of spiritual observation and experience as to be legitimate object of faith and material for doctrine. Our object at present, however, is not to define God but to define the Gospel, and our contention is that the Gospel is definable in facts that taken together make up the truth of the Trinity.

The first condition and constituent of the Gospel is the fact that God in Himself is love. How do we know that God is love? I believe that actually or historically we know it in Christ in whom the fact of the divine love is consummated and manifested. But in the light now of Christianity I believe that it is also philosophically demonstrable that goodness or love is the essential principle and the ultimate end of the universe. How God is love, not only in antecedent nature but in the actuality of self-fulfilment in the world, may be readable too in nature, after the light thrown upon it by Christianity, but in fact it is known in its reality only in Christ. Love is no more in God than in us an abstract disposition or affection. All the love we know is in concrete relations and the forms of affection determined by the character of those relations. Human love is marital, parental, filial, etc. out to the wider and widest forms of national, racial, and human affinity and affection. The concrete form in which alone we can know God as love is expressed by our designation of Him as eternal Father. That gives shape and definiteness to not only our conception, but the reality itself of His relation to us and ours to Him, and no less of how that relation is to be fulfilled. The full reality of fatherhood comes about in actuality only in the full realization of sonship, and that therefore must be God s meaning and end for all that is in the universe of His self-expression. We begin so to anticipate the truth that is to be expressed in such statements as that God has foreordained or predestined us to sonship through Jesus Christ unto Himself, that God has foreordained us to be conformed to the image of His Son, and many others to the same effect. But before we come to these unfoldings of the divine nature and purpose, let us reflect upon the following antecedent truth.

The beginning of all distinction between a pantheistic and a theistic conception of the world lies in recognizing the world as the expression, not of God Himself or, as we say, "of His substance," but of His Logos, His Thought, Will, Word. The Logos of God, then, is not God (*a theos*); we distinguish Him. And yet certainly the Logos is God (*theos*); we identify Him. Moreover, when once we have conceived and accepted God as eternal Father, we are in position to assume that the Logos, not merely as the principle of the divine self-expression but as God Himself self-expressed, must manifest Himself universally as Son or in sonship; since universal and everlasting Sonship is the only self- expression of eternal and essential Fatherhood.

The first constituent, therefore, of the Gospel is the fact in itself of the divine Love in Fatherhood. The second is, the equal fact in itself of the actualization of the divine Fatherhood in creature–or, definitely, in human–Sonship. The love of the Father fulfills and manifests itself in the grace of the Son. Love is grace *potentid*; Grace is love *actu*,–just as Fatherhood itself is Sonship potential, and Sonship is Fatherhood actualized. When we have once seen all humanity perfected as son in Jesus Christ, it is not hard to see in Him the whole creation so perfected in man as its head and as heir of its destiny. And then still less hard is it to see how we could never have known God as Father if He had not so fulfilled and manifested Himself as Son.

The hesitation and reluctance to see all God, and highest God, not only in the humanity but in the deepest human humiliation of Jesus Christ, is part of the disposition to measure exaltation by outward circumstance and condition instead of by inward quality and character. We find it impossible to recognize or acknowledge God in the highest act of His highest attribute. We cannot listen to the thought that it is with God as it is with us, that it only is with us because it is with God, that self-humiliation is self-exaltation. Not only in this way do we refuse to know God Himself as love, but we refuse to understand the universe as love. If we would but surrender our reason as well as our heart and will to God in Christ, we should cease to prate as we do of the mystery and the incomprehensibility of things. We could see how our Lord could say of the cross itself, Father, the hour is come. Glorify thy Son, that the Son may glorify thee. We lose thus the supreme lesson of human experience: Not merely to conjecture that somehow good is the final goal of ill; but to know by actual trial just how the supremest ills are the necessary steps to the highest goods. As St. Paul says, the cross of Christ is foolishness and a stumbling block only to the earthly wise and the self-righteous. To them that are saved, or are ever so little being saved, it is the wisdom of God and the power of God. To know God in Jesus Christ is to know the divine Logos, through whom alone God is knowable. It is to know him, not in His inferior activities of physical creation, nor yet in His higher capacity of lawgiver and law in a world of intelligent reason and free will. Rather is it to know Him in the act and process of that self-communication of love, grace, and fellowship, which is the basis and condition of the only real knowledge.

The third constituent of the Gospel is the fact in itself of the fellowship of the Spirit. Truly, our fellowship is with the Father and with His Son Jesus Christ. The possibility or potentiality of such a real unity and community with God must exist somehow beforehand in our nature as spirit, or in the natural relation of our finite spirits to the Father of spirits. But the actuality of spiritual relation or intercommunication which we call fellowship is no fact of nature but an act or interaction of spirits. It is not for us to say how, theoretically, spirit can act upon spirit; all that we can do is to understand how, practically and actually, spirit does act upon spirit. The most perfect expression of the actual action of the divine upon the human spirit is contained in the words, The Spirit beareth witness with our spirit, that we are the sons of God. Let us assume the objectivity or truth in itself of the eternal Fatherhood that is to say, not only Father-relation but Father-spirit, love, will, purpose or predestination, etc. of God in Himself. Let us also assume the objective reality as matter of fact of all that we have claimed to have happened in Jesus Christ: viz., that in Him as Logos God revealed Himself in the universe, and that in Him as Son God fulfilled Himself in humanity. In other words, let us assume that all that God is in Himself as Father has evolved itself through nature and man in the universal and everlasting Son-ship realized in Jesus Christ; God in Christ as Son is *actu* all that He is *potentia* in Himself as Father. When we have assumed all that body of objective truth the truth in itself of the Father and the Son what remains still to make it the Gospel to ourselves? Undoubtedly something remains. All the reality in the universe can be no Gospel to us so long as it remains objective, or until it enters into living relation with ourselves. Of course, it can never so enter unless there is in us the natural potentiality of entering into relation with it. But equally certainly that potentiality can only be actualized by ourselves. What is necessary within ourselves to give effect to all that is true without us is a corresponding response, or a response of correspondence, on our part. That correspondence is, I repeat, not a fact of natural relationship, but an act of spiritual communication or self-impartation. When the Spirit bears witness with our spirit, that we are sons of God, it is not only God who communicates the gracious fact, but it is God who awakens the humble and grateful response, and puts it into our heart to say, Abba, Father. If we cannot thus know God subjectively in ourselves, we cannot know God objectively in Jesus Christ. And if we cannot know Him in His Word and by His Spirit, we cannot know Him at all.

As we can know the eternal and universal Sonship incarnate in Jesus Christ only in the perfection of the human sonship realized in Him in other words, as we can know the Word or Son of God only in the man Christ Jesus, so we can know the Spirit of God only in ourselves or in our own spirit. We cannot know any spirit other than our own otherwise than through a certain oneness or identity of it with our own. There must be both an inter-penetration of the two as distinct and the identification of them as one. Hence the common demand upon men to be of one spirit. What a subject of reflection then, and of realization or actualization, is there for us in the fact of our fellowship, our participation, with the Father and the Son in the unity and identity of a common Spirit. It is in this eternal Spirit that God Himself is God and is Love. It was in this eternal Spirit that the whole creation in humanity offered itself without spot to God in the person of Jesus Christ; and in that consummate act fulfilled His relation to it through realizing its own relation with Him. It is through this eternal Spirit, which is God's and Christ's and ours, that we pass from ourselves into Christ and through Christ into God.

We have seen that there could have been no Gospel of God to us except one of objective Word and subjective Spirit. All life is defined as internal correspondence with external environment. We saw, I think, long ago that as it is the function of the divine Word aptare *Deum homini*, so is it that of the divine Spirit *aptare hominem Deo*. On the same line we may say, that as eternal life is given to us in Jesus Christ to be received, so is it given to us by the Holy Ghost to receive the life. Our Lord said of the promised Spirit, that its function should be to bring us to Him. There would be nothing to which to come if there were no objective fact and gift of life, there would be no coming to the life if there were no subjective preparing for and drawing to the life. How then finally does the Spirit fit us for Christ and fit us to Christ? It is the act and operation of the Spirit, first, that from the beginning, though yet a very far off, we can already know Christ as our own. That is the power of faith, which lives by God's Word and takes what that says as though it were. To faith Jesus Christ is the divine, not only revelation but reality of itself from the beginning of the foreknowledge of God in the eternity of the past to the end of the predestination of God in the eternity of the future. To faith Jesus Christ is all the eternal love, the all-sufficient grace, the perfect fellowship or oneness-with-it of God, which is salvation ex parte *Dei* or *salvailo salvans*; and no less in Jesus Christ the perfection of our own faith, hope, and love, our own holiness, righteousness, and life, our own death to sin, and our own life to God, which is salvation *ex parte hominis* or salvatio *salvata.* The Spirit thus brings us first to a perfect correspondence of faith with the fact of our life of God in Christ. But just because faith means life, that is, knows, desires, wills, and intends it therefore it is it. God already imputes, as He will impart, and faith already appropriates, as it will possess, the life which is so believed in. So believing in it we have it already in faith, and as surely shall have it at last in fact. Attuned to Christ by the anticipatory spell of faith, hope, and love, we shall be by a natural process of spiritual assimilation transformed into His likeness in act, character, and life, until coming to see Him perfectly as He is we shall be wholly what He is.

It has not been my object to add to the solution of the speculative problem of the Trinity. I have only aimed to show practically and spiritually that if at all we are to know and worship God in reality as our God, we must do so as Christianity has always done in Trinity. We must worship God in the Father, and the Son, and the Holy Ghost. Because God is, and is operative for us, not alone in one but in all these. We cannot but distinguish the Three; it is only in the completeness of their threefold operation that we can perfectly know the One.

Week Twenty, Reading Assignment for Year One

This section on Micah is extracted from John J. Collins's longer text, *Introduction to the Hebrew Bible*, because Micah is not addressed in the *Shorter Introduction to the Hebrew Bible*, our current text for Year One.

Micah[69]

Roughly contemporary with Isaiah was Micah of Moresheth, a small town about twenty-three miles southwest of Jerusalem. According to the superscription of the book, he prophesied in the days of Jotham, Ahaz, and Hezekiah, and his oracles concerned both Samaria and Jerusalem. In contrast to Isaiah, Micah was a rural prophet and not so closely engaged with the Davidic dynasty. As in the case of all the prophetic books, however, we must reckon with a process of edition and supplementation that may have gone on for centuries. A clear example of this is found in Mic 4:10, where Zion is told to writhe like a woman in labor, "for now you shall go forth from the city and camp in the open country; you shall go to Babylon. There you shall be rescued, there the Lord will redeem you from the hands of your enemies." The initial prophecy that the city would be undone, and that its inhabitants would have to camp in the open country, may well have been uttered by Micah. It is quite compatible with the critique of the ruling powers by the rural prophet. The extension of the prophecy to include the Babylonian exile and the subsequent restoration must have been added by a postexilic scribe, who felt impelled to update the oracle in the light of subsequent history.

The actual extent of the supplementation of the oracles of Micah is a matter of controversy. One scholarly tradition, developed in Germany in the late nineteenth century and still widely influential, attributes only material in chapters 1–3 to the eighth-century prophet, and that with minor exceptions, most notably the prophecy of restoration in 2:12–13. These chapters consist primarily of judgment oracles. The more hopeful oracles in chapters 4–5 are usually dated to the early postexilic period. Chapters 6–7 are also regarded as later additions. At least the conclusion in 7:8–20 was added to adapt the collection to liturgical use. This kind of analysis may go too far in denying the prophet any hope for the future. At least a few passages in chapters 4–7 are likely to come from the eighth century. In contrast to this approach, some recent commentaries have tried to defend the essential unity

69. John J. Collins, *Introduction to the Hebrew Bible* (Minneapolis: Augsburg Fortress, 2004), 321–324.

of the book (Hillers, Andersen and Freedman). There can be little doubt, however, that the oracles underwent a process of transmission and that the book, like those of the other pre-exilic prophets, was given its present form after the Babylonian exile.

The Social Critique

The opening oracle invokes an old tradition of the theophany of the divine warrior. In Judges 5 the imagery of storm and earthquake were used to express the terror caused by YHWH going to help his people in battle. In Micah they describe the terror of YHWH coming to judge his people. The wrath is directed against both Samaria and Jerusalem. The focus on the capital cities is significant. The offenses are primarily charged to the ruling class. Jerusalem is derisively called a "high place." Micah makes no distinction between the guilt of the two kingdoms. In 1:6 he prophesies that Samaria will be made a heap. In 3:12 he predicts that "Zion shall be plowed as a field; Jerusalem shall become a heap of ruins." The latter prophecy is cited in Jer 26:18, where its nonfulfillment is explained by the fact that Hezekiah repented. Micah says that he will go naked and barefoot as Isaiah did, but where Isaiah symbolized the captivity of Egyptians and Ethiopians, Micah's action is a gesture of mourning for the destruction of Judah. The statement that "it has reached the gate of my people" recalls the invasion of Sennacherib (cf. Isaiah 1), but it more likely refers to the Syro-Ephraimite war, in view of the date ascribed to Micah and his concern for Samaria as well as Jerusalem.

The initial charge against Samaria and Jerusalem is idolatry. Jerusalem is compared to a high place; Samaria is accused of prostitution (cf. Hosea). More typical of Micah, however, is the accusation of injustice. The statement that "they covet fields, and seize them; houses and take them away," refers to the same phenomenon noted in Isa 5:8, which is addressed to those who add house to house and field to field. The punishment will fit the crime. Their own houses and fields will be seized by the invaders. Micah's condemnation of the exploitation of the poor is more biting even than that of Amos. The rich "tear the skin off my people and the flesh off their bones; eat the flesh of my people . . . chop them up like meat in a kettle" (3:2–3). The punishment to come will be a response of YHWH to the cry of the poor. Like Amos, Micah disassociates himself from the professional prophets (nebî'îm, 3:5–12). These people, we are told, give oracles for money (3:11; rulers and priests are similarly venal). They cry "peace" when they have enough to eat, and mislead the people by saying "surely, the Lord is with us" (3:11). If Isaiah saw this Davidic slogan as ambiguous, Micah sees it as a misleading illusion. We have no narrative of the call of Micah as we have of Amos. It seems safe to assume that he did not consider himself to be a nābî'. Like Amos, his preaching encountered opposition and some people tried to suppress it (2:6). It has been noted that the formula "thus says the Lord" occurs only once in chapters 1–3, and that Micah sometimes speaks in his own name (3:1). Nonetheless, he also speaks in the name of the Lord (e.g., 1:6: "I will make Samaria a heap"), and he claims to be filled with power, with the spirit of the Lord, to denounce the sin of Israel (3:8).

The critique of the cult in chapter 6 is also in line with what we have seen in the other eighth-century prophets and is plausibly attributed to Micah. This passage is cast in the form of a rib, or legal disputation, and can be viewed as a covenant lawsuit. God reminds his people Israel that he brought them up from the land of Egypt and redeemed them from slavery. There is a clear implication that Israel should have responded by serving the Lord with justice and has failed to do so, but the offenses and consequent punishment are not spelled out. While the exodus played no part in the preaching of Isaiah of Jerusalem, it figured prominently in the oracles of Amos and Hosea, even though Amos, like Micah, came from the southern kingdom. Micah too addressed Israel as well as Judah. Many scholars assume that the appeal to the exodus here is the work of a Deuteronomistic editor, but this is not necessarily so.

Micah 6:6–8 considers the misguided reasoning of an Israelite, or Judean, worshiper. The assumption is that God will be impressed by the cost of the sacrifice. Even human sacrifice is contemplated. As we have seen in connection with Genesis 22, human sacrifice was practiced in ancient Israel and Judah. King Manasseh of Judah, son of Hezekiah, was said to have made his son "pass through fire," which is to say that he sacrificed him as a burnt offering (2 Kgs 21:6). Human sacrifice, however, is much less likely to have been an option in the postexilic period. Micah's critique of sacrifice is essentially the same as that of the other prophets we have considered. It indicates a misunderstanding of what YHWH wants, which is "to do justice, and to love kindness, and to walk humbly with your God" (6:8). Most of the positive oracles in chapters 4–5 are likely to have been added by postexilic editors, when the time of judgment had passed and the need was for consolation and hope. Micah 4:1–5 repeats an oracle found in Isaiah 2:1–5, with a variation in the concluding verse. The imagery of tôrāh going forth from Jerusalem and the peoples streaming thereto fits better with the aspirations of Second Temple Judaism than with what we know of the eighth century. The oracle probably circulated anonymously. That it is associated with two eighth-century prophets is striking, but probably coincidental. A more difficult case is presented by Micah 5:2–5, which predicts the advent of a ruler from Bethlehem of Judah, the ancestral home of David. Many scholars take this as a postexilic prediction of a restoration of the Davidic line, and the obscure statement in v. 3, "the rest of his kindred shall return," can be read as supporting this interpretation. But the focus on Bethlehem, as opposed to Zion, may be significant. Micah of Moresheth may have felt that the Davidic monarchy could be redeemed if it returned to the humble roots symbolized by the ancestral village. The prediction of a ruler from Bethlehem would then be a rejection of the ruling king and the Jerusalem court, but not of the Davidic line. The oracle would still have been read in a messianic sense in the postexilic period. In the later context Assyria would be understood as the archetypical enemy. The fantasy of a final defeat of invading nations appears frequently in the later prophetic and apocalyptic books (e.g., the prophecy of Gog in Ezekiel 38–39).

Resources for Spiritual Autobiography and Listening

Spiritual Autobiographies—Some Guidelines

A spiritual autobiography is your life story–the telling of your journey told with the purpose of discerning and proclaiming how your experience has shaped your relationship with God. Each year in the program you are asked to recall your life story. Later, you are given an opportunity to share what you think is appropriate with your seminar group. A different structure is provided for your use for each of the four years of the program. These structured methods allow you to look at the whole sweep of your life. Constructing your autobiography provides a firm foundation for the continuing work of integrating the content of your year's study with the events of your life. Your experience is a primary resource for your theological education; the yearly review of your life story enables you to hear how the timbre and direction of that story has changed in the last twelve months. Your call, discernment, vocation, and ministry are imbedded in your spiritual journey. This process of telling and retelling your story helps those themes come more clearly into your consciousness.

A spiritual autobiography may contain both religious material–significant people or times within the religious community–and everyday material like people and times in your life that have influenced who you are now and how you understand God's presence or absence in your life.

The work you do on your spiritual autobiography is private, "for your eyes only." This allows you to be free, without concern about how others will interpret either the context or expression.

Preparing a spiritual autobiography each year provides a way to deepen your understanding of both the Christian life and ministry. By virtue of your baptism you were called to ministry, guided and pushed by personal gifts, passions, skills, experiences, and interests.

Once you prepare your spiritual autobiography, you need to decide what you want to share with your seminar group. Martin Buber, a twentieth-century philosopher and Jewish theologian, is reputed to have said that he could never hold a significant conversation with another person until he had heard the other's life story. The purpose of sharing autobiographies is to build trust and understanding within the group and to begin to make connections within your own story. We need the experience of hearing other life stories to know that we are not alone in God's world. By sharing appropriate stories of our lives we form learning communities that can challenge and support us throughout our lives.

Your mentor will relate her or his own story and help the group structure the time for sharing of autobiographies. Most groups give each member **around ten minutes** to tell his or her story, followed by time for the rest of the group to respond. Spiritual autobiographies are the focus of most of the seminar time for the first few meetings of the year. This is a special time for your group. This component of your group's life will carry you to the next phase of your year together. This may be the first time to tell your story in this way. It may seem a bit daunting at first. Remember that you should offer what you feel comfortable sharing in the group. This is not an opportunity for "group therapy" or psychologizing, so the group should not engage in raising questions about motives or probe for information beyond what you share. Feel free to say "no" or to say that you do not wish to explore questions that others may raise out of curiosity or concern.

Sharing your "spiritual autobiography" is a way to say, "Here I am," and to join your EfM group as a full participant. Over the years in EfM you will probably find that your spiritual autobiography changes. You may find yourself free to talk about things which were previously guarded. You also may find that your freedom to "be yourself" will grow as your personal story, the life of the group, and the story of God's people relate to each other.

Holy Listening

VocationCARE is a program in ministry discernment and design, a sister program to EfM in the Beecken Center of the School of Theology/Sewanee. The acronym CARE stands for

- CREATE *space to explore Christian vocation together;*
- ASK *self-awakening questions together;*
- REFLECT *theologically on self and community; and*
- ENACT *the next faithful step.*

VocationCARE Model for Story Telling/Holy Listening[70]

Tips for Telling Your Story

EXAMPLE:

Tell a story about why you do what you do, love what you love, care about what you care about.

BE SPECIFIC

Talk about what actually happened. It helps to begin stories with "One time . . ." or "I remember a time when . . ."

BE DESCRIPTIVE

Use images, feelings and places to provide texture, color, and thick description to your story. Use the 5Ws: who, what, when, where and why.

BE SELF-REFLECTIVE

What was the occasion of your discovering that *this* was what you loved, cared about, or loved doing? Was there anyone with whom you shared this discovery? How did it feel to know this about yourself?

Tips for Listening to Another's Story

UNDIVIDED ATTENTION

Make eye contact with the storyteller and give him or her your full attention as if there was nothing else more important than listening to his/her story.

70. Adapted from the Fund for Theological Education's *FTE Guide to VocationCARE* © 2012, pp. 18–19. Used with permission

HOLY LISTENING

Listen reverently as if you were in the presence of the Holy and witness the truth of this sacred story. Hold the space with your presence and receive the precious gift in this story. Imagine you are listening with God's ears.

JOURNALING

As you journal: What images, key words, or phrases stand out as meaningful to you? Is there a question you might ask your partner that would move the conversation deeper into "the heart of the matter"? What did you enjoy or find yourself wondering about?

Resources for Reflecting Theologically

A theological reflection in EfM begins in one of the four sources: personal experience/**Action**, the **Tradition** of the faith, personal beliefs/**Position**, or **Culture**/society.

The movement of theological reflection is: **Identify** a focus, **Explore** the focus, **Connect** the focus to other areas/sources, and **Apply** learning.

A reflection takes on theological strength by viewing the image/picture, issue, or matter through some theological lenses, asking questions concerning the nature of the world, the relationship of God to the world, the nature of repentance and forgiveness, the nature of human community, or the quality of redemption and restoration of relationship. These are also known as **theological perspectives**, sometimes identified by the traditional systematic terms Creation, Sin, Judgment, Repentance, and Redemption/Resurrection. Theological perspectives may also be framed in everyday language that carries the themes of the traditional terms, such as wholeness, brokenness, recognition of brokenness, reorientation, and restoration.

Theological reflection remains only an interesting exercise if learning is not embodied in ministry. What can be carried forward from the reflection?

Bibliography for Theological Reflection

Killen, Patricia O'Connell and John DeBeer. *The Art of Theological Reflection.* New York: Crossroad, 1994.

Paver, John E. *Theological Reflection and Education for Ministry: The Search for Integration in Theology.* Ebook. Aldershot, England and Burlington, VT: Ashgate Publishing, 2006.

Thompson, Judith, Stephen Pattison, and Ross Thomason. *SCM Studyguide to Theological Reflection.* London, UK: SCM Press, 2008.

Theological Reflection Process Chart[71]

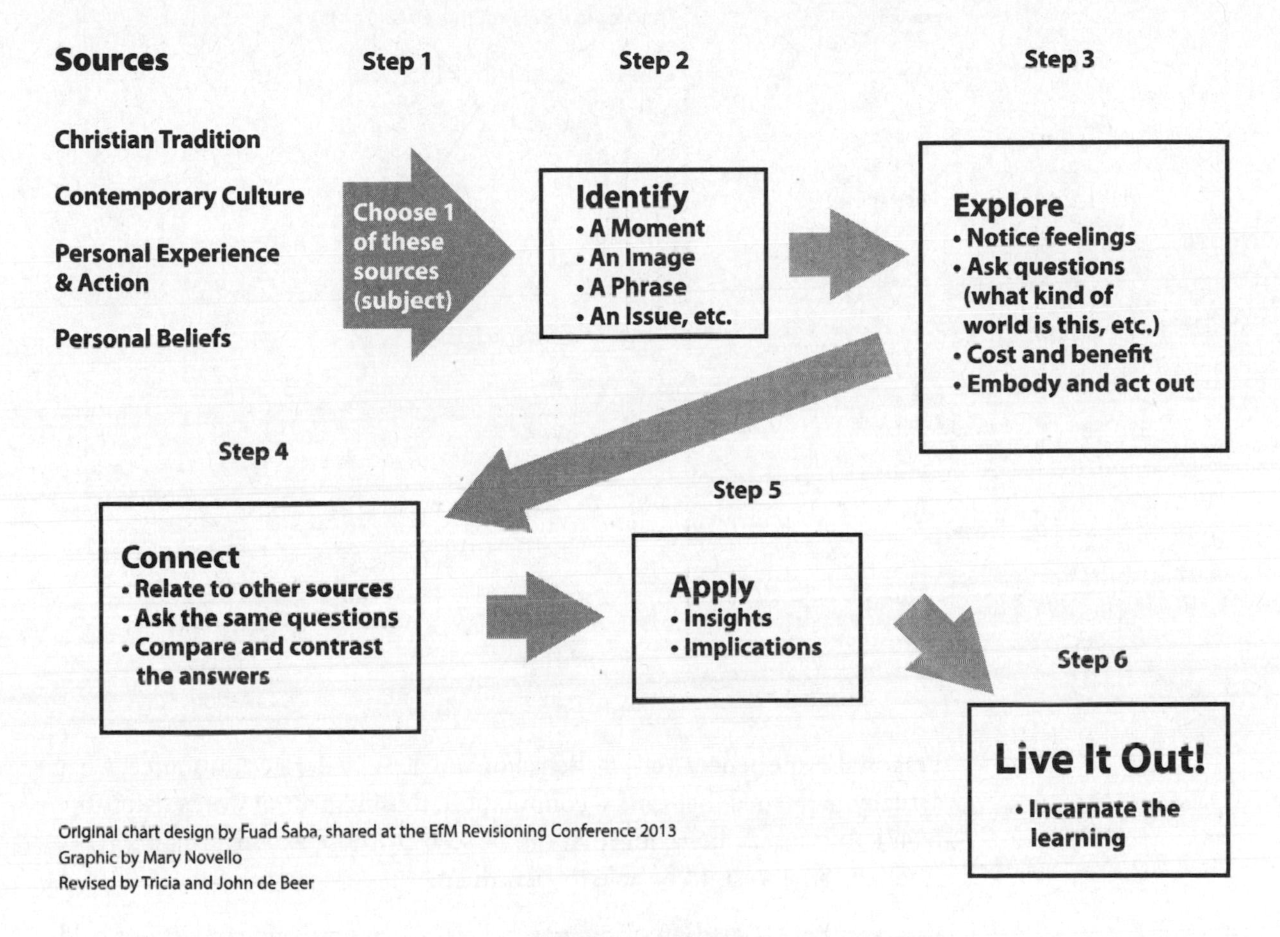

Original chart design by Fuad Saba, shared at the EfM Revisioning Conference 2013
Graphic by Mary Novello
Revised by Tricia and John de Beer

TR Process Chart

71. Like many of the resources in the EfM program, this one is the product of a collaborative effort. The original process design was developed by EfM mentor Fuad Saba and shared at the Re-visioning EfM conference in Sewanee in July 2013. The graphic presentation was designed by Mary Novello, EfM Coordinator for the Diocese of Western Michigan. Tricia and John deBeer, EfM trainers, further refined the language.

Framework for Theological Reflections[72]

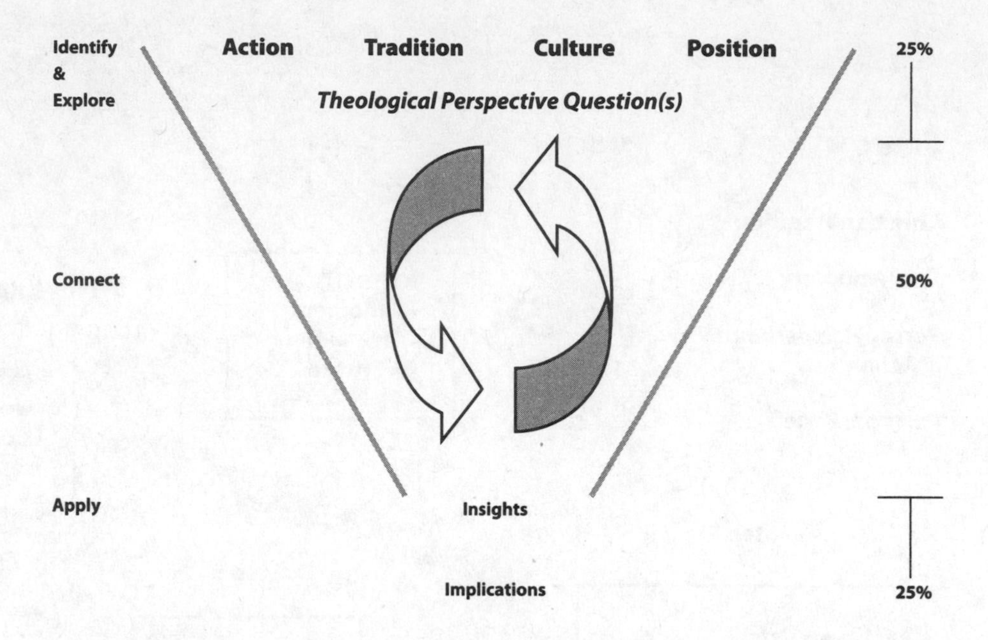

	Internal	External
Group	Tradition	Culture
Personal	Position	Action

Personal Experience/Action–Behavior and activity define this source; what actually happened that can be communicated using neutral words (RRG-B, p. 47). Actions are behaviors that can be seen by those external to ourselves. A video camera has to be able to view them.

Personal Belief/Position–Opinions, beliefs, viewpoints, and convictions held by a person constitute the position pole of the four-source model (RRG-B, p. 47). The important opinions are those that directly influence our behavior.

Faith Tradition–Whenever the language, concepts, terms, or images in a conversation come from the Bible or some other document or story that is part of the Christian lore, then one is drawing from the Christian Tradition source (RRG-B, p. 46).

Culture/Society–This source of the four-source model refers to a very large body of material. Literature, music, paintings, and other artifacts are part of the Culture Source (RRG-B, p. 46). Other parts are movies, television shows, and books. Focus on the aspects that influence your Positions and Actions.

72. Created by Joshua D. Booher.

Unpacking the Framework for Theological Reflections[73]

When two words are placed together, for example "theological reflection," the second word is the primary or focal word. In this case, we are engaging in a reflection. A reflection indicates there are two things. The first is the item (our lives) to be reflected and the second is the item the first item reflects off of. For it to be a "theological" reflection, one of the two items has to originate from our Tradition source.

There are four sources from which you can begin a theological reflection (TR). To help my own understanding, I have them in a two-by-two grid (see chart). The rows are us as individuals (Personal) and us in a group (Group). The columns are things that only we can know (Internal) and things that can be seen from the outside (External). In this grid, things about us that can be seen from the outside are our behaviors or Actions. The things about ourselves that only we can know are our Positions. Things about a group that a person outside a group can see is the Culture of the group. Things about a group that are primarily known only to people inside a group are the Tradition of the group. Though not perfect, this grid helps to show that the influences on our behaviors come from us or a group we are in and/or from inside or outside ourselves. This helps to explain why these four sources help us work our way through a TR. They cover all the influences in our lives.

Though you can start a TR from any of the four sources, for it to be a theological reflection one of the first two sources has to be Tradition. For this example our point of origin will be a personal action.

After identifying the story from your life that you want to reflect on (Action), you need to ask a theological perspective question to explore the story. This question helps to align the mirrors to get a more accurate and meaningful reflection. These questions can take on many forms, from creation/sin/judgment/repentance/redemption to love, grace, salvation, transubstantiation, and transfiguration. Often a good theological perspective question that can be used will arise during the text reflection portion of the seminar.

To be a "theological" reflection, after exploring the Action source from the theological perspective question, the group needs to explore the Tradition source. This allows the Tradition source to "reflect" and inform the Action source. Once a piece from the Tradition source has been identified, ask the EXACT SAME theological perspective question of it.

---

73. This framework was designed as a training tool to help mentors understand the overall map of the TR process and as a supplement to the four-source model so that when a TR is not proceeding well or there is confusion the mentor has a mental framework to help participants get back into the process and to assess what else needs covered to complete the TR process. EfM participants may also find the tool helpful as they work with individual reflections in the Reading and Reflection Guide and group reflection in their seminar.

Asking the EXACT same theological perspective question is the best way to ensure that you align your two mirrors correctly. For instance, asking, "What is your age?" and, "What year were you born?" get to related information, but do not line up exactly. To get from one to the other you have to execute mental arithmetic. The same would be the case if you ask of the Action source, "What was the world like in this story?" and of the Tradition source, "What was Creation like in this story?" As the mentor you might mean the same thing by these two questions, but the participants are likely answering different questions.

Once the group has explored the Tradition source with the exact same theological perspective question, you are ready to move on.

To have a reflection, you only need two things: the item to be reflected and the item doing the reflecting. So, at this point, we have set that stage. Our life story (Action) is being viewed against the mirror of our Tradition. The mirror was aligned by asking the exact same theological perspective question of both sources. At this point, the actual reflection begins. Everything before this point has been setting up the reflection by exploring the Action source and the Tradition source.

Now, the group will sift through the material that has arisen in the two explorations and see where there are points of similarity (Compare) and differences (Contract). Begin discussing the similarities and differences.

After the Compare/Contrast discussion, you can move directly to the Insights/Implications. You have done everything required of a theological reflection. You have examined the point of origin (Action), the point of reflection (Tradition), and how they reflect upon each other. However, to have a richer reflection, bring in the other two sources. You do this by seeing how the sources resonate with the discussion through the lens of the theological perspective question. Don't go sequentially through the sources, though. Allow the sources to speak to each other as resonates arise.

Then, as time and/or energy start to wane, ask the group what insights and implications have arisen for them in this discussion.

Other Comments on Framework Application

This framework matches the RRG's four step model of Identify/Explore/Connect/Apply. In the Identify step, you are choosing the point of origin. You Explore the point of origin by way of the theological perspective question. You then Connect to the Tradition source. You also Connect to the other sources as time and energy allow. Finally, you Apply your learnings by way of Insights and Implications.

In addition, TRs have limited time in which to be completed and you want to make sure to give each section enough time. Through my experience, this is done by allowing 25 percent of your time to get through the Tradition theological perspective question discussion. At the 25 percent mark, you should be starting the compare/contrast of the two Explorations. (This covers Identify/Explore and the beginning of Connect.) At the 75 percent mark, you should stop wherever you are and go to Insights/Implications. (This is Apply.) Going to Insights/Implications at the 75 percent mark allows time to go into some detail in identifying learnings and applications from the discussion. This leaves the middle 50 percent (25 percent to 75 percent) for having a good, rich, flowing discussion. In my experience, this middle 50 percent is the heart of the TR. It is where the strongest energy is and where the learnings and insights occur. So, you tighten up the beginning 25 percent to allow more time for the heart of the TR. This is done by being more directive and not overanalyzing the first few steps. Then, when you reach the Compare/Contrast point, you step back and let the conversation flow more freely.

Questions tend to stop the flow of a conversation as participants have to reorient to what is being asked, think about the question, and restart the conversation. One way to avoid this problem is to make statements. Statements allow the participants to either follow the statement or stay where they were. If they are ready, they will move on by following the statement's content. If they are not ready, they will stay with the content they were previously discussing. For instance, if the group is discussing comparisons and contrasts and you think it is time to add content from the Culture source, you could make a comment relating the Culture source to the discussion. If other participants are ready they will follow your lead. Otherwise, they will continue discussing comparisons and contrasts.

All of the sources are very broad. It is good to find a way to narrow them to a more manageable size. The key is to focus on what aspects of the source influence your behavior. For example, in the Culture source, there are a lot of areas that don't influence my behavior. However, what I learned from my parents, my favorite books, and school does influence my behavior. So, when discussing the Culture, those are the areas I will focus on. Phrased another way, the way I look at sources is through the lens of "What from *Source* influences the way I think about *Theological Perspective Question*?"

Examples of Theological Reflection

Theological Reflections from Volume C

Because the focus of Volume C is on becoming spiritually mature, most of the theological reflection exercises begin from the Action/Personal Experience source. Examples of reflections beginning in other sources follow.

Theological Reflection Beginning with a Personal Experience (1)

Identify a focus.

In writing, describe the conflict you recalled in the Respond section. This places you in the Action/Experience source of your life; you recall something you've experienced or done.

Narrow the narrative by looking for a point in the conflict that had high energy.

Name your thoughts and feelings at that point of energy.

Draw a picture of a metaphor that illustrates what it was like when you had those thoughts and feelings. Think about color, sensation, heat/cold, location in your body of energy or tension. When you have/had those thoughts and feelings, it's as if. . . .

Explore the focus with theological perspectives.

Continue the reflection using your picture and considering these questions.

In the picture you created, what kind of interaction do you see?

How is that interaction revealing goodness or brokenness?

What kind of relationship does God have with those in that world?

What kind of relationships exist in that picture?

What crises are suggested in that picture?

What would persons in that kind of picture-world hope for?

Connect to other sources.

What personal beliefs (Position source) come to mind as you reflect on the picture and the world it captured?

Who or what in the Christian story (Tradition) or the world around you (Culture) helps you make sense of the world in the picture? In those sources, who are the wisdom figures or groups to help or guide you in a moment like you pictured?

Apply learning.

What prayer would you offer to God as a result of your reflection?

Name two areas in which you have the opportunity to minister in your life.

How will this reflection make any difference as you live in those areas?

How has your EfM study given you a way to view the circumstances of your life?

Theological Reflection Beginning with a Personal Experience (2)

Read through the entire reflection outline first. Let your mind and heart receive images and memories naturally. Keep clear for yourself what the overall movement of reflection is: Getting a focus, Exploring the focus theologically, Connecting other "voices" that confirm or challenge the focus, and Applying the results to ministry in daily life. A written outline might suggest a lock-step approach, which cannot be further from the intention. Reflection is conversation, either between the individual and God or a group and God. Allow that conversation to unfold in its own way, using the outlines as guides to deepen prayerful consideration.

Identify a focus by starting from Personal Experience, describing a moment in your life when you sensed that you were maturing spiritually, even if it was just a hint of that sense.

Pick the particular moment when something occurred that gave you a sense of maturing spiritually.

Name two or three strong feelings you had at that moment and two or three thoughts at that time of awareness.

If you recall first a feeling, identify a thought that was present with that feeling. Likewise, if you recall a thought first, identify a feeling that connects with the thought. This is sometimes an easy way to get at the distinction between thoughts and feelings for a reflection.

Now form the metaphor. Take those two or three thoughts and feelings and make them into a picture or image. Ask yourself, "What is it like when I feel/think that way?"

Work to get an image that is not simply another experience. Something like, "It was like falling in love," could be an actual experience you had. If so, just think about that time, too, but still work for a metaphorical expression. A metaphorical example of thoughts and feelings that contain joy might be something like, "It was like joining a celestial dance," that is, a symbolic representation of thoughts and feelings.

Explore the focus (image or metaphor) first by telling the story of that image. Write the story.

Apply theological perspectives to the image/story. What kind of world does your image-story describe?

What is creative or good about that world?

What would damage or disrupt that world?

How are God and that world related?

Connect the focus to other sources by asking how your image relates to Culture, Christian Tradition, or Position (personal belief). For instance, is there an example of your image happening in your local community or geographic region? Is there an example of that image being threatened in your culture in some way?

Is there an example of your image in the stories or prayers of the Church?

Make notes about the connections that occur to you.

What do the connections imply for spiritual maturity?

Apply insight and learning to ministry. Would you want to bring your image more fully into the life you lead? If so, what support would you want?

What would prevent you from extending the image into ministry in the world?

What commitment are you willing, even hesitantly, to make about ministry in light of this reflection?

Theological Reflection Beginning with a Personal Experience (3)

Identify a reflection focus.
Recall a time in your life when you believe you experienced the Presence of God.

Make some notes about the experience.

Locate the central moment of the experience, when your awareness of God's Presence was most vivid.

Name two to three attendant thoughts and feelings in that moment.

"It was like_________." Draw a picture that represents that moment's thoughts and feelings or make a brief statement of six to nine words.

Explore the focus image or statement.
Bring theological perspectives to the reflection.

Study the image or statement in silence. Let the "voice" of the image or statement become present.

What questions about the image/statement surface for you? List those and your responses.

Identify the type of theological questions those are. That is, are the questions about the nature of the world, the nature of God, the relationship of God to the world, the nature of mercy, of grace, of hope, and so forth?

Connect to other sources of meaning in your life.

When life is like that image/statement for you, how do you make sense of the experience?

What wisdom do you draw on for understanding? Who or what have you studied in the Christian tradition or the world around you that can "speak" to you or teach you about a moment like that?

What do you deeply believe about the experience you had? What doubts and hopes are present for you? Where do those feelings originate?

Apply insight/learning.
Sit quietly with the image, exploration, and connections, perhaps lighting a candle as you reside with the reflection.

What prayer begins praying in you? Try to write that down.

How does the theological reflection support or challenge one commitment in your life?

Theological Reflection Beginning with a Personal Experience (4)

Identify a focus.

Write about your journey of spiritual maturity in the last five years.

Review your writing. If you described any aspect of your experience in image language, try to draw that image and use that as the focus for the Explore phase. If not, select one key point in your journey and create a picture that expresses that point. Just using a phrase that conveys a metaphorical or image idea works well, too.

Explore the focus.

Sit quietly with your image or statement and then identify which theological perspective(s) the metaphorical expression contains.

Describe how the image reveals something of compassion, justice, or human flourishing.

Add consideration of anything in the image that reveals damage or brokenness.

How does God fit into the image?

Connect

Consider what other sources may contribute meaning to the reflection.

Return to the writing you did at the beginning of this reflection. Mark any of the following that you may have mentioned:

Culture–Did you refer to any books or stories you have read, movies you have seen, social environment that supports or challenges you, social norms that help or hinder you?

Christian Tradition–Did you recall any stories of the Bible, or hymns, or prayers of the Church?

Personal Beliefs–Did you make any statements of conviction, hope or doubt in your writing?

How have those areas helped you recognize God's presence in your image?

Apply

Relate this learning to ministry in your daily life. What do you see in a new way? Is there any area of your life that the reflection draws you toward in ministry?

How does this reflection contribute to listening with the ear of your heart, your commitment to place, or your continual conversion?

Theological Reflection Beginning with a Personal Experience (5)

This variation of theological reflection has sometimes been referred to as the "microscope method" because it describes the refining process that helps focus intently on a beginning point for theological reflection. Typically, the method begins in someone's experience and systematically focuses the circumstance to one fleeting moment in which to open the self or group to the eternal. In this form of theological reflection, we move into the particular to discover the eternal.

Identify a focus from which to reflect:

Recall and recount a time when you were confronted with a barrier of some sort. Describe the circumstance in as much detail as possible.

Notice when there were significant shifts in energy in the event and identify the one moment of greatest energy for you. Let all else fall away and mentally stand just in that discrete instant.

List two or three primary feelings and two or three key thoughts you had *at that tiny moment.* Decline any internal mental invitation to explain, justify, or interpret. Just let yourself accept your key thoughts and feelings of the moment.

Let yourself feel the feelings and notice where in your body they are. What is that like? Do they create a sensation of heat or cold? What color do they have? Settle into those thoughts and feelings and create a picture of what it's like for you when you experience that combination. For instance, is it like a tea kettle whistling because pressure has built up, or like walking barefoot on rocks, or like hanging from a limb high off the ground?

Write or draw a picture of what it's like when those feelings and thoughts are present. From this point forward, the reflection is on the image or picture-world that represents your thoughts and feelings, not on the original incident.

Theologically explore the world represented in your picture.

Stay inside the picture-world for this exploration. How does that world reveal something about wholeness or goodness, or about brokenness?

What does someone in that picture-world have to recognize in order to know there is brokenness? What would that person have to change in order to move towards wholeness?

What would it take to restore wholeness?

Connect by letting your mind freely move through and around the image.

What does your image-world call to mind for you? Are there events in the world around you that relate to the image and help you make sense of those kinds of moments?

If you've been thinking of some scripture passages or a hymn or prayer, stop and look those up. This is a very important part of theological reflection. How do any of those connections help make sense of this kind of moment?

What do you believe about living in a world such as the image captured? What helped to form that belief? Do you sense any other possible beliefs?

Apply to daily life. Theological reflection provides support for living a life of maturity in faith and action.

In what ways might this reflection inform your behavior when you again have an experience that raises these thoughts and feelings? Make notes about how reflecting theologically on this moment helps you integrate belief and behavior and raises any kind of possibilities for you in ministry and maturity.

There may be opportunity during the group's seminar time to explore the theological reflections of various group members. There may be time to do a group reflection around a central theme of the group's choosing. If so, what do you notice about the difference(s) between reflecting alone and reflecting in a group?

Theological Reflection Beginning with the Christian Tradition

Identify the focus or a primary point of your EfM study this week.

Explore the primary point by identifying the theological perspectives of the world, sin, judgment, repentance, and/or redemption reflected in that focus. Apply any of these or similar theological questions to your consideration.

What view of the world is present in that focus?

What brokenness or sin does that focus address or reveal?

What questions or crises does that focus respond to or contribute to?

How does that concern or focus lead to repentance or reorientation?

How does that concern lead to restoration to a creative life?

What does the focus say about forgiveness?

What concern about God does the focus address?

Move to the other sources

Connect by stating how the focus is present in today's world *(Culture)*.

What book or movie has dealt with this focus?

Compare and contrast the connections to the world around you with the above exploration of the focus.

What issues or concerns do you become aware of?

What personal experiences (Action) have you had that relate to this focus?

State one or two personal beliefs (Position) you have about the focus that surfaced in this reflection.

How did those beliefs form?

When has it been difficult for you to act on those beliefs?

Apply

If you could do just one thing about the concerns that surfaced in this reflection, what would that be?

Theological Reflection Beginning with the Christian Tradition (Scripture)

Identify

The following passages involve the people of Samaria, a group that fostered strong feelings among the Jews. Carefully read the passages and identify two or three topics common to both.

> When the days drew near for him to be taken up, he set his face to go to Jerusalem. And he sent messengers ahead of him. On their way they entered a village of the Samaritans to make ready for him; but they did not receive him, because his face was set toward Jerusalem. When his disciples James and John saw it, they said, "Lord, do you want us to command fire to come down from heaven and consume them?" But he turned and rebuked them. Then they went on to another village.
>
> *Luke 9:51–56*

> But wanting to justify himself, he asked Jesus, "And who is my neighbor?" Jesus replied, "A man was going down from Jerusalem to Jericho, and fell into the hands of robbers, who stripped him, beat him, and went away, leaving him half dead. Now by chance a priest was going down that road; and when he saw him, he passed by on the other side. So likewise a Levite, when he came to the place and saw him, passed by on the other side. But a Samaritan while traveling came near him; and when he saw him, he was moved with pity. He went to him and bandaged his wounds, having poured oil and wine on them. Then he put him on his own animal, brought him to an inn, and took care of him. The next day he took out two denarii, gave them to the innkeeper, and said, 'Take care of him; and when I come back, I will repay you whatever more you spend.' Which of these three, do you think, was a neighbor to the man who fell into the hands of the robbers?" He said, "The one who showed him mercy." Jesus said to him, "Go and do likewise."
>
> *Luke 10:29–37*

Note: Though the above scripture passages are quoted from the NRSV translation, reading the passages in a variety of translations may increase the sense of meaning.

Focus the passages by considering where the key energy/heart of the passage is, what the passages seem to be about.

Develop an image in words or a drawing that brings the point of the passages into focus.

Explore the image or central idea of the passages, using questions from the theological themes of Creation, Sin, Judgment, Repentance, or Redemption, such as:

- What kind of community does the image-world/theme suggest (Creation)?
- What might get in the way of relationships in that image-world/theme (Sin)?
- What could make those in that world realize there's something wrong; what choices are there (Judgment)?
- What would represent a change of direction (Repentance)?
- What might a new, life-giving creation look like (Redemption)?

Connect

Note: Connecting happens best if some freedom is allowed. Listen to each of the "voices" or "sources" below and let your responses emerge in any order. You may not make a connection in one area; that is okay. That may occur at a later time, or not at all. Mainly, allow your inner life to speak, connecting you to these areas of potential meaning and revelation.

Personal Experience–When has something happened in your life that is like the world of the image/metaphor? For instance, if the image created for the passages is "extending a party invitation," when have you given or sent such an invitation?

Compare your experience with the preceding theological exploration. How do your experience and the image relate to one another?

Contemporary Culture/Society–Who or what has taught you something that is helpful when life is like the image? In our world, how is there opposition to that image? How is there support for it? Where is God extending party invitations in the world in which you live?

Christian Tradition–What other scripture passages or church history events remind you of the image or central point of the passages from Luke?

Beliefs/Positions: What key issues do the metaphor and personal experience and contemporary culture raise? State your Beliefs and Positions relative to those issues.

Apply meaning and purpose to the reflection by identifying learning and clarifying questions.

How do the beliefs and insights of the exploration support you in ministry?

Notice where you might want to make some changes in action or viewpoint about the matter covered in the reflection.

Write a prayer in response to the discoveries in this reflection.

Theological Reflection Beginning with a Dilemma

First, read through this method a time or two before working with it and then try applying it to a dilemma from your past.

Identify

Describe a time when you faced a dilemma in decision and action. For the purposes of this reflection, the incident should be one that is already completed, with no decisions pending.

> Ex.: When my son died suddenly I was given the option to view his body in the morgue before he was taken for cremation. I was so torn and so deeply in sorrow and pain and shock. I could barely absorb this loss. The thought of seeing him that way was horrifying. I wanted only to think of him as alive. I guess to deny the death. And yet, I wanted to see him one more time. I chose not to view.

Name the turning point in your incident once you have written about the experience.

What's the central moment of your incident? Where is the tension greatest? What was happening? What were you thinking and feeling at that moment?

Describe the central moment and your thoughts and feelings at that moment.

State the central dilemma at the moment of greatest tension. Often a simple statement of the dilemma works better than an image in this type of reflection. Dilemmas tend to get represented metaphorically as "walking a tightrope," or "between a rock and hard place," but these are metaphors for any dilemma and too generic to work well. The specific dilemma in an incident needs to be clarified and clearly stated in universal terms. Universalizing is a corrective for giving advice or overly focusing on one person.

To help get to the dilemma statement, list statements about what you wanted at the moment you felt the tension or what interests were at stake at that moment. You will likely have several "I wanted" statements.

> Ex.: I wanted my son alive. I wanted to see him. I wanted to protect myself from the pain. I wanted to remember him as he had been. I wanted this to be a dream.

Select the pair of statements that best represents the central dilemma. Record the dilemma statement as "I wanted _____ **and** I wanted _______."

Note: A dilemma is a tension between two things a person wants, not between an "I want" and "I don't want." It is a challenge to get to two "I want" statements that clearly reflect the dilemma. The dilemma is between two goods, but a choice has to be made.

Most important step: Record the *universal* dilemma. For instance, if my dilemma is between using recently received birthday money for myself and bailing out an indigent friend's child who is in jail for the first time, the universal nature could perhaps be stated as "the dilemma is between taking care of self and helping others." Universalizing is especially necessary when reflecting in a group in order to avoid advice-giving and problem-solving.

Note: If this were a group reflection, each person would identify a moment when they, too, experienced the same universal dilemma. In a group, this is another way in which a tendency to continue to focus on the presenter can be redirected.

Explore the universal dilemma by considering what it is like to live in that dilemma/tension.

Use Cost/Promise (Risk/Hope) or Theological Perspectives as a tool to explore the universal dilemma.

COST/PROMISE

Name the costs (risks) and promises (hopes) of each side of the dilemma. For instance, what is the cost of taking care of oneself and what is the promise of doing that? Likewise, what are the costs and promises of helping others?

OR

THEOLOGICAL PERSPECTIVES

Questions exploring theological concepts can be used either with an image or a dilemma statement. For instance, in the universal dilemma between taking care of self and helping others, it would be possible to consider what that dilemma reveals about justice, compassion, and human flourishing.

Use only one or two of the following question examples when exploring:

What are the power dimensions of the dilemma or image? Who has power? What has to be yielded?

What sacrifice(s) might be called for? What are the temptations of the cross, of powerlessness? To whom or what is power yielded?

How is power transmitted to the powerless party? What is required in order to enter the cycle that leads to empowerment? What builds endurance?

What tomb is left in the image or dilemma?

How does resurrection or hope occur in the image or dilemma?

Connect to other ways this universalized dilemma has been engaged in our Christian story or the culture around you or in your personal beliefs. *Remember, these connections can come in any order. This is not a rote exercise, but a reflection. The purpose of laying out the sources is only to help remind you of these areas if one or more do not come to mind on their own.*

CHRISTIAN TRADITION

Identify some stories from scripture or church history that relate to the dilemma. In the stories of the people of God, who has been in the same dilemma? Or perhaps some prayers or hymns come to mind that relate to this reflection. Look up what you recall and spend time with the story or account or prayer or hymn. How does the connection help or challenge you in this dilemma?

Compare and contrast what our Christian Tradition and the initial experience have to say about the universal dilemma. What choices would the Tradition support? Not support? Why?

CULTURE/SOCIETY

How is the universal dilemma you identified experienced in our culture? Have there been news stories about it? Have you read a book or seen a movie that dealt with that dilemma? Is there a political dimension to that dilemma?

POSITION

What do you believe about the issues raised by the dilemma? How were your beliefs in conflict in the dilemma? What do you hope for regarding the dilemma? What formed your beliefs about this matter?

Apply

INSIGHTS AND QUESTIONS

What do you see in a new way now? What have you learned about facing this dilemma? What questions remain for you in this kind of dilemma?

IMPLICATIONS

Identify how the reflection has helped you to listen with the ear of your heart, bolstered commitment to place, and/or contributed to continual conversion for you.

What do you want or need to do? Do you feel a call or a tug to do something specific? Consider social implications, actions you could take, what else you could or need to learn, support that would help in the midst of such a dilemma, and where you could find that support.

Theological Reflection Beginning with a Social Concern

Philosophical anthropology studies the nature of humankind. Questions of identity, both individual and communal, comprise the field of study. Theological anthropology addresses human nature in relation to God. Both philosophical and theological anthropology address related questions: What is the end (*telos*) of human beings? What does human flourishing involve? What is "the common good"–the actions, values, and policies that allow people to flourish? In theological terminology, what is God's vision for all people? Such questions involve thinking about the meaning of terms such as the Kingdom of God, heaven, and the *eschaton* (end-time).

The following theological reflection outline provides a way to consider philosophical and theological anthropological matters.

Identify a focus.
Develop a list of social concerns that are presently being deliberated in your Culture/society. The items on the list might come from politics, news media, documentaries, current cinema, or advertisements.

For example:

- Environmental concerns
- Universal health care
- National security
- Distribution of wealth
- Economic wellbeing

Select one topic from the list you create and reflect theologically on that voice from the Culture source. You will have a chance to make additional connections to the voice of Culture when you add the Connect movement to your reflection.

Explore some dimensions of your selected social concern. For example:

- Notice what is revealed about human nature in the identified concern, both individually and corporately. What human values seem to be operating around the social concern? Describe what the identified social concern seems to assert about "the common good"; that is, if the concern you are working with is "economic wellbeing," how does that concern relate to the common good?
- What characteristics of God are present or absent in that concern? Possibly, a social concern around national security could reflect God's characteristic of protector. What about God's self-emptying?
- Identify the deep hopes that are present or implied in the nature of the social concern.

Connect

Describe various ways the identified social concern gets manifested at the present time. For example, if universal health care is the identified concern under reflection, then identify the ways in which that concern has come to the foreground in the culture/society where you live, such as:

- U.S. news report on congressional action
- Canadian experience of universal health care
- English experience of universal health care

Where do you hear God's voice in your social structure, or your culture?

Learn something new. Find a way to hear the voice of Cultures/societies other than your own, such as how other countries handle the same or similar concern. How do varying cultural groups handle such a matter, perhaps even within the same country? Please resist the temptation to "talk off the cuff" about another place or people; rather, try to talk to someone from that culture or look up information that you could consider authoritative and reliable.

Personal Experience: Name concrete ways in which the issue has intersected your life. For example:

- Retirement brought change in how medical insurance was obtained
- Got ill and had to receive medical attention over an extended period of time
- Health of a friend's parent deteriorated and he/she required extended health care
- Visit to emergency room of hospital and noticing who was there and why
- Change in a person's life that required addressing the need for medical insurance

When have you had personal experience related to that concern or issue? What emotions have you experienced as that concern has intersected your life: fear, frustration, sorrow mixed with gratitude? Name your thoughts and feelings in relation to the focus you have selected.

Personal Belief/Position: What seems to be at stake in the reflection as you have explored and connected to the identified concern? What statements of conviction are you willing to make? What is alive for you in this matter?

- State what you value and hold important that is touched by the identified social concern.
- State your best vision or hope for the world. For creation.

Tradition: Listen to the voice of Christian tradition, especially the way Christian tradition speaks to the questions of God, common good (reign of God), or human nature.

What specific stories from the Christian tradition speak to the concern? Note what scripture stories, perhaps ones you remember from your childhood, give shape to the concern.

As you access the various voices in Personal Experience, Christian Tradition, Culture(s), Personal Beliefs, what rings true for you or seems new to you? Express, as best you can, any intuitive sense of what "should" be, "ought" to be, could be, or "must" be done relative to the social concern. In other words, what matters to you about this?

Describe actions that you could take that might contribute to the reign of God, the common good, in the matter of the social concern on which you reflected.

Apply

Apply the insight and new awareness from the reflection within the context of the social concern you named above.

How do the dimensions of the social concern point to the common good?

In what way does participation in the social concern/issue contribute to a vision of God's reign?

How does human flourishing revealed through the reflective theological conversation point toward action and behavior and practices?

In other words, what are you going to do (ministry) with what you have considered?

What would support you? Where/how will you reach out for that support?

Theological Reflection Beginning with a Personal Position

Identify a focus.
Begin with a focus on the value of music and poetry in worship and prayer.

Explore the focus.
Make a statement or image that reflects a connection between music and poetry and prayer or worship. For instance, someone might express that he only likes a certain type of music in worship because another kind destroys the sense of peace and beauty. Or another person might create an image that depicts people singing or playing instruments and the music notes floating outward towards God and the world.

Explore your statement or image theologically, using a few of the questions provided, or create your own questions for the image:

How does the overall statement or image reflect wholeness or goodness?

What view of the world is contained in your statement or image?

What view of the relationship between God and creation exists in your statement/image?

How would someone experience God in that statement/image?

What might disrupt someone's relationship with God and others in that focus?

What view of restoration to wholeness is contained in the focus?

Connect to other sources.

State your personal belief that undergirds your initial image or statement.

How do your personal belief and the exploration above coincide and how do they conflict?

What troubles you about the comparison? What comforts you about the comparison?

Find one or two scripture references to the place of music and poetry in liturgy and worship. Or, select one or two hymns to connect to. How do those hymns relate to your focusing image or statement and to your position? How do they relate to the exploration?

What view of the world around you is contained in your personal belief statement, in the image, in the hymns you chose?

Apply what is learned to daily life.

Once a person takes a stance or affirms a position, implications for ministry begin to emerge.

What do you see for your ministry as you live day to day?

Close by composing a prayer adapting the structure of Jewish prayers:

Blessed are you, O Lord God, ______________________
(description of God),

for you ____

and make us ___________________________________

through _____________. *Amen.*

Theological Reflection Beginning with a Provocative Word[74]

Identify

Select a word that has impact. For the purpose of this reflection and the practice, try the word "DESIRING."

What revelations on the meaning of the word do you have? Anything it denotes or connotes?

Explore

Next, ask the six "journalist's questions" about the feeling the word conveys:

WHO was involved when you were feeling ______________________?
(Action . . . tell the stories from your life)

WHAT image comes to mind about the feeling(s) __________________?
(Image . . . explore the metaphor–its reflection of wholeness, brokenness, recognition, reorientation, and/or restoration)

Connect

Go to the other sources we use to help explore meaning.

WHERE does this feeling come from and WHERE is it found in society?
(Source/Culture)

WHEN does this feeling come up in the Bible, lives of saints, hymns, and so forth?
(Source/Tradition . . . explore the world of tradition)

WHY is this feeling manifest in our lives?
(Source/Position)

HOW might God redeem any negatives in this?
(Hope in Christ)

Consider insights and implications.

WHAT have you learned for the next time you feel _________________?

Apply

Write a collect using the outline:

Dear God . . .	**(naming of God's aspects)**
You . . .	**(connect situation of the image to that aspect)**
We pray that . . .	**(petition of our hearts)**
So that . . .	**(result we desire)**
Amen.	

74. Adapted from a design by Patricia Bleicher, EfM mentor.

Theological Reflection Beginning with a Wide-Angle Lens

Why this title? The image of a wide-angle lens is used because this reflection begins with a variety of perspectives, then focuses on a thread/theme/idea/image that connects them. An individual starts by finding the threads or themes present–in this case in something he or she reads or watches. The key for use by an individual requires initiation from something that could produce several themes or ideas (in this case, two or more articles on a topic of interest). In an EfM group, the reflection's beginning point can be themes from the spiritual autobiographies, themes from the week's reading, themes from any on-board time of the group, or some other starting point from which a variety of perspectives can be elicited.

The key is first to list the themes in what is under consideration, then find a thread that runs through the themes.

Identify

FIND A COMMON THEME OR THREAD

Begin with the articles chosen for the Respond section above.

What are the common themes or elements which emerge?

Is there a central question, struggle, or issue contained in the articles?

State the central thread as a simple statement, image, metaphor, or issue.

For instance, a review of several articles could reveal themes of challenge of the *status quo,* support of a particular view, and/or revelation of something new. Asking "What ties some of those themes together" yields a thread that may have run through the articles.

Explore

THEOLOGICAL PERSPECTIVES

Write about what's going on in the image, issue, or statement you created in the Identify step above.

Sit quietly and let the image or statement and your writing rest in you.

What questions does your image or statement raise?

What questions does that image or statement answer?

Identify the perspectives contained in the questions, that is, wholeness, brokenness, recognition, reorientation, or restoration.

Connect

This is the point at which one looks at the various sources in life to help find meaning in matters of daily life and ministry. The object is to find connections between the image, statement, or issue and other aspects of our life that teach us something.

CONNECT TO CULTURE AND SOCIETY

Focus on one or two areas of your culture or society so that the reflection will not be too broad. These connections might come from your local community or the larger world: your work environment, the education system, the health care system, your grandmothers, movies, TV, literature, art, songs, artifacts, architecture, government, or the press, to name a few.

Pick just one area of our contemporary society with which to connect. For instance, what does the world of employment teach you about the theme you have identified? Or, what have you learned from the news media in your culture/society that helps you or challenges you regarding the theme?

How does the selected area of culture/society speak to or about this thread?

CONNECT TO CHRISTIAN TRADITION

- Identify biblical passages or other elements from Christian tradition (scripture, hymn, prayer, church history document) in which this common thread is evoked or brought to mind. Read the passages.
- Select one passage that seems to address the image, statement, or issue.
- Examine the passage:
  - Note how the passage offers insight into the image, statement, or issue you are considering.
  - Note how the passage challenges the image, statement, or issue.
  - What does the passage mean to you?

COMPARE AND CONTRAST CULTURE/SOCIETY AND CHRISTIAN TRADITION

From the perspectives of each, what kind of a world emerges?

Where do these perspectives join or compete? Where do they clash or contrast?

Note what seems to be "at stake" as you compare and contrast your Culture and Tradition connections.

CONNECT TO PERSONAL EXPERIENCE

When have you experienced something that relates to what seems to "be at stake" above?

CONNECT TO BELIEFS, POSITIONS, AND AFFIRMATIONS

What positions or affirmations do you hold in relation to what is at stake?

Identify how that belief formed for you. Was it from personal experience, from something you learned in your faith tradition, or from the cultural messages you have inherited or encountered?

What "gaps" are there for you between what you believe and how you act in relation to the theme considered in this reflection?

Apply

IDENTIFY INSIGHTS AND PERSONAL IMPLICATIONS

What have you learned about coherence of belief and behavior?

What are you personally called to do differently, to affirm, or to change?

What skills did this reflection help you learn in thinking theologically about something you read or watched?

DECIDE ON SOCIAL AND CIVIC CONSEQUENCES

What actions will you take to carry out the implications you have discovered?

Consider how this reflection supports you in living in a multicultural world.

Resources for Community Life

Group Life: The Seminar

The Nature of Groups

We all live in groups. Whenever two or three gather together, we have a group. Because we take this so much for granted, we often fail to note that groups have lives. They begin, they grow, they encounter changes and mood swings, they calcify, they end. When we pay attention to the life of the group, we can keep patterns healthy and vibrant. We can make them into creative centers for learning and productivity. Other groups may degenerate into destructive patterns that feed on negativities, breed destructive behaviors, or just simply become ineffective, unproductive, stale, and dissatisfying. These groups usually collapse in conflict or abandonment.

The goal of the EfM seminar is to discover our theology with others on a common path. We know that certain considerations must be met in order for this to happen in a group that maintains a productive and creative life.

The key element of any seminar is **TRUST**. Without it every discussion becomes a defensive encounter and learning is limited by tactics of self-protection. An effective seminar develops because the leadership provides a venue in which leadership can be shared, responsibility for the common wellbeing can be assumed by everyone, and each person can enter the discussion with a sense of value, acceptance, and the ability to make distinctive contributions. Such a pattern does not just happen. It grows in an environment of caring and nurturing. Its growth validates that we learn more effectively by cooperation and enthusiastic participation than by competition and argumentation.

Essential Elements

We have determined that certain elements need to be present in the life of a seminar to make it effective and satisfying as **a learning environment**. Seating in a seminar should be arranged with no one dominating the group as if chairing a meeting. Members should be able to see each other, and the room should afford a sense of privacy. Different styles may dominate. Put aside barriers, such as a table in the center of the room, that may reduce personal communications. Seminars do not work well with interruptions such as might take place in a large hall open to the public. Restrooms and hospitality can be very helpful, including access to liquids, at the very least water. Nourishment that maintains a sense of comfort and wellbeing are suggested.

EfM offers participants an opportunity to share their "spiritual autobiographies." **Self-revelation** is a part of every encounter, when we state our names, shake hands, and offer information about ourselves. Typical information beyond our names includes our address, occupation, and family status. Of course we also reveal a great deal in non-verbal ways by appearance, body posture, and tones of voice. All these features highlight our encounters everyday. To develop a seminar group requires that we reveal a bit more. What we reveal depends upon our own comfort level in a group. Some personal information is obviously not appropriate in a seminar group, but members must make decisions about "how free" they can be. Usually this is an evolving process, like a marriage. As we grow in trust and support for one another, we reveal more and become more open. Secrets tend to restrict our freedom to express ourselves, resulting in a smaller and narrower world view. We cannot grow by ourselves, and we also cannot grow if we fail to participate. Self-revelation is our participation. Feedback from others is how others can contribute to our learning process.

While we begin with Spiritual Autobiographies in EfM, this is only one aspect of our continuing self-revelation and growth. Theological reflection only works well if it speaks to events in our lives. We can find it difficult to engage in theological reflection unless we can reveal enough of our lives to examine with the theological tools we acquire through the process of study.

A mentor has certain leadership functions assigned by the task, but **shared leadership** has more to do with style than with function. Shared leadership means that a group takes sufficient time to arrive at a consensus, that is to say a willingness of all to pursue a certain course. Consensus does not mean that all agree, but it does mean that everyone is willing to pursue a given option. Sharing the leadership requires that group members check with each other. Those who are most vocal need to give place and to encourage those who have less to say, but may indeed offer significant contributions. Shared leadership means looking out for one another, taking time for one another, and recognizing that unless we move together, our seminar will end.

No seminar works well unless there exists **a common enterprise**. This is the subject of our inquiry, in this case the theological enterprise in all its complexity. Our common enterprise includes the history of theology and the sources for our faith, the Bible, the experience of the people of God throughout history and through liturgy, and the interpretation of those experiences that have been handed to us in countless libraries as well as through a shared tradition of experience.

In academia the pattern or discipline used in seminars frequently follows that of the lecture hall. Instead of faculty, seminar members offer papers or "talks" which may be critiqued and discussed. For participants such seminars are often dry and uninteresting, unless either the subject is scintillating or the discussion takes on a polemic level that energizes at least some of the participants. We do not believe, however, that disputation as a technique to manage a seminar is very helpful.

The **general pattern** for conducting an EfM seminar is as follows:

- There is time to catch up with one another. This is kept short unless there is a crisis.
- There is time to worship together. The kind of worship will depend upon the needs of the participants.
- There is time to discuss the lessons, not in detail, but to note highlights, ask questions for clarification, and elicit themes and information that catch or surprise students.
- There is time to engage in reflective work such as a spiritual autobiography or a theological reflection; or time to examine spiritual needs, to plumb for theological meaning, or to examine the meaning of Christian ministry.
- This is a time to harvest the fruits of the seminar. Often we learn without knowing it and we fail to use what we have discovered. We have to name our discoveries in order to truly "own" them. It is important from time to time to ask: What have I learned? What are the implications of what I have learned? What must I do to put what I have learned into practice? What difference will what I have learned make in the way I am now? Tomorrow? In the future? What difference will it make for us, our families, our friends, our church, our communities?
- There is adequate time for breaks and refreshment.

We advise that the group produce a set of statements about the purpose, expectations, and norms by which it will work (e.g., the time to begin and to close each session). It also helps if everyone agrees to a schedule about various tasks associated with the seminar.

Social groups and work groups usually create opportunities to **celebrate** life. This is also true of an EfM seminar group. Remember special events in the life of the group with appropriate festivities. Just how and when this is done will vary from group to group. These celebrations may include a meal and alcohol may be served; however, whenever alcohol is served, the group must be sure to offer non-alcoholic beverages in an equally attractive manner.

Celebration may provide an occasion to bring in significant persons who are not part of the group. Spouses or special friends may be included so that they will have an opportunity to meet the group.

We often fail to say goodbye properly, to grieve for what will be no more, to celebrate what we have enjoyed and to give thanks for what we have received. Celebration may be part of **closure**, but closure is more than simply enjoying festivities. Only when we mourn are we ready to release and move on to the next opportunity. We do ourselves and others no service when we fail to mourn, for that failure means that we remain fixed to the past and our creativity diminishes. Certificates, diplomas, remembrances we exchange in token and in words, all serve as epitaphs and tombstones for the past. It is important that seminar groups find ways to express closure adequately.

Tools from Kaleidoscope International

The following processes for gracious communication are from the Kaleidoscope Institute with whom EfM has been in a collaborative relationship since 2011. Learn more about KI at www.kscopeinstitute.org

The Cycle of Gospel Living

The difference in attitude toward the powerful and the powerless was very clear throughout the ministry of Jesus. Jesus never told the poor and powerless to sell all they own and give to the poor. That would obviously be an absurd thing to say. Jesus healed them, loved them, ate with them, touched them, comforted them, blessed them, served them, encouraged them, taught them, and liberated them by his own suffering, death, and resurrection. Finally, Jesus breathed on them to infuse them with the power of the Holy Spirit–the power to teach, heal, and forgive in the name of God. On the other hand, Jesus never told the rich and powerful that they are blessed. Instead, Jesus warned them and challenged them to serve and to humble themselves. He reminded them of what the law and the prophets had said.

The Gospel invites the powerful to take up their cross and follow Jesus. Salvation for the powerful comes from the decision to give up power and take up the cross. The Gospel, however, never asks the powerless to choose the cross because the powerless, by the condition of their powerlessness, are already on the cross. There is no need for them to choose it, just as there is no need for the poor to give up what they have and give to the poor because they are already poor. Because the powerless are already on the cross, salvation comes from endurance and faithfulness in the hope of God's deliverance through the resurrection.

Choosing the cross and the resurrection of Jesus are part of the same Gospel story. But we interact with the different parts of the story differently depending on our place of power in a particular situation. As a Chinese American working in the Episcopal Church, I often find myself in situations where I am set up to be powerless. For example I am sometimes invited to be the token Asian in a meeting. When I am in this kind of situation, I actually spend some time before I enter the meeting to get in touch with the empty tomb, the resurrection side of the Gospel. I tell myself that I am blessed and a child of God no matter what happens. I ask God to breathe the Holy Spirit through me to give me strength to endure and power to speak and challenge the system I am about to enter.

On the other hand, as a trainer and consultant I also find myself in situations where I am given power and authority to influence others. In my preparation for each training session, I spend time reflecting on what it means to choose the cross. I tell myself that I am a servant to the participants. I tell myself that even though I may be treated as an expert, I must be humble. I tell myself that my job is to work myself out of my job by giving my knowledge, skills, and power away freely, so that at the end of the session the participants will know what I know and my services are no longer needed.

It is crucial to determine in a given situation which side of the cross we are on if we are to experience the wholeness of the Gospel. No one can stay on one side of the cross all the time. That would be neglecting the wholeness of the Gospel. Living the Gospel involves moving through the cycle of death and resurrection, the cross and the empty tomb, again and again. The moment I am resurrected into new life of empowerment, I must begin to think about serving and giving away my power and take up the cross again, or I stand the chance of abusing my power. The moment I take up the cross and become powerless, I must begin to think about faithfulness and endurance and look toward empowerment through the empty tomb. It is in this dynamic of death and resurrection, cross and empty tomb, Lent and Easter, that the Gospel comes to life in each one of us.[75]

Law uses this diagram to illustrate his Cycle of Gospel Living.

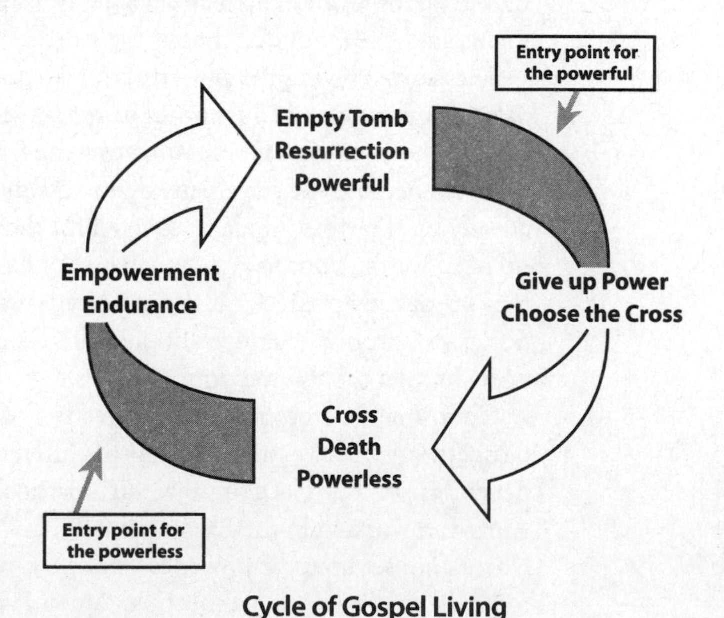

Cycle of Gospel Living

75. Eric H. F. Law, *The Wolf Shall Dwell with the Lamb: A Spirituality for Leadership in a Multicultural Community* (St. Louis: Chalice Press, 1993), 41–43.

Mutual Invitation

In order to ensure that everyone who wants to share has the opportunity to speak, we will proceed in the following way:

The leader or a designated person shares first. After that person has spoken, he or she then invites another to share. (Whom you invite does not need to be the person next to you.) After the next person has spoken, that person is given the privilege to invite another to share.

If you are not ready to share, say "I pass for now" and we will invite you to share later on. If you don't want to say anything at all, simply say "pass" and proceed to invite another to share. We will do this until everyone has been invited.

We invite you to listen and not to respond to someone's sharing immediately. There will be time to respond and to ask clarifying questions after everyone has had an opportunity to share.

(adapted from *The Wolf Shall Dwell with the Lamb* by Eric H. F. Law[76])

As you practice Mutual Invitation you are enacting the Gospel Cycle of Living. The person speaking is powerful. The persons refraining from speaking have given up power, but will take it up again when invited. A person who passes has the power to offer power to another through invitation. Notice and reflect on this cycle as you become more adept and comfortable with the process.

76. Atlanta: Chalice Press, 1993.

Respectful Communication Guidelines

R = take RESPONSIBILITY for what you say and feel without blaming others

E = use EMPATHETIC listening

S = be SENSITIVE to differences in communication styles

P = PONDER what you hear and feel before you speak

E = EXAMINE your own assumptions and perceptions

C = keep CONFIDENTIALITY

T = TRUST ambiguity, because we are not here to debate who is right or wrong

(from *The Bush Was Blazing but Not Consumed* by Eric H. F. Law)

I agree to uphold these guidelines for the time we have together.

Signature ____ Date ______________